Jacqueline Blakeway is a Psychotherapist, Master/Teacher in Magnified Healing, Soul Reader, Psychic Counsellor, Motivational Speaker and Author. Her extensive experience in the areas of personal and spiritual development has enabled her to inspire and assist hundreds of people to achieve their full potential in life. Jacky sees herself as 'An Awakener' during this important time of planetary transformation and currently guides others toward their true spiritual purpose. She lives in 'blissful simplicity' on the Costa Blanca, Spain with her two beautiful children, Jessica and Temujin.

The sequel to this book, 'God is Definitely in Charge' is currently a work in progress and due for publication in Spring 2008.

www.jacquelineblakeway.com

Praise for Jacky Blakeway

Readers of this book will appreciate the lucid manner with which Jacky's writing presents a truly compelling account of a uniquely personal experience. She provides just enough of the professional data to lay the foundation for a unified approach to the subject matter, which will be of great interest, not only to those involved in healing, but also those engaged in the practical daily work of psychotherapy and wider mental health issues. This underlies, of course, her enthusiasm portrayed in the book for developing creative, highly individualised approaches to healing and personal development and I commend the book to you.

Dr. Paul Birley, Ph.D., MA, B.Sc.(Hons)
United Kingdom Council for Psychotherapists,
Registered Psychotherapist

Acknowledgements

Thanks go to the following people without whom this
book would not have been possible.

To Kate Smith: For your love & friendship, relentless research and
for always being there for me, (and for the phone
calls from Thailand that Martin doesn't know about
…whoops!).

To Jayne: For your empathy and for travelling this part of my
soul journey with me… you are truly loved.

To Christine & Steve Hastings, Andy Laverick, Martin & Dawn, Colin,
Claire and Andy:

Thank you for your love and support and for
reminding me of the importance of family.

To Malcolm: For Jess's childhood memories, more precious than
you will ever know.

To Don: For acknowledging my need to grow … and in that
respect loving truly, properly.

To Sal: My dearest friend and soul traveller … and for being
able to make me laugh … no matter what!

To Christopher: For the therapeutic value of listening, for making the
Spanish connection and for your friendship and
generosity.

To Kath: The most stalwart friend a person could wish for.
Thank you for your endless support … and for
helping me to understand the difference between a
computer and a microwave!

To Amon-Ra: God bless you for your healing.

To Tony, Ram & Sid:

For the helpful advice and healing when I
most needed it.

To Ann Drury: For my introduction to the healing arts and
for your service to the light.

To Paul Birley: For giving me the platform from which to work and for your love and commitment to others in the field of personal development.

To Robin Sieger: For your encouragement, much appreciated help on this book and for your words of wisdom.

To Kenny Pask: For the catalyst you were and for your love and dedication to spirit.

To Hazel: For writing an insightful 'Foreword' and for your generosity, support and belief in my message.

To Mr Seal: My inspiration for creative writing and a credit to the teaching profession.

To Steve & Ann Yates, Roz, Helen & Ann, Caroline, Doris, Kath R, Pam & Sue, David, Carolyn & Marilyn, Alma, Wendy, Freda, Nancy, Joyce, Kathy, Margaret, Marie, Christina, Jane, Val & all at Q.E.D:

For letting the vision live on and for your dedication to the light.

To Anita & Peter: For the generous use of the 'Coach House', a haven of love and light. Thank you for your support.

To Diane: For extending yourself and for giving your time to counsel Jess unconditionally, thank you.

To Geoff Addis: A testament to courage... May you rest among the Angels.

To Liz & Rob: For your practical support, friendship and for always being there.

To Anne: For letting me 'borrow' your landscape, for a photo shoot that was so much fun! ... and for your generosity and friendship.

To Trini & Manuel: For your help and kindness and for making us feel truly welcome in a new country. *Gracias.*

To my mum: My Angel in the heavens

To Fran & Sarah: For your generosity, words of encouragement and for being two of the loveliest goddesses I know.

To Ken & Hayley, Trevor & Brenda, Lauren, Kelly and all at Libros:

For having the courage to follow through on your vision... and for believing in mine. God bless you.

To Carol Cole: For a wonderful editing job. Thank you for your patience in working with the most computer illiterate person you've ever known and for making this part of the process relatively painless!

To Muku: Thank you for the venue of 'Everest Tandoori' for my launch and for your beautiful friendship.

To Anton & Emma: For your love, support and for sharing your wisdom ... and to Anton who, despite the challenges, came through on the book cover for me – Maestro I salute you - truly inspirational!

To Johan, Ina, Tibo & Maro:

For your wonderful friendship and kindness and for the joy you will bring to our July and August every year for a lifetime.

To Jess: For your insight beyond your years, attempts to console and messages of hope ... and for always being a ray of sunshine. I love you.

To Sarah, Chris, Jane, Lisa & Michael, Edwina, Janet, Gay, Lucy, Margaret, Diane & Gary, Lynn & Geoff, Jeanette, Karen & Tracy, Saemus and Doreen:

For your friendship and for being my support network in Spain.

And finally to Temujin: A blessing from God and my hope for the future.

ISBN 1-905988-08-7   978-1-905988-08-2

Published by Libros International

www.librosinternational.com

Cover design by Anton Kornblum
www.akorndesign.net
www.mayatime.net

This book is dedicated to my dad with love. Thank you for the help when I needed it most, for loving me ... and for knowing how hard I tried.

God Works For Me Now

Jacqueline Ann Blakeway

Libros International

FOREWORD

By Hazel Courteney, Columnist, Broadcaster and Author of 'Divine Intervention' and 'Evidence for the Sixth Sense'

This book is greatly needed. Spiritual books may be the fastest growing sector in the book market, but books that deal specifically with Spiritual Emergency (when spiritual awakening becomes a physical and/or mental health crisis) remain rare. Much courage has been needed by Jacky to relate her harrowing experiences during her partner's intense spiritual opening and her story makes riveting reading.

I first heard from Jacky when her partner was at the height of his experience. They found me via my book, 'Divine Intervention', which tells of my near death experience and subsequent spiritual emergency. I once believed that what had happened to me was totally unique – but as soon as my book was published I quickly realized that intense spiritual awakenings are becoming more commonplace and that there is a desperate need for both the public and health professionals to become more aware of this phenomena and its myriad of associated symptoms and potential causes.

Jacky was desperate for help – as her partner seemed to have 'completely lost the plot'. He was claiming to be 'the Saviour of all mankind'. As soon as I spoke to Jaya, which I did on several occasions, I quickly realized that his ego had taken control and that his underlying personality had been greatly amplified by his awakening. My heart went out to him, as I too had once entertained such misguided thoughts – but I understood better than most how truly different you feel and act when experiencing heightened states of awareness.

How Jacky coped and survived to tell this tale is little short of a miracle. Her work as a Psychotherapist and Healer and her excellent intuitiveness enabled her to identify that her partner's awakening had triggered NPD, Narcissistic Personality Disorder.

Spiritual awakening can be a magical process, which is everyone's natural birthright – or it can be a baptism of fire.

Every mother offers her own unique story of her child's birth – and yet there are always similarities in the majority of births. The same can be said of Spiritual Emergency which can trigger hugely diverse symptoms, from the person becoming super psychic, to tremors, hearing voices, extreme personality changes such as NPD, violent swings in temperature, a feeling of being 'all knowing', visions, terror, complete bliss and so on. Everything becomes a paradox.

From all the doctors, health professionals and psychiatrists I eventually interviewed, it quickly became obvious to me that a large proportion of people now diagnosed as suffering from conditions such as psychosis or schizophrenia are being misdiagnosed, and that the parameters describing such conditions are becoming more and more blurred. But, thanks to the work of eminent doctors such as Stan Grof, a professor of psychiatry based in San Francisco who has spent fifty years studying spiritual awakenings, at long, long last, there are now a few more research papers making their way into mainstream health care. More awareness is needed urgently in all sectors, and this book will be of great use to anyone who wants to expand their knowledge of intense spiritual awakenings.

After all how would you cope if a loved one suddenly awoke and claimed that 'God worked for *him* now' and at the same time began having incredible visions and insights?

We are all spiritual beings having a physical experience – and this book will help you and others to more fully understand and integrate who we really are and what we are truly capable of, into our everyday lives.

Hazel Courteney
February 2007
www.hazelcourteney.com

AUTHOR'S NOTE

This is my true story. All of the events detailed in this book can be verified through police records, court correspondence, taped conversations and private letters. In order to protect the identities of certain individuals, some names have been changed.

For the purpose of this story, my partner has been called Jaya Kham Daridra, Jai for short. This name was chosen for its symbolic meaning (given below) and in order to maintain the authenticity of his origins.

Jai or Jaya is a Sanskrit/ Hindi word meaning "Hail!" or "Victory to Him!" or "Glory to Him!"

Kham (Kham Brahm) A sanskrit term meaning "all is *brahman*" - an Advaita expression from the Vedas; it states that nothing else exists but *brahman* because everything is *brahman*.

Daridra (Daridra-Sheva) A Sanskrit term, *Daridra*, meaning "poor".

Sheva: "service, pledge, worship", service to and care of the poor and needy.

As taken from 'The Rider Encyclopaedia of Eastern Philosophy and Religion' first published in the UK by Rider in 1989.

I researched, unaided, the mental health issues I have discussed in this book. In this respect, the opinions I express or the conclusions I have drawn concerning these issues are my own and based entirely on my findings.

Throughout my spiritual journey and, in particular, during the time span of this extraordinary experience, I have read many, many books relating to spiritual matters and mental health issues. I have an excellent ability to retain information and, wherever possible, I have attributed the sources of certain phrases imprinted on my mind to their respective authors. If there are any that I have failed to acknowledge, I apologize for the oversight as no ill intent was meant. I remain indebted to the authors' works I have mentioned in my bibliography and for whose prolific writings this book is the worthier...

LIST OF CHAPTERS

PART ONE *'THE EMOTIONAL JOURNEY'*

PART TWO *'THE AWARENESS AND UNDERSTANDING'*

PART ONE

'THE EMOTIONAL JOURNEY'

PROLOGUE

The Vision

My heart pounded violently as I pressed 'play' on the recorder. "I should have given this to you six months ago," I stammered through the floods of tears.

There was a tense silence between the two police officers as Jai's chilling words began to fill the room...

"Do you know He's given me the greatest power of all the Masters, Jacky? Do you know why? You know when I sat around the table in the grand halls of the kingdom of Heaven, yeah? I was sitting there with Krishna, Buddha, Mohammed, Hitler and Jesus ... and He said all the darkest work has to be done ... He said *all* the work has to be done, so all the Masters put their hands up ... But when He said *that* I kept my hand down. But then He told them what the work was ... and it involved everything dirty and good, yeah?

"And then the Masters put their hands down, and they said, '*We can't do that*'...Jesus said, '*I can't be nasty to people, I'm compassion!*' Buddha said, '*I can't eat meat!*' Mohammed said, '*It's not a job for me!*' and Hitler said, '*Those swine! Give me a day and they'll pray for inner death!*'

"But do you know what I did then, Jacky? I put my hand up and Krishna said to me, '*Why didn't you put your hand up before?*' So I said to him, '*Because, Lord, there's no place I'd rather be than at your feet.*'

"Then Buddha ... *he* said to me, '*Why are you putting your hand up now?*' And I said, '*Lord, there's nothing I'd rather do than be at your feet and do your work!*' And he smiled at me and I put my hand up again ... and I said, '*Lord, there's no*

21

*work I'd rather do than your **dirtiest** work, the work no one else is prepared to do!'* and He really looked at me and He said, *'For **that** I call you 'Jaya'*...

"Now, the meaning of 'Jaya' is 'Glory to Him!'... And then the Lord, He said, *'With that, I'll give you a surname 'Daridra', because I know you mean what you say ... **that you have pledged yourself in service to the poor and needy!'***

"And this man who now speaks in front of you is **Jaya Daridra, 'Victory to Him',** who'll never give up until he gets *every* single soul back to God, which *ever* way it takes. The way he enjoys the most is the *nice* way; that way people will enjoy it *with* him. ... But then, if they don't listen, it'll be the *fun* way, and he'll take them *away* the fun way. If they still don't listen, he'll use the *angry* way and then they'll get back. But if the anger doesn't work; then the **power** will come and I'll show them what I can do! If that doesn't happen, I'll destroy them and then they'll have to get back ... do you understand?

"That's the start of it, baby! So I'm in full control of my energy ... Because the reason I've got it is because I can control it. **No** other **person** on the planet could control it. You know why? Because all the Masters got it *wrong*. When they put their hands up they were eager to come down because everyone wants to please the Lord, you know? But I never did, 'cause I got the answer right first time and He's always testing **us** Masters as well you know. Don't think that you're not being tested at *all* times... you're being tested at all times!

"You know the same day that Nostradamus said that the world would blow up; well, **I'm** the man who's **blowing it up,** in the *nicest* possible way. But if I have to be **bad**, I'll be **bad**, and blow it up in the **baddest** way! Saddam Hussein thinks *he's* bad? I could destroy Saddam Hussein! President Clinton think's he's a 'jucker' ... I can out-juck Clinton! Tony Blair thinks he's clever? I'm cleverer than Blair any day! Do you understand what I'm saying? **I'm** the man that Nostradamus talks about. Aries was his sign, yeah? Aryan was his descendant, **yeah**? And tomorrow is the day that Nostradamus said the *world* would blow up, as you know it. Upside-down, 'cause I'm gonna turn it around!

"*Me!* ...**and do you know why I'm so sure?** ... Because I'm the only person who's prepared to take a gun, *put* it in *another* man's hand and say **shoot** me! And what the **fuck** will everyone say? **'No way'**, they'll say, because that's the way *they* are. They're cowards and they're fearful, so they make little excuses ... but this guy will take **any challenge!** 'Cause a man who's **true** will take **any challenge!** He'll take a good challenge; he'll take a bad challenge ... but these people who are pretending to be good ... they'll say **No** ... but I say I am God.

"Then, because I can do **anything** ... you **can't shoot me,** but I can shoot **you!** And that makes me ... God! That's what makes me **victorious!** But you know, as I talk, people will say 'he's arrogant!' But I **know** that I'm sitting in **His** lap. So I can say what the **fuck** I like, and I can't be touched 'cause what **I say ... goes!** 'Cause that's the **power** I have. *You* don't even know it yet. **But I promise you one thing, baby! The world will know it** *one* **day, and it's a** *glorious* **time we're living in ... a** *glorious* **time! You know why? 'Cause it's gonna be all fun ... it's gonna be happy. It's gonna be hallelujah!"**

The menacing tone prevalent throughout his monologue now gave way to a deafening crescendo. A feverish torrent of words, utterly devoid of emotion, spilled from the tape...

"**But if anybody ever** *fucks* **with** *me*! ... *This* **motherfucker is the** *baddest* **motherfucker that God has** *ever* **sent down to sort out** *all* **the motherfuckers; the motherfucker of all motherfuckers ...** for pretending they're good guys ... do you understand? 'Cause *I'm* the *man*, baby! You'd better *believe* it – *I'm* the **man!** You were right, Jacky; you've unleashed a **monster ...**"

I watched the colour drain from the officers' faces.

"We've heard enough," one of them said starkly. "That's all

we need to convince the CPS to keep him in custody."

He paused and in a loathsome tone added, *"That is one twisted fuck."*

My heart sank. Tearfully, I handed over the tape. I needed to vomit.

It was Tuesday, 1st May 2001; the day I finally realized that this was a situation I could no longer control.

CHAPTER ONE: 'IN THE BEGINNING'

'Where love rules, there is no will to power.
And where power predominates, love is lacking.
The one is the shadow of the other'

Jung, Carl (1875-1961)

This is not a love story. But it is a story about love. The people who enter and exit our lives are like actors playing out our personal story. Some leave a faint impression on our memories…others the most unimaginable scars. So it was with Jaya Kham Daridra. A story that was written five thousand years ago began to unfold and this vision marked its beginning. For Jai, it marked the beginning of a descent into a bottomless pit of need and self-destruction …

In the beginning …

Jai walked into my life and the tiny therapy room I rented twice a week from the local hairdressers on November 25th 1998. Dressed in a bright yellow, hooded sweat top and black jogging trousers, with his fingerless gloves he looked every inch of his generous six-foot frame, like a film extra from the 'Rocky' movies.

I noticed he had a habit of bowing his head forward and hunching his shoulders. It gave him an air of pronounced humility and I remember commenting on it. Jai's friend and mentor, a gentle Italian man in his late fifties, introduced him to me with these words, "He's a bit of a rogue, but he has a good heart."

I carried out Indian Head Massage and Reflexology. His prime objective was to de-stress, learn how to relax properly and still his 'monkey mind'. His sixteen-hour days, he told me, left him 'crashing' in front of Sky television late into the night, his only method of unwinding.

Sometimes my work enabled me to use my 'psychic sense' as a way of unlocking the deeper issues a client may consciously or unconsciously be suppressing. Right from the start, I *knew* there was a deeper mystery to him than just the presenting problems for which he'd come to seek my help.

I found Jai's boyish charm enchanting. Here was a man who, on the surface, had seemingly mastered the physical plane, having opened his first successful newsagent's at nineteen years of age and yet, beneath this worldly exterior, I sensed there was a small child struggling to come to terms with the harsh realities of life.

I felt at ease with Jai right from the beginning. We talked about *everything*: the meaning of life and of love; we talked about our faith, the universe and God. We shared our dreams, our goals, our hopes and our aspirations. I'd never met anyone before him who viewed the world with such childlike and passionate enthusiasm.

I suspect it was this ease that allowed me to kid myself early on that the attraction was purely cerebral. Quite simply, from our very first meeting, there was something about Jai that drew me to him magnetically … irresistibly.

I knew he was married; it wasn't as though he tried to conceal it; quite the reverse. He talked fondly about his wife, her beliefs, her daily spiritual practices and her devotion to him. I thought they must have a 'marriage made in heaven' and that this was a relationship built on such strong foundations that nothing could shake it.

For the next four or five months our treatment sessions continued on a once or twice weekly basis. Jai was hardly ever on time for an appointment and I found myself only mildly irritated by this, dismissing it as the downside of his busy schedule. Many times I caught myself hovering at the hairdresser's window anticipating his arrival, waiting to catch a glimpse of his yellow sweat top as he turned the corner from the car park. I would feign my disinterest at his lack of punctuality by pretending to be absorbed in some book or other.

Often our conversations formed as much a part of the session as the treatment itself. Once, whilst working in his 'auric layer', I felt strongly guided to impart a 'past life' impression I'd seen with my psychic eyes. I 'saw' him as a warrior in full Mongolian garb. "You rode with Ghengis Khan," I told him. Seemingly excited by this, he told me a clairvoyant three years earlier had given him the same information in a reading.

I'd long learned to trust my own inner wisdom. My fourteen-year journey of self-discovery had included years of 'sitting' in a development circle during my involvement with the spiritualist church. In Australia I'd trained with an Ayurvedic Master in the art of meditation and, as an enthusiastic student, I soon learned how correct breathing and selective concentration enhanced my ability to 'still the monkey mind'. It was in these still moments that I somehow connected to a deep inner guidance that became a source of transformation in my life.

Jai on the other hand didn't find it easy to still the mind; he was a man who thrived on external stimuli. The more I came to know him, the more I became aware of his short attention span, his impulsive nature and his excess of energy. In the beginning, I didn't see these qualities as either negative or problematic. On the contrary, enthusiasm is infectious and Jai's passion for life was a pure joy to be around.

I was blissfully unaware at that time of what lay ahead …

Soon I caught myself replaying our sessions over and over in my mind, reviewing our conversations and, before long, I was aware that my thoughts were consumed with him. Kate, a close personal friend and my researcher for this book, would cast me a wry smile after I'd managed to somehow steer the conversation which had begun on a completely different topic once again back to Jai.

She would suggest that I had feelings for him and I'd then spend the next hour or so convincing her otherwise. I would hear myself saying things like, "Of course I haven't" "Besides, he's out of bounds" and "We've just got a kind of *connection*".

Back then, I had no idea what a poor job I was doing of convincing myself.

Someone once wrote, 'Love is like driving into a blizzard; you are snow-blind, there is silence, yet you still move on'. There's no doubt in my mind that love *chooses* us. Like the proverbial butterfly, if we chase it, it will escape us … stay still for a while … and, often when we least expect it, it will happily come to rest upon our shoulder.

Love is magical when it finds us. Had I in some mystical way found in Jai the soulmate I'd been searching for all my life?

Certainly, up until this point, the yearning for true love in my own life had been fraught with difficulties. Following the breakdown of my eight year marriage in 1985 at the age of twenty-nine, I threw myself into one love affair after another; misguidedly believing that to love again would erase my sense of failure and restore my faith in relationships. In fact the opposite became my reality. I realized I'd carried the emotional residue from my previous relationship into each new entanglement and, as a result of not dealing with it, had sabotaged any hope of success.

By the time I'd reached the age of thirty-five, a single mother with a string of broken love affairs behind me, I realized I knew very little about love at all! It was time to direct my attention inwards, time to explore my own inner world and discover why I had created barriers to the perfect relationship I longed for.

This period in my life marked the beginning of an intense

journey of self-discovery. I read avidly, positively craving esoteric books that explored the answers to some of life's deepest mysteries, never ceasing to be amazed how the 'right' information always seemed to present itself just when I needed it!

A book which had a major impact on me at the time was Dr. M. Scott Peck's book 'The Road Less Travelled' and, in particular, the part of the book in which he brilliantly explores the mystery of love.

'Of all the misconceptions about love, the most powerful and pervasive is the belief that 'falling in love' is love or at least one of the manifestations of love,' says Peck. Romantic love, he states is a 'myth', perpetuated by our culture and has 'its origins in our favourite childhood fairy tales, wherein the prince and princess, once united, live happily ever after'.

I wondered if with Jai I was now simply nurturing a romantic notion born out of the 'myth' Peck talks about. All I knew was that, when I met Jai, it was like meeting a kindred spirit and, over the twenty sessions or so that he came to see me, an inexplicable intensity and unspoken attachment developed between us.

I don't believe our meeting was an accident. There are no 'chance' encounters; rather that each person who crosses our path has come into our lives for a reason, sometimes to work through shared karma, sometimes to teach us things about ourselves.

When we were well into our sessions and he knew me a little better, Jai confided that a clairvoyant had predicted he would 'meet a woman dressed all in white who would teach him the principles of meditation'. When he saw me dressed in a white uniform offering to help him focus and still his thoughts in meditation, he thought the prediction had come true! As the relationship between us developed, neither of us believed our meeting was the hand of chance.

James Redfield writes about chance encounters in his hugely

successful book, 'The Celestine Prophecy'. It has changed many people's lives, as it did mine when I read it in 1996. Interwoven in the book, a suspense-filled tale about the disappearance of an old Peruvian manuscript, are nine 'insights' or 'truths' that Redfield predicts we must grasp in order to propel ourselves forward on our own evolutionary pathway.

In the third insight he says this: 'The old Newtonian idea is that everything happens by chance, that one can make good decisions and be prepared, but that every event has its own line of causation independent of our attitude. After the recent discoveries of modern physics, we may legitimately ask if the universe is more dynamic than that. Perhaps the universe runs mechanistically as a basic operation, but then also subtly responds to the mental energy we project out into it.'

Reading 'The Celestine Prophecy' gave me a new understanding of the changing events in my own life. I began to make sense of the connections and like pieces of a puzzle ... people, places and events all began to fit together. The more aware I became of the signs, the more my life flowed with ease and a sense of purpose. It seemed that with every new experience and synchronistic event, the further I journeyed towards my destiny.

We can *all* begin to experience life in this way. When we become aware of the profound sense of being in the right place at the right time, our lives become transformed. Meditation teaches us how to concentrate, still our thoughts and observe our inner guidance. In this way we become more open to synchronicity.

I meditated regularly and at different times achieved different levels of consciousness. Often, in a deeply meditative state, I would receive 'flashes of insight' or be hit by a sudden new or creative idea. Occasionally I'd have 'visions'. These I defined as extraordinary experiences and I viewed them for the healing potential they offered.

Sometimes I found myself experiencing a 'far memory' or past life.

One such extraordinary experience took place on 16th March 1999 whilst attending evening meditation at the spiritualist church. I relate this 'vision' along with others in this book, as they have a significant place in the telling of my story.

Earlier that day, Jai had telephoned me to ask me if I wanted to participate in a 'fast' the following day. Apparently it was an important date in the Indian calendar. I told him I had a busy schedule and didn't think my body would be able to take it. I am the sort of person who needs food at regular intervals, otherwise I start to feel faint and dizzy. So I answered, "Perhaps another time."

That evening, in circle, my meditation lasted a full fifty minutes and our facilitator remarked how long it had taken to 'bring me back' to full waking consciousness. I'd accessed a level quite different from ordinary relaxation, one in which I felt almost suspended in space and time and with no awareness of my body or surrounding environment.

In this state I became conscious of a 'far memory' and 'saw' myself on horseback, my arms encircled around the waist of the rider. I was wearing a tunic type garment and moccasins as befitting a Native American Indian woman and the word 'Navaho' sifted into awareness. The rider turned towards me and I looked deep into his eyes. It was Jai, who I instinctively *knew* was my husband. I observed some stone-built dwellings, a holy place with a Mexican 'feel' to it and, in the palm of my hand, I tenderly cradled a small silver talisman and an eagle feather. Even though I had never visited the place in my life, I had a sense of being in New Mexico.

Then, in my vision, I was swiftly transported to the Canadian Rockies, beside a great lake. I 'saw' myself on the side of the bank, now a very old woman with long grey hair, like gossamer, flailing in the breeze. My entire body rocked back and forth, arms forming a tight cross against my chest as

I watched myself wailing … wailing as the mortal remains of my dead husband were being ferried across the great lake in a stone canoe. Against the backdrop of a pearl grey sky, I watched as his spirit arose and departed from his body, carried on the wind like a billion tiny sparks of light …

When I returned to full waking consciousness, I felt a depth of calm and stillness I'd never known before. It was customary in circle to 'share' insights or information with the rest of the group. This time, however, I felt the need to be silent, as though what I had 'seen' was so deeply personal that to impart it would feel like a betrayal.

I felt I'd been blessed.

I knew it wasn't necessary to 'prove' the vision with historical data, for it was the healing that the memory subsequently brought to my life that was important. Even so, I was curious. I knew very little about Native American Indian culture and, whilst browsing through the historical bookshelves of my local library a few days later, I picked up this information:

The Apache and Navaho tribes spread across the plains of New Mexico, living in stone or clay dwellings called 'pueblos' which were considered advanced for their time. They wore breech cloth, leggings, moccasins and feather or rabbit robe. Apparently, 'fetishes' were talismans of good luck, exchanged between tribal members. Eagle feathers were used as part of the battle dress. The male in the household was dominant and polygamy was practised in the marriage. The Navaho male was very 'warrior-like'.

Two further pieces of information stuck in my memory: firstly, the Navaho male reached 'manhood' at the age of sixteen on the eve of a fast. I remembered how Jai had rung me in the late afternoon on the 16th March to ask if I wanted to take part in the fast the next day. The other thing I made a note of at the time was that the people imagined 'the soul must be ferried over a great water in a stone canoe …'

My findings confirmed what I already *knew*: that I'd

accessed a soul memory far too significant to ignore. As a spiritualist, I was already convinced that the soul incarnates lifetime after lifetime, often reconnecting with our karmic counterpart to complete unfinished business or release painful or negative emotions that no longer serve us.

Strangely this vision was to have an even greater impact on me when I returned to it later in my healing and at another place in this book.

In late March 1999, our sessions were interrupted as I took a well-earned rest with my then seven-year-old daughter, Jessica, at the resort of Santa Ponsa in Majorca. The temperature was a comfortable seventy degrees and our days were taken up around the hotel pool as we swam, read and basked in the sun's healing rays. I returned home on Good Friday, April 2nd 1999, tanned and relaxed.

Within a few short hours of being back in the flat I already had that 'post holiday blues' feeling. Outside, the blinding brilliance of the sky beckoned. The temperature was unusually high for the time of the year and, within a couple of hours, I'd thrown together a few clean clothes and provisions and hooked up my little caravan. Without a backward glance at the two suitcases of dirty clothes that lay unpacked in the hallway, I headed for the Malvern Hills.

I was unaware at this point that my life was about to change forever.

Malvern was for me a kind of retreat, a place of peaceful stillness. Wild hillsides adorned with a random array of flowers and grasses formed a spectacular backdrop to our campsite at Castlemorton. A mere fifty miles from my home in Sutton Coldfield, this was nature in extreme contrast to the bustle of city life and at its most glorious.

Easter Saturday was taken up with one of my uncle's famously long country walks. On Sunday, my dad drove

Jessica and myself to the Priory Church in the centre of the town.

On this particular Easter Sunday I sat down and said a prayer. Not just because I was in church but because I have *always* prayed. As a small child I prayed a lot. I remember a feeling, a kind of 'knowingness' that something existed that was infinitely greater, beyond that which I could see in the physical universe. I don't know where this feeling came from; I never stopped to question it. I just *knew* there was a God.

In times of sorrow and great difficulty, I always prayed harder and it was as though my faith released me from my suffering. Just as if God somehow reached into my life and lit the way forward in a field of darkness. With experience and maturity and a conversion to the spiritualist faith came the certain knowledge that God exists in all things and is simply love … in all its boundless glory.

On this occasion my prayer was for some direction in my life. I knew I wanted to be of service, but my greater purpose was unclear to me…and, as always, I prayed for more peace and understanding in the world. In the quiet, cool stillness, a voice, not inside my head but somewhere outside me, said, "Give up the meat."

Just that. No blinding vision, just a voice, clear and distinct.

Nothing extraordinary in this, you may think, just a simple prayer answered. Yet add to this something that happened to my brother, Martin, at the same time, on the same day, and you cannot help but ponder if more than just coincidence was at work here.

Despite the ten-year age gap between us, Martin and I had developed a deep closeness ever since embarking on our world trip together in 1991. In my meditations I have 'seen' that we have shared many incarnations together and he too had long come to accept the power of synchronicity in his own life. I was unaware that he had gone away for the Easter weekend to the Lake District. On his return, he related this experience to me.

"I was in a deeply relaxed state," he said, "and in my mind's eye a vivid image containing all the animals of the kingdom unfolded before me. They seemed to be coming at me from all angles. I was suddenly repulsed at the sight of myself in a loincloth, poised with a spear, aimed right at my target, ready to go for the kill. Then they all seemed to halt right in front of me except one, an elephant. It moved closer, then stood still, bold, defiant, just looking down at me. I remember thinking, why an elephant? Elephants are herbivorous. That was it! When I awoke I was struck by an overwhelming feeling that I should stop eating meat."

Two events on the same day, at the same time, miles apart and yet so amazingly connected that they actually produce the same outcome. How do you explain this? I don't believe it was mere coincidence. I believe these events were *meant* to happen, just as much as the paths of two people are simply destined to cross.

I was missing my soul mate.

Travelling home from Malvern, my thoughts were filled with Jai. The more I saw of him, the more convinced I was that our lives were somehow interwoven. I had missed our philosophical discussions and now I was eager to tell him of my newfound vegetarian status. My opportunity came the next day, when he kept a previously arranged appointment for an Indian head massage. He told me how much he admired my decision to become a vegetarian; that in God's eyes it was always the *intention* that counted and that I should not be too hard on myself if I slipped.

"After all," he remarked, "people in the West are used to meat-based diets. It must be extremely hard to give that up."

I couldn't have known at the time the significant effect this decision was to have on my life. I took his casual remarks to be sensitivity on his part. In retrospect I now know that if I were *still* eating meat, Jai and I would never have formed a relationship. It was as simple as that. Ironically, I found nothing easier in my life than my decision to stop eating meat and, from that day to this, I have never slipped.

We talked non-stop, positively basking in each other's energy. Jai commented on how much a suntan suited me and that I was 'glowing' with health as a result of my break. I felt a particular closeness to him on this day, maybe born out of the enforced absence. It was always customary practice at the end of the head massage to allow the client to 'lean' his or her head gently backwards against the therapist's upper chest.

On this occasion, I let him 'rest' a while longer than was usual. There was nothing sexual or intimate in this action on my part, just a closeness born of a deeper familiarity. But, in the months that followed, it was an action that was to have brutal implications on our relationship. Although I didn't know it at the time, it transpired that this session was to be our last 'professional' meeting as client and therapist.

Over the next few days, the telephone became glued to my ear. Jai rang me at every opportunity, often after he'd closed the shop at midnight. We talked for hours, sharing our past experiences, our daily happenings, our insights and our dreams, the bond between us growing ever closer.

When one person is moved to share their most traumatic memories with another, a unique and unshakeable link is created between them. I knew, in the dark recesses of his mind, Jai nurtured a deeper pain that he had not fully come to terms with in his adult life ...*his father's suicide.*

How we react to such a traumatic event is indicative of whether or not we have come to terms with it. Accepting it and moving through the pain associated with it creates enormous inner strength and deep healing usually follows. Failure to come to terms with trauma of this nature causes the mind to repress the memories attached to it. In my psychotherapeutic work I use the analogy of the 'onion layers', as each painful event gets layered on top of the one before. The survival mechanisms we develop somehow get us through our lives.

Ironically I was to write a profile on Jai in the coming months using these words, *'His early upbringing was hard and unforgiving but the scars of endurance from his early childhood and teens only served to mould the deeply philosophical man he is today'*. They were words that would come back to haunt me.

Although Jai talked about his past with relative ease, I had no conception of the despair he was masking. Neither could I have known the impact that this unresolved pain would have on his life when it eventually sought its release.

Despite the growing closeness, still neither of us spoke about how we *felt* about each other. Underneath, I began to silently suppress the guilt that welled up inside me, guilt born out of a mutual *need* to share our innermost thoughts.

The turning point in our relationship came on Thursday, 8th April 1999. I'd encouraged Jai to make an appointment on this day with a 'soul reader' by the name of Kenny Pask. I'd received a 'reading' from Kenny a year earlier and during one of our conversations I had told Jaya all about it. Kenny is an extremely talented and gifted individual whose work has taken him the length and breadth of the country and who now lives and works in Spain.

Kenny has the ability to 'see' into the akasha, the etheric memory of the universal energy field. In esoteric terms the information held in this 'energetic memory bank' is called the akashic record and holds the energetic 'blueprint' of our every thought, deed and action that has ever happened, or indeed ever will happen. Working in tune with the akasha, a gifted person may 'access' past life memory or information stored in the 'auric field' and impart it so as to enhance an individual's spiritual growth. I'd found my session with Kenny fascinating and inspiring. He told me many things that on a deeper level I already *knew*, such as some of my previous incarnations and my soul's deeper purpose.

Now Jai was telephoning me to ask if he could come round to my flat. He was eager to share the contents of his 'reading' from Kenny. Listening to the tape together back then, I remember it was full of positive and encouraging statements. Kenny told him that his spiritual path would eventually lead him to teach, that others would benefit from his deep philosophy and that much could be achieved by helping his 'own people'.

Jai interpreted this to be the origins of his birthplace, Uganda, and that it was his destiny to help the poor, starving and needy people of the Third World countries. "Krishna is behind you and Sai Baba is standing right next to you," Kenny said in his down-to-earth Norfolk lilt. "With those two guys guiding you all the way," he added, "how can you possibly fail?"

Those words were to take on a prophetic meaning in the months that followed...

That same night I gave Jai a gift. It was a small sandstone elephant. I had bought a pair at a craft centre two days earlier, remembering he'd told me it was his birthday that day, April 6th. I kept the other elephant for myself. The elephant has deep symbolic significance in traditional Hindu culture, believed to be 'the remover of obstacles' and generally considered a positive symbol. Jai was deeply touched by the gesture, but commented that he rarely celebrated his birthday in the traditional sense ...*It was also the anniversary of his mother's death.*

As he stood by the door ready to leave later that evening, I hugged him tightly.

I don't think I will ever forget being encircled in the grip of his powerful arms and the feeling it gave me.

I wanted the moment to last forever.

It was a mid-morning telephone call a week later.

"You know I missed you while you were away," he said. I remember mumbling something completely irrelevant about getting back on track with our sessions and he interrupted me.

"No, Jacky, I mean I *really* … missed you."

We had never before spoken about our feelings towards each other and now these emotionally charged words, delivered with such sincerity, literally brought me to my knees. I sat on the floor in the hallway of my flat, leaned against the wall and silently cried.

"I don't know why but I feel strangely protective towards you," were the only other words I can remember him saying between my muffled sobs that day.

I knew then only one thing, and the one thing I'd been hopelessly denying for months: that I was falling for this man and I was utterly powerless to do anything about it …

CHAPTER TWO: 'LOVE IS BLIND'

'When love beckons to you, follow him;
Though his ways are hard and steep.
And when his wings enfold you yield to him; Though the sword
Hidden amongst his pinions may wound you.
And when he speaks to you believe in him;
Though his voice may shatter your dreams
as the north wind lays waste the garden'

Kahlil Gibran (The Prophet)

Telling me he'd *missed* me was hardly a declaration of undying love on Jai's part! Yet hidden beneath those words there was a sentiment, so loving and tender, it made my heart stop, just for a second. From this moment on, my life was to change beyond recognition; I'd fallen *passionately* in love with this man.

And love is blind.

To say our sexual relationship began in a most unorthodox way and to say no more would leave you, as the reader, wondering … *And me, less than honest with myself.*

Actually, Jai put a proposal to me: that we practice 'Tantra'.

So there are no misunderstandings here, this was not a bolt out of the blue to me. We'd discussed it, although I confess my knowledge was sketchy. I knew only that it is a wholly disciplined path that combines meditation with sexual practices. In saying this little about it, I do the spiritual practice of Tantra a grave injustice.

It wasn't quite the proposal of a practised seducer and yet there was something so incredibly seductive in Jai's unshakeable confidence. He believed wholeheartedly in everything he did … and said.

Every ounce of rationality went out of my mind as all those months of denial just melted into blazing desire.

I wanted him.

"Yes," I said.

Lord Byron once wrote, 'Pleasure's a sin and sometimes sin's a pleasure'.

Up until that day on Monday 12th April, the only sin had been in my thoughts. We hadn't even held hands.

Now we were making love.

If you were to ask me at what point did I *know* Jai and I would become lovers I would not be able to answer. But, on some level, I *did* know.

For a brief period, our lovemaking was to take on a strangely ritualistic quality. He insisted on white cotton bed linen. I didn't have any, so he bought some, pristine white and new. He lit candles and incense … and placed them directly in front of a picture of Sai Baba. I didn't question his rituals; there was something wholly sacred and beautiful in what he was doing. After all, he rationalized, God *was* everywhere … and sexual arousal between two human beings was merely an expression of energy.

It's a known fact that many profound spiritual experiences have occurred during intense and overwhelming lovemaking and, if practiced properly and reverently, Tantra allows us to open the energy channels within our bodies. This can lead to heightened sexual awareness and expanded states of consciousness. In much the same way that the spiritual seeker yearns for enlightenment, so human beings naturally yearn for ecstatic union with each other. As such, Tantra can be viewed as a pathway leading us towards union with the divine.

Whether in our lovemaking we were actually achieving Tantra or not wasn't important; there was no doubt that our *intention* and our approach to it was wholly reverent. It was an approach that seemed to suit Jai, whose intensity and abundance of energy could be channelled through sex whilst still allowing him to feel close to God.

The thing was that Jai had already *found* God. Quite literally.

Not only had he found Him, but he had also *recognized* Him to be God. Something Jai believed every other mortal on the planet had failed to do and, just as if this unique knowledge gave him right of ownership... somehow he believed God belonged to *him* now.

Quite simply, Jai had the whole God issue worked out. God was residing in the form of Sri Sathya Sai Baba, the spiritual teacher, born in Puttaparthi, Southern India, in 1926.

Jai had told me during one of our therapy sessions about his visit to Sai Baba's ashram in Prasanti Nilayam, Puttaparthi. He had interrupted his honeymoon to visit there with his new wife some ten years ago. As Sai Baba moved between the crowds giving *darshan* (blessings), Jai had fixed his glance. 'Are you *really* God?' he'd asked of him earnestly in his mind. Baba's look ripped through him like a razor-sharp blade. 'Yes, I am,' came back the silent response ... And in that moment of searching, touched by divinity, Jai was paralyzed with fear ... the overwhelming fear of his own unworthiness.

I'd heard about Sai Baba before I met Jai. Devotees will tell you that when you are moved to investigate this religious teacher, relatively unknown in the West, that this is Baba himself giving you his 'calling card'. My 'calling card' came when Ann, my tutor with the College of Healing, passed me a book to read entitled 'Sai Baba, The Holy Man and The Psychiatrist' by Dr Samuel H Sandweiss. I confess it piqued my interest in this Indian mystic known for his healing powers and ability to materialize objects out of thin air.

Jai invited me to the Sai Temple in Perry Barr, Birmingham. I was moved by the warmth and devotion of the people and found myself drawn to attend worship there every Friday evening. Worship took the form of bhajans, the singing of devotional hymns to God.

There was something about the rituals and beliefs of the Hindu faith that deeply resonated with me. It was like 'coming home'. I was being reminded of the sacredness and interconnectedness of all beings, the eternal cycle of birth, death and rebirth (samsara) and the path of liberation (release from samsara). Sai Baba devotees are encouraged to live by the five 'Human Values': Right Conduct, Truth, Love, Peace and Non-Violence. They personified a way of being that I constantly strived for in my daily life and a way of being which brought me closer to God.

Most of the wonderful experiences that have transpired on my spiritual journey were as a result of my willingness to remain 'open' to different religions and alternative religious practices. After all, 'all roads lead to one'. Although I'd discovered a sense of comfort and peace with the spiritualist movement, I didn't feel exclusively attached to it. Its basic tenets, the notion of the soul progressing through lessons and learning over many lifetimes, seemed to fit with me. I also liked the idea of 'personal responsibility': that we are each responsible for our actions and that in those actions there is a consequence: *what we give out, we get back*.

But these were also the basic tenets of the Hindu faith and accepted by Sai Baba devotees. Recently, Sai Baba, the man, has come under a great deal of public and personal scrutiny. The nature of this bad press has some relevance later in my story. For now, whatever feelings I may have had toward the 'messenger', Sai Baba himself, his 'message' was timeless. That is, 'There is only one language, the language of love'.

The *extent* however to which Sai Baba was to invade *every* area of our lives from this point on ... I could not possibly have imagined.

For Jai's love of Sai was like a time bomb waiting to explode ...

For the next six weeks, we hid our love from the outside world. But there was a sparkle and exuberance about me that was difficult to conceal, from those closest to me at least. The first time we publicly displayed our feelings for each other was at the end of May, at a birthday party for one of my brother's friends. That evening I clung to Jai like a limpet clings to rock. It was the first time he stayed with me … all night.

It was the night that was to seal the end of his marriage.

Five days later, on Thursday, 27th May 1999, Jai arrived on my doorstep at midnight, bin bags in tow. I will not disclose the chain of events that led up to this finale, so as to exclude his wife from my story. I have prayed many times since for her forgiveness.

That night there was a most ferocious storm. The sight of this awesome spectacle is etched in my memory. As I watched the lightning dance across the horizon from the elevated position of my fourth-storey windows, I could well understand how, in ancient times, violent storms were considered to have religious connotations. In Greek mythology, thunderbolts were thought to have been thrown by Zeus, father of all Gods, to punish the arrogant.

As I listened to the roar of thunder pierce the night sky, I couldn't help but wonder if God was indeed angry with us …

How Jai came to involve me so deeply in such a short space of time is a question I've asked myself a thousand times. But deeply involved I was.

And so was my daughter, Jessica. In a nutshell, Jai literally 'steamrollered' into her life. Jess had met him only three or four times before he began living with us permanently and she was to comment a year later at the age of eight, "Mum, he was right in my face from day one."

Up until this point, Jess and I had enjoyed a particularly close relationship. First time motherhood at the age of thirty-six had literally struck me like a thunderbolt and I admit the whole 'baby talk' stage didn't come naturally to me. Rightly or wrongly, I communicated to Jess in a manner far beyond her years. Perhaps this was because she was incredibly bright and confident from an early age, excelling in her school work and displaying a natural ability towards music, dance and drama.

By the time she was about four or five, I was heavily involved with the healing arts and talking openly to her about meditation, our energetic make-up, celestial beings, the spirit realms and God. She always seemed comfortable with my explanations. I remember a time at the age of six when she proudly displayed her collection of polished stones and crystals to a prospective client, recounting their names and healing properties!

The greatest trauma in Jess's life came at the age of four and a half, when in 1996, my mother died from lung cancer. My younger sister and I helped nurse her from the time of diagnosis until her death several months later. The pain of watching my mother suffer in such a way stayed with me for a very long time. When I look back on that time now, I take comfort in the knowledge that, in *losing* my mother, I *found* myself in that my mother's death served as the catalyst for my own healing. Knowing that I was loved and cherished gave me the strength to cope as well as grow from such an experience.

And my mother *knew* how to love.

To Jess, she was a second 'mum' in the absence of any 'real' father. Jess *adored* her. We assume that children are resilient, that they will 'get over things' much quicker than adults. I was far from prepared for the impact this loss was to have on my daughter at the time and the pain that it has caused her in her life, even today.

Children, especially when they are small, thrive on normality and routine. Change, particularly in the wake of trauma, is detestable to them and now here I was, two years after her beloved nanny dying, thrusting a potential stranger into her midst and expecting her to embrace him with open arms. The last thing Jess needed in her life back then was a man she hardly knew laying down the law, as Jai often did, although in his mind with the best of intentions. At worst, their relationship became a battle of wills; at best, an unspoken tolerance of each other.

Despite this, for a while at least, our lives seemed blissfully idyllic.

Shortly after Jai moved in with us, my landlady served notice on the flat I was renting and we were forced to seek new accommodation. We took a year-long lease on a beautiful, furnished, four bedroom, detached house in Sutton Coldfield. It was a residence that far exceeded my expectations.

I completed the year-long Hypno/Psychotherapy course I'd begun with Centre Training School, passing the examinations with merit and I started to attract clients to work with. It was the creative rewarding work I was born to do and I truly felt I was being of service. With the financial security that appeared to come with Jai, it seemed that, for the first time in many years, I was creating the kind of life I'd dreamed of.

Looking back on those first early months of our relationship, I realize I was intoxicated by Jai. His was an intense, all-consuming love and I felt *adored* by him. Equally he positively *basked* in the attention I gave him. It's a wonderful feeling to find a partner whose beliefs and dreams echo your own. Even though I knew a time would come when inevitably our perceptions and ideas were bound to clash, I believed our love was so deep and real that it could weather any storms of disagreement in our relationship. The truth was I became enmeshed in Jai's world.

And his was a world of dreams.

Jai's greatest dream of all was to make his mark in the

business world. It seemed to me he'd already done it, having four profitable News and Convenience shops in a 'shared' partnership with his brother. A shared partnership it might have been, but they certainly didn't share common business aims and I was soon to discover that Jai's relationship with his brother was as complex and unstable as were his business dealings.

And, in those, I believed and trusted everything he told me.

Jai loved the world of business. He was never happier than when bouncing an idea around with a colleague and then trying to enlist their help and cooperation to get it off the ground. He once told me he spent his days 'hustling'. I had no idea what that meant. I just knew I'd never met anyone before him who seemed to have made an occupation out of the pursuit of wealth. It was what drove him through his sixteen-hour days; the endless ring of the cash register recording yet another sale and counting the day's takings lain out on the dining room table in our home until the early hours of the morning.

It puzzled me how he reconciled his love of money with his spiritual beliefs. "The world *needs* to see me as wealthy and successful," he exclaimed. "How else can I help the starving millions?" It seemed a noble and worthy claim and by no means self-serving.

But then there was the gambling.

He made no secret of it, at least not at first. I wasn't aware, however, of the *extent* to which he gambled. Casually asking him one day why he did it, he simply replied, "For the buzz." It wasn't something I had personal experience of; no one in my family or anyone I had ever known had gambled. I did know from my psychotherapeutic work that it stemmed from a deep-rooted pattern of emotional deprivation … and it was most certainly addictive. The gambler's belief system is somewhat hedonistic, 'I want it all and I want it now' and there was no doubt that Jai wanted it all … patience was not a word that entered his vocabulary.

Within two months of our living together, he'd traded his battered old car for an almost new black Saab convertible that bore the personal plate JAI 900V. He led me to believe it was bought and paid for; that he had called in a debt, a twenty-five thousand pound debt to be precise, for which the car was the pay-off.

Although it was obviously a beautiful machine, Jai knew me well enough to know that the trappings of the material world held no interest for me; a car was a car after all. Several times over he told me that it was not to satisfy any personal need in *him*. "People make judgments," he would say. "It is a need in *them* to see me with a car of this standard." Status symbol or no, it was obvious from the first day of ownership that Jai *adored* that car.

If there was one other thing that matched Jai's love of the casino, it was his love of fast driving. Not that he was particularly reckless, but he did like to push the limits and take unnecessary risks. A couple of times the police followed him home having spotted him jumping a red light or exceeding the speed limit. He liked to live life in the fast lane and yet, somehow, he always managed to use his sharp wit and undeniable charm to manipulate a situation to his advantage. It began to dawn on me that he was … *a born actor.*

He had this amazing knack of being able to diffuse in seconds a potentially volatile situation, such as my frustration at his inability to turn up on time for *anything*. It was hard to resist his boyish charm, the adulation and the flattery … and an armful of roses, *always*.

Initially the highs far outweighed the lows. Jai had the ability to live in the moment unequalled by anyone I had ever met and I found his spontaneity exciting and refreshing. Eating out with him was always a treat. He knew every restaurant that served high quality, authentic Indian food and he knew how much I loved Indian cuisine. His seemingly never-ending circle of friends ensured there were always 'extras' at the table. Oddly though, despite Jai's popularity, I don't remember a single time when someone else picked up the bill.

In those early days I suppose I was desperate for my family and friends to embrace and accept him the way I had done. How could anyone fail to see the qualities in the man I had fallen in love with? How could they fail to be seduced as I had been by his charisma, his enthusiasm for life, his generosity, his strong beliefs and his love for humanity?

Walking away from the school entrance one day, I was finding it hard to conceal the look of joyful contentment on my face. I was a woman 'in love' after all. An acquaintance turned to me and said, "I hear you have a new man in your life, Jacky. It shows."

My face broke into a delicious smile.

"How have your family accepted him?" she went on, "y'know, because he's …"

"Because he's what?" I enquired back.

"Well … because he's … *Asian*," she added nervously.

"Oh … is he?" I said, fixing her gaze. "I hadn't noticed."

Jai's origins weren't an issue with most … except my dad. To say my dad embraced him with warmth would be an overstatement. He was polite and pleasant, but guarded. My dad believed he'd weighed Jai up from the first evening he spent in his company, the night of my forty-third birthday.

I'd booked a table at a Greek restaurant in the city centre for a small group of family and friends. I'd chosen the venue more for the atmosphere rather than the food; the Greek dancing and traditional plate smashing routine was always a good party starter. The evening finished around midnight and everyone went their separate ways, except my dad. Jai had asked him to accompany us to the casino.

It was my first time in a casino that night and I suppose a part of me was intrigued. My dad and I watched as Jai played the tables, three or four at a time, placing bets of a hundred pounds in one go. In the time it took us to consume one drink, maybe half an hour or so, he'd lost over a thousand pounds.

Whether it was his nonchalant attitude to the money, or the seemingly arrogant air with which he played the tables that irritated my father that night, I'm not really sure. I know one thing: my dad was never to forget that first evening and the low opinion he'd formed of Jai.

Ironically, when I look back I see that all Jai was trying to do was *impress* my father. I underestimated how much of a challenge it was for him to cross the cultural bridges and fit into my world. After all, I'd readily accepted his world and felt quite at ease with his customs and traditions. I had no idea at the time that he'd spent most of his life simply 'trying to fit in'.

Although Jai volunteered little about his childhood in those early days, what he did volunteer was crucial to gaining a full understanding of the man I'd come to view as both complex and fascinating.

He had suffered much emotional pain and he knew all about *oppression*. His early upbringing had only served to teach him that we live in a society contaminated with prejudice and hatred. Being forced to leave his Ugandan homeland under the Amin exodus in 1972 had undoubtedly left its scars and most would have buckled under the tests and trials that life threw his way.

Yet it was as though Jai used every harsh experience to 'sharpen his sword' and strengthen his character. I marvelled at his ability to bounce back despite all his setbacks and difficulties. Listening to him, I concluded that this must be due, in part, to his sheer optimism, his self-confidence … and his unwavering belief in God.

I listened to Jai a great deal in those early days, talking endlessly about his beliefs, his goals, his dreams and his aspirations. It's not easy to truly 'listen', especially when we don't feel like it. Often my therapeutic work left me feeling tired and drained and sometimes I would crawl into bed before he came home just to catch an hour or two of sleep. I'd come to know and *accept* that whatever time, day or night, he would demand my attention. "I need to bounce an idea off you," he'd say.

I wish back then I'd listened more to Jai ... and that maybe by paying attention to the spaces between the words ... I might have heard what he was *really* saying.

In hindsight, all the vital clues were there. When we're so emotionally involved with another person, we tend to overlook a flaw in their character or a strange pattern of behaviour. It's the 'rose-tinted spectacles' scenario when, for a brief while, our adoration for a person allows our judgment to become hazy. I couldn't fathom why he felt the constant need to test me.

Once, toward the end of our therapeutic relationship, I was forced to cancel an appointment he'd booked that day. "I had a narrow escape on the road yesterday," I told him on the telephone. "One of my tyres is practically bald and I have to get it changed right away." He seemed fine with the explanation albeit a little disappointed that our appointment wouldn't go ahead as scheduled. Later that afternoon, I happened to glance out of my flat window to see him walking around my car, examining my tyres. It was more a 'feeling' I got as I watched him, a sort of 'hunch'. He'd suspected that I'd lied to him.

When we distrust another human being, we are really saying something about ourselves. Somewhere along the line, we placed our trust in another person and that trust was abused in some way. Jai seemed to have trust issues in just about every area of his life. He didn't trust his employees, his business associates, his friends, even his own brother. "My whole life I've put my trust in people, Jacky, and they've always let me down," he told me.

And so the tests kept coming.

I once heard him on his mobile to his best friend. "I can't fault her, man. She *must* be an angel. I keep testing her and she keeps passing."

I suppose I ignored it just as I ignored a great deal of Jai's odd behaviour, - until one evening which set the alarm bells ringing in my head.

Jai rarely took time out from his punishing work schedule to do the things 'normal loving couples' do, like staying in with a takeaway and a good movie. When we did, I treasured those moments. The rest of the time I spent waiting around like some lovesick puppy for his key to go in the door, a feast prepared for him, even at two in the morning.

On this particular evening, I was lounging on the sofa, my head in his lap and tired from the day. My back gave out the odd twinge of pain from carrying out numerous massage treatments that day. "Get me a cold drink, will you, please?" he asked in a demanding tone.

I whined and asked if he could get it himself, a little irritated by his lack of sympathy for my aching back. After about fifteen minutes or so, he rolled me off his lap, got up, and poured himself a large glass of squash. I thought nothing more of it.

But during the next three or four days, his mood grew increasingly sombre, almost cold. Everything I asked him was met with a 'yes' or 'no' answer. I was unaware of anything I'd done to upset him and was as loving and attentive as I had been from the start of our relationship. That Friday evening, we'd planned to go to bhajans at the Sai Temple as usual and then, after the service, spend the remainder of the evening together over a meal in town. Knowing we were going out, I'd made an extra special effort to dress up.

Jai *always* liked to talk in the car; it was his favourite space to 'bounce ideas' but, on this particular evening, during the journey there, I was given the silent treatment. Finally I broke it, asking him what was wrong and why he was being so off with me.

"Come to think of it," I remarked, "you've been moody since last Tuesday when we stayed in together".

He threw me an intense look and his jaw stiffened. "You know what it's about," he yelled. *"Think hard."*

"No, I don't!" I felt a sickly knot rise in the pit of my stomach. "All I can think of is you went strange on me when I refused to get up and get you the …" my voice trailed off. "Please don't tell me all this is about a cold drink?" I could hardly believe the absurdity of the question.

It was our first blazing row. Up until that point there had been minor disagreements, but this now escalated into something I could barely comprehend. Now *everything* was wrong with me. Clearly I didn't respect him enough; otherwise I would know that it was a woman's role to please her man. This was what was wrong with the whole world; women had forgotten how to treat their men properly.

Obviously something had gone wrong in my upbringing; probably my father's fault for not correcting me enough. As for what I was wearing, did I not know what was considered appropriate dress for bhajans? Did I not understand that Indian women are humble souls? Did I have any idea how inferior it made them feel, seeing me so glamorously dressed? What on earth was I thinking of wearing an ankle-length sarong skirt and heels? But then, if I didn't show respect for my father, how could I show it to my man. Even worse, how could I possibly know how to show respect to God. It was a vicious torrent of criticism that went on …and on … and on.

I felt like I'd been showered with machine-gun bullets.

There was no meal after bhajans. As he pulled into the drive at our home, I'd barely exited the passenger seat before he sped off at breakneck speed into the night. I was left feeling as though I'd been punished for some grave and unforgivable misdemeanour.

In truth, all I had done in his eyes … was fail the test.

It was barely daylight when I was awoken the next morning by Jai, standing imposingly over me by the side of the bed. My first thought was to ask him where he'd been all night but I quickly reviewed that; *maybe not a good idea.* He was as impeccably dressed as he had been the night before. The only telltale sign of the passage of time was the light stubble of early growth around his chin line.

"Hello," he said cheerily, "how's my queen?"

Neither of us mentioned the row the night before. His mood was relaxed, almost buoyant. Within twenty minutes he had showered and was dressed in casual clothes and we were headed for the park.

The mood swings, the intense emotions and the inexplicable anger.

It was to become an all too familiar pattern.

When you are so in love with a person, I guess it makes it much easier to forgive their faults. Back then I put Jai's irrational mood swings down to the intensity with which he approached *every* area of his life. He explained it away as 'his passionate nature'. Certainly the passion had its compensations… life was never dull!

One thing Jai was fiercely passionate about was Dove St News. Although I was flattered by it, it puzzled me that someone who appeared to have such a sound command of the business world went out of his way to seek my opinions on *everything*.

Granted, my extensive experience in human resources had taught me much about people management and a business is only as good as the people in it. Jai's main problem seemed to be in controlling staff turnover. That's not to say that he was a poor man-manager, quite the reverse; I'd never encountered such a strong leader and natural motivator of people as I'd found in Jai. He pushed his staff to the limits and, when occasionally he found an individual who rose to the challenge, he gave back wholeheartedly.

On the other hand, when someone let him down, badmouthed him, or stole from him as they often did, he absorbed it as a personal injury and showed no mercy. I quickly learned that Jai was not someone you would ever want to make an enemy of.

I devised a staff induction programme for him and helped him set up a training initiative to combat his shops' shrinkage problems. Despite the growing turnover, his natural wastage, breakages and theft problems were extraordinarily high. Most of the time he seemed to turn a blind eye to it, concentrating more on generating sales volume than tackling the problem of what he was losing in profit terms behind the scenes.

As an 'ideas man', Jai was extraordinarily talented and often willing to forego the daily grind to concentrate on some great new idea he'd had to increase sales volume. Watching him, as I often did, at the 'helm', he was like a captain steering his ship, dexterous, vigilant, sharp and full of energy, and his greatest skill was the way in which he handled his customers. He could bring a smile to the face of someone who that very morning had buried their grandmother!

In the brief contact that took place in a single transaction, Jai had the ability to make you feel as though you were the most important person in the world... and his customers loved him for it. Often his pricing policy attracted criticism, even insults, and yet he remained undeterred. Somehow he always managed to win them over with his sharp wit and candid humour... and few could resist that mischievous and disarming smile.

Jai was indeed clever.

By far the cleverest manipulator of people I'd ever encountered.

In the beginning I supported every business idea he had. He relied on my encouragement and adulation and positively thrived on the challenges he set for himself. He was without doubt a 'visionary' and I found myself telling him so *often*. That's why it puzzled me when his ideas often failed to come to fruition, as though there was something lacking in his ability to turn them into reality.

I suppose I failed to realize in those early days the detrimental effect that being a bankrupt played in terms of his reputation and, ultimately, his progress. The simple truth was that Jai relied heavily on others' financial investments to launch his business projects. And there weren't many people who shared his 'fly by the seat of your pants' attitude towards business. Occasionally he found one, someone who was prepared to trust his instincts, even if for Jai that meant, in doing so, it placed him heavily and forever in their debt. It wasn't a position he liked.

Not one bit.

August 1999, less than six months into our relationship together, marked an event which was to alter the course of Jai's life forever...

Dove St News was voted an award for 'Best Marketing Strategy' in the News and Convenience category, sponsored by Westway's food chain. The nominations were linked to outstanding growth in the industry over the previous year and there was little doubt that Jai's flagship was producing phenomenal results. Westway's were intrigued; surely this could only be achieved through strategic planning and sound business acumen?

Out of the hundreds of retail outlets nominated for awards, three were chosen to participate in the production of a short film outlining their personal success story ... Dove St News was one of them. It was a prestigious award giving Dove St a professional boost and putting Jai firmly in the retail spotlight.

I'd come to know Jai's city centre shop a little over the many hours I'd spent patiently waiting in the car after his 'quick five minute pop-in' would turn into an hour or two. City street life at night was mesmerizing. I'd watch the endless stream of humanity, as various in types as the products on sale, constantly flowing until closure at midnight.

The shop interior was hardly a grand display of retail elegance. Without a night shift operating, the enormous sales volume barely left time for stock replacement, never mind cleaning and tidying.

Yet Dove St had a magnetism I cannot explain. With its orange neon sign, it shone like a beacon in the darkness ... *drawing its customers to it with an undeniably palpable and potent energy.*

Now the media crew were in place and, unable to find an aesthetic reason for its operational success, they turned their attention to the man at the helm, Jai. He must after all be doing something right. How else could he achieve such an enormous sales volume?

Suddenly Jai had a camera thrust in his face at every opportunity, following him around 'in action' for several days. Soon they began to build a personal profile on the man who was fast becoming an enigma to them; captivated by his boundless energy, his positive outlook on life and his deep philosophical truths.

The decision to film Jai in his private surroundings was unplanned. But now the film crew were entering our home, driven in the pursuit to gain another angle on the man whose marketing prowess both intrigued and mystified them.

Jai positively basked in the attention. I'd never seen anyone so at ease with the camera. Asked what his five year projected business plan was, he confidently replied, "We *will* have nine hundred shops." It was an ambitious aim considering the present business stood at five outlets and one that justifiably might have invited criticism. Yet behind the camera lens, with confidence and charisma positively oozing from him, no one dared to challenge Jai's unwavering self-belief.

I was as guilty of being in awe of him that day as the rest of the film crew. They got an interview they hadn't bargained for; loaded with Jai's deep-rooted philosophical views on life and death, success and failure, human relationships and family values ... and, above all, his special relationship with God. Several hours of filming later, the raw material was on its way to the cutting room. The result would be a ten-minute intensive interview, highlighting the key ingredients to Dove St News, and Jai's personal success story.

It was a 'wrap' as they say in movie speak ... *and the day that marked the beginning of Jai's love affair with the camera.*

It didn't cross my mind that I wouldn't receive an automatic invitation to attend the awards ceremony planned for late that October. But, oddly, Jai had to use all his powers of persuasion to obtain a ticket for me; a ticket that meant an all-expenses-paid weekend in London. Naturally Jai's brother, Nara, was part of the celebration; theirs was a shared partnership and the success of Dove St was also due in part to Nara.

Jai explained this oversight to me as 'petty jealousies'. "The world can't bear to see how much in love we are. People are jealous of our relationship," he said. An irrational explanation to say the least and yet, in Jai's eyes, the only conceivable one to explain the lack of courtesy towards me.

We travelled down to London the night before the ceremony, enjoying a romantic dinner at a Cantonese restaurant on the banks of the Thames. I felt closer to Jai on that night than I'd ever felt.

The next day at the ceremony we found ourselves seated at opposite ends of the auditorium. Guests were apparently not allowed to sit next to recipients of an award, even though there was ample seating for us to sit together. I think it irked him more than me. Prior to the day, Jai had been at a loss to know what to wear for the occasion. I encouraged him to wear 'traditional dress', as befitting his culture. He chose to wear his 'wedding ensemble', a cream and gold embroidered long tunic and loose fitting trousers that he'd worn on his wedding day to his first wife. It didn't occur to me to mind. My classically tailored cornflower yellow dress and jacket perfectly complemented his suit.

When we emerged from the hotel room into the foyer that morning, I wasn't sure whether it was admiring glances we were attracting or rather that we stuck out like sore thumbs. Everyone else was dressed in business black! We didn't care. Jai looked every inch like an Indian prince and I was his princess.

The ceremony was opened by an extremely enigmatic and humorous guest speaker called Robin Sieger. At that time Robin had recently published a book entitled 'Natural Born Winners', a sensitive and inspirational guide in which he explores the human characteristics that typify natural born entrepreneurs and highly successful people.

In the wake of the film show, Robin commented on Jai's performance by saying, "I've heard more business wisdom from this man in the last ten minutes than many of the experts in the past ten years." Here was a perfect stranger talking about the man I adored and I was bursting with pride.

However, if Robin could have known how that accolade was to contribute to the chain of events that followed he might well have swallowed his words that day...

The four-course meal was fabulous, followed by the most entertaining and funny after-dinner speech I've ever heard. After a while, I was hardly able to distinguish whether my euphoria was due to a natural 'high' from the positive atmosphere of the event or, in part, to the wine that flowed copiously throughout the meal.

Back at the hotel we settled into an evening around the bar accompanied by the media crew responsible for the production of the short film on Jai. More drinks flowed. An Indian meal was arranged for later that evening. In the bar I found myself seated next to Rita, a slender, slightly boyish-looking Asian woman in her late twenties who had headed the team. What Rita lacked in size, she made up for in personality. She and I had somehow 'gelled' during the filming at our home, having shared spiritual beliefs and finding that we had a great deal in common.

Halfway through the evening, she leaned over to me and in a half whisper said, "You're besotted with him, aren't you."

"Of course," I replied; then, with a pronounced sincerity in my voice, added, "He's the real deal, you know."

It was an odd thing for me to say, but partly prompted by her less than complimentary remarks to Jai during filming. Rita had teased him that the success of Dove St was gained 'by default', as if sheer luck had been on his side, rather than apportioning it to any business prowess on his part. I had detected a 'rub' between them early on, although she was clearly captivated by Jai's charm and charisma.

"No, Jacky," she replied, almost clinically, "*you're the real deal.*"

The words seemed to drop like a brick from a fifty-storey building. There was a tense silence. Jai fixed my eyes with a hostile glare indicating it was time to leave.

I made a polite excuse that we were going to shower and change for evening dinner.

We never returned.

We'd barely entered the lift on the way back to the room before he began demanding to know what the conversation had been about. "I'll tell you later," I answered, knowing that to repeat her words might evoke a response I was neither prepared for nor capable of responding to.

"Tell me now!" he demanded with an increased intensity in his voice. My head began to swim from the effects of the alcohol.

I begged him to let it go, but in the split second of putting the key in the door, a raging torrent of abuse poured forth like a dam bursting open. Jai's eyes blazed with fury and I began to tremble. Like a lamb being led to the slaughter, the more he raged, the more silent I grew.

In the next instant, he'd grabbed his overnight bag and thrust his belongings in it.

"Where are you going?" I muttered feebly. He didn't answer, having already dialled his brother's mobile telephone and, speaking in Gujarati, issued a demand for Nara to meet him in the lobby of the hotel.

"How do I get home?" I whimpered between my tears as he headed for the door. "I've no money."

Forty pounds fell on the bed with a contemptible wave of the hand. "Find your own way back," he said.

And with those words he was gone.

For an hour or so I sat on the bed in numbed silence. I could barely comprehend how the weekend had gone from heaven one minute to hell the next.

What followed was a steady stream of telephone calls to the hotel room that began at midnight and continued until 3:30 a.m. A ten-minute conversation was followed by time for me to absorb what he had just said and time for the effects of the alcohol to wear off. Each call a careful analysis of the whole weekend's events, a detailed dissection of every conversation that had taken place, who had said what, and with what facial expression or tone in their voice. Initially I found myself trying to blame the alcohol. Eventually I found myself apologizing.

Ultimately I placed the blame squarely at my feet.

The final telephone call delivered a direct order. "Take a freezing cold shower, sober up and get the next available train home."

King's Cross station at five in the morning is not somewhere you want to be hanging about, particularly alone and with the next train's departure time another hour and a half away. The freezing cold shower had done much to sharpen my senses, but now the icy chill of the early autumnal air seemed to penetrate to my core.

It was nearly 9 a.m. when I finally arrived home. Although dazed, I could feel the flames of anger welling up inside me. Whether the hot salty tears I tasted as Jai fervently kissed my face over and over that morning were real or not, I was far too tired to fathom.

I fell into a deep and dreamful sleep, as he clung to me like a suffocating vine.

I suppose, looking back, I just didn't want to acknowledge his controlling behaviour. I believed I'd found the perfect relationship and the perfect man for me and I glossed over all the telltale signs, blissfully unaware of what lay ahead.

Instead, I threw myself into my work; it was a pattern I'd long developed whenever I was seeking to bury subconscious fears. There was no doubt that I was helping others to face debilitating patterns in their own lives and this felt truly rewarding and, yet, the more I was being of service the more my own wounds were emerging to the surface to be healed. I couldn't have known at that time how my work was to sustain me ... *and see me through the darkest period of my life.*

Back then, in the early throes of our relationship, I'd longed for a spiritual venture that Jai and I could participate in together. We'd talked endlessly about opening a spiritual centre, a place where we could host talks and workshops, share our knowledge and provide others with a platform to do the same. Jai began seeking out a location and a venue. Site finding was something that came naturally to him and, within a few short weeks, we'd secured some spacious second floor offices close to the town centre.

The ball was set in motion and I was on a roll, fuelled with ideas and bursting with creativity. The birth of Sai Workshops was to take another nine months to come to fruition ... *and they were to be the most turbulent of my life.*

The idea of using the name of 'Sai Workshops' came to me in a dream. Conscious of not wanting to be seen to promote any favoured religious beliefs, I used the word Sai as a pneumonic. 'Skills in Action in Industry' was designed to appeal to the large corporate companies, promoting workshops for the business world. 'Self Awareness for Individuals' was aimed at the spiritual aspirant and those interested in self-development and personal growth.

During those early months our home had become a shrine to the Indian Avatar who, up until that point, I had little real knowledge of and yet had come to invade even our most perfunctory routines. Pictures adorned every wall of our house. We watched videos together and explored his teachings. Jai would not leave home for work each morning without first kissing Sai Baba's countenance in the large, prominent picture that hung by our front door and then placing vibhuti (sacred ash) on his own brow, at his third eye centre.

A total of sixty-six books written about the Indian mystic graced our bookshelves, some of the titles repeated three or four times over. "We need some spares to give away to people," he told me, and they were. Street sellers coming to the door would be given an unsolicited copy of Sai Baba's life and teachings to take away with them. No one was spared from the urgency of Jai's message, not even the window cleaner!

Quite simply, Jai vehemently believed that Sai Baba was the singular embodiment of God in human form on the planet and that Jai himself was the *only* soul who had recognized Him. Sai Baba is considered to be an Avatar among his followers, an incarnation of Divine consciousness here to teach us love, wisdom and compassion. Whilst I was open to Sai Baba's teachings, it irked Jai that I didn't 'grab him' as he had done. "You've got limited understanding, Jacky," he said to me rather condescendingly on more than one occasion. "One day you'll recognize him as I have."

Believe me I tried. In the beginning I cannot deny there was something immensely touching about Jai's sheer devotion. Yet I was still wary of any kind of 'guru worship', believing that blind faith or the surrender of our spiritual welfare to another was merely a way of avoiding taking responsibility for the difficulties in our own lives.

Despite that, I became involved to an extent with the Sai Centre in Perry Barr, Birmingham, acquiescing to take the Friday evening class for the five to seven-year-olds whenever a teacher was absent or an extra pair of hands was needed. It was rewarding work which allowed me to be creative. Guiding a dozen or more six-year-olds in the practice of 'silent sitting' and helping them tap into their own creativity took me back to my own Sunday school days, to which I attribute the roots of my own faith and a firm belief in a benevolent, albeit invisible, God.

Isn't it always when you least expect it that life has a habit of speeding up? And at those times it's even more important to look after the body's physical system. Christmas 1999 was one of those times and, with my energy levels and immune system at an all time low, I was hit by a bout of flu that literally knocked me off my feet.

Looking back I can see how I drew illness to myself. A punishing work schedule and prolonged lack of sleep were taking its toll; add to that an extremely demanding partner ... and every ounce of vitality was being drained from me.

Our first Christmas together didn't turn out to be the romantic, peaceful break I'd anticipated. Jai kept the shop open until midnight on Christmas Eve and reopened on Boxing Day morning, serving 'mulled wine' to his customers whilst promoting the idea of shopping for those forgotten gifts and culinary needs. As my energy levels were depleting, his were going into overdrive. He began to spend nights away from the home we shared. If I protested, as I sometimes did, he would justify his absence with an endless list of new 'contacts' he'd made, new ideas he'd set in motion and a perpetual stream of hangers-on he'd collected that were soon to become a trademark for the way he lived his life. I was struggling to maintain any kind of routine, drawn into a world of 'busyness' that seemed to take over our lives.

Life seemed strangely out of balance. On the one hand there seemed to be an outpouring of genuine love from Jai and he appeared to want to spend every waking moment in my company and then, on the other, he almost went out of his way to distance himself and vacate my life for days on end. I would be left with this 'void', the bereft feeling of having been the centre of his world one minute and a segment of it the next.

When he did spend time at home, he slept for whole days. It was difficult to keep any sense of momentum; one minute he seemed to exude an excess of energy that was almost impossible to keep up with and the next he would sink into long languorous days, filled with sleep and inactivity. Deep down I knew there was something wrong, but I couldn't put my finger on it.

It struck me as odd that he felt impelled to spread his knowledge of 'Ayurvedic' principles to anyone who'd listen and yet they were not disciplines he carried over easily into his private life. I noticed an excessive craving for junk food and sugar. Sometimes having Jessica with him on a shopping trip gave him the perfect excuse to fill the cupboards with crisps, chocolate, cakes and sweets.

Despite still suffering from a post-viral flu infection I was determined the millennium would not pass me by without some form of celebration. I was ecstatic therefore when my brother decided to host a party for a huge number of family and friends. I saw it as an opportunity to attend a family occasion as a 'proper couple', to show off to the world how much in love I was and to give Jai the credibility I believed he deserved.

In less than two hours, however, he was making his excuses

that he needed to be at the shop, 'driving the workforce', and here I was on the millennium, the most important landmark I'd ever get to see in my lifetime, the beginning of a new century... alone. Once again he was off ... disappearing, like an alley cat, into the night.

It was in late January of the year 2000 that Jai declared to me in a telephone conversation that he'd taken 'offices' near to Birmingham city centre. When I asked him why, he told me he 'needed to spread his energy' and needed a place where he could hold meetings and put his ideas into action.

An office to me conjured up the image of just that, a room with a desk and filing cabinets, maybe a space above a shop front that provided a place from which he could quietly work. It was several weeks later that I discovered the 'office' was a two bedroom terraced house for which he told me he was paying a hundred pounds a week in rent.

Jai displayed no worries about money; he didn't need to...I fretted enough for the both of us. I agonized over how we could sustain two homes, a total of twelve hundred pounds just in rent, as well as finance the workshops, the initial expenditure for which was already mounting into thousands. The payment of all the domestic bills was down to me. I assumed it was because Jai was unable to open a bank account owing to his bankruptcy. The simple truth was he took no responsibility for the financial aspect of our relationship and placed no restrictions or controls on his daily expenditure.

This blasé attitude towards money was to create a turbulence that infected and even outlived our entire relationship.

As for the workshops, what began as an intended 'joint' venture very quickly became my sole responsibility. Jai's hands-on involvement ceased from the moment we secured the premises. Despite the many twists and turns from its conception to its birth, with the landlord doing a complete U-turn at one point, I was still convinced that Sai Workshops was destined to come to fruition and I forged ahead with its opening.

We clashed right from the outset over the workshops, even something as fundamental as its 'intention' caused the basis for an argument between us. Jai saw it as a business, one that, if handled properly, would "turn over a hundred thousand pounds in its first year." To me, the workshops were a wholly spiritual venture and, whilst I appreciated they had to support themselves, the prime intention was to share knowledge.

It was not just me with whom Jai seemed at odds on a daily basis. He was constantly at loggerheads with his brother over the running of the shop. Hell-bent on driving the business forward, Jai wanted to explore new ideas and began urging his brother to free up a cash injection commensurate with his expansion plans. Nara took the opposite stance. He wanted nothing more than to keep the business tight, to safeguard a thriving nest egg and so steadfastly refused Jai's frequent requests to take financial risks.

As a result of these differences... an unspoken rift began to develop between them.

Over the weeks that followed I noticed a marked increase in Jai's moodiness. I put this down to his increased stress levels and urged him to address his erratic sleep patterns and dietary habits. He became increasingly argumentative, picking fights with me for little or no apparent reason.

I remember one evening as I washed the dishes. "Didn't your mother ever teach you to wash up properly?" came the offhand remark, as he stood behind me, criticizing the fact that I had failed to rinse the crockery with clean, cold water after washing them. I couldn't understand why he was making such an issue of it and replied that I'd always was hed up this way. In one sweeping gesture, he pushed me away from the sink and poured neat washing up liquid all over the clean dishes. "If we're going to eat soap, we might as well eat loads of it!" he scorned.

The dishes remained there for two days until the detergent, like congealed glue, had to be practically scraped off.

Other things began to gnaw away at me. I began to view his apparent disregard for any sense of time as a significant issue in our lives. It constantly felt as though Jess and I had to somehow fit around *his* schedule. Whenever he arranged an evening out, on every single occasion without exception, he would calmly turn up some two, even three hours later than the appointed time and wonder why I seemed slightly irritated! Getting information out of him about his whereabouts was like quizzing a Russian spy and was often met with frequent displays of annoyance. In short, I had no idea where he was or what he was doing, day or night, and I simply wasn't allowed to ask.

I found myself constantly placating his daily impatience, restlessness and bouts of frustration by showering him with my love and displays of intimacy. When he was responsive and in a loving mood, I became "the best wife, the best mother, the best lover ..." There were times of deep understanding, mutual respect and overwhelming closeness.

And there were times when I thought I would drown in the intensity of his emotions...

Whatever else was happening in my life, my therapeutic work was keeping me calm and focused on a daily basis. Any doubts or anxieties that I was on the right track were swiftly removed when I meditated and called on the higher realms for guidance. In March of that year I ran a workshop entitled 'Past Lives – Resolution & Healing'. Jai attended and uncharacteristically shared a childhood experience that had clearly had an impact on his life.

'I was sitting on a seat at the back of a bus with my parents, having recently arrived in the UK from Uganda. I'd have been six years old. My parents began to argue violently. I moved seats to be nearer the front. I remember sitting there alone,

quietly pondering my future and being struck by the overwhelming feeling that I would never find anyone to love me. That in my worthless existence, no woman would ever want to marry me…'

It was a telling story and one that Jai had explored with the help of a hypnotherapist several years earlier. How much healing had taken place during that one and only session I'm not sure. I do know that it was a belief system that had stayed with Jai for most of his adult life and one that had created barriers to his acceptance of love in his life.

Now, in the first year of our relationship, Jai was having difficulties reconciling the guilt he felt at having left his wife. Somehow or other he made me feel that I was entirely to blame for it. Surely a man isn't anywhere he doesn't want to be, I told him. But it suited him to heap the guilt on me, saying that 'I had seduced him' and 'lured him away from her'. In some way I think it cleansed him.

During strained moments in our relationship, he would tell me how wonderful she was, how loving and devoted a wife she had been. Then at other times, often when things were going well between us, he would refer to her as 'frigid', 'cold' and 'misguided in her religious beliefs'.

Of course, his accusing words cut like a knife and the guilt gnawed away at me but I hadn't gone out actively seeking a married man to fall in love with. As I have said before, the experience chose me. When I reflect on how the two of us ever came together, I *know* that I genuinely fell in love with Jai. For his part, I believe he was attracted to me because of the way I made him *feel*. For the first time in his life, he felt truly appreciated, wanted, needed and *loved*.

Certainly the *work* of loving Jai, being *with* him on a regular basis was no picnic! I thought that if I could help him dissolve some of the pains of his early experiences, he might regain some emotional freedom and his life would move forward. For the most part he seemed in denial, particularly regarding the emotions he'd buried surrounding his father's suicide.

One evening, a mutual acquaintance came to dinner at our house. Ray was a trained NLP (Neuro Linguistic Programming) practitioner and I had enlisted him as a potential speaker for when the workshops opened. Whilst the three of us sat in our living room quietly chatting, Ray casually turned to Jai and said, "I sense you're holding a lot of anger towards your father." For a few brief seconds, I thought the unwelcome comment might have attracted a fiery response. But the opposite happened. Jai looked thoughtful for a moment, then replied quietly, "No, I don't feel anger. In actual fact I have a deep respect for my father's courage."

In that instant I felt his father's spirit enter the room. Occasionally, it happens that way. People often ask me during psychic readings to give them a message, then and there from their deceased relatives. It doesn't work like that of course. You can't 'call up spirits' as though they were hanging on the end of a telephone; you can only draw them to you with your thoughts and, if it is appropriate to the enquirer, a message will be given.

"Your dad is here," I said to Jai. "Quick! Find me a pencil and paper." I began to 'psychically' draw what his father was showing me. Rolling hills formed a beautiful backdrop to a floodlit swimming pool, all around were straw-topped huts shading picnic tables. His father had his back turned towards me, appearing not to want to show his face. I felt an overwhelming sense of sadness and remorse as though he was lost in some vast and empty wilderness.

When Jai looked at the picture I'd drawn, he recognized it to be Africa. His father was bringing me a memory of the place where he was happiest in his life, when he worked as a leisure attendant in the great outdoors in Uganda. "He is stuck, Jai," I said. "He needs help finding his way to the light."

Some of my healing work in this physical lifetime is to assist disincarnate entities or earthbound spirits who have departed from the physical world but have no comprehension of the 'afterlife'. I help to 'guide them back to the light'. It is worthy and rewarding work and I feel privileged to be able to work for spirit in this way.

There are many reasons *why* a deceased person remains earthbound. Sometimes it can happen when a life has been cut short abruptly or when death has been violent. Such strong emotional attachments like fear, anger, bitterness or remorse act like leaden weights upon the soul. Suicide is viewed in most spiritual traditions as going against God's natural law and is almost certain to keep a soul trapped in his own negative karma.

I sensed that Jai's father needed to be freed from the negative emotions that had caused him to take his own life in the first place. The following day Jai and I set a prayer in motion, which we recited daily for one hundred and eight days (the number of the different names for God). Shortly after the final prayer, Jai's brother had a dream, *a dream where his father flew in through an open window* …We took this as a sign that our prayers had not been in vain and that his father's spirit had finally found its release.

At this point in my life I was certain of one thing. *I* needed a rest and we *both* needed a holiday. So, throwing financial caution to the wind, I booked a week away just for the two of us in Fuerteventura, the Canary Islands, in early April 2000.

I wish I could say that it made everything right, but it didn't. Everything about the resort and the hotel was fine and, for my part, I quickly and easily switched into holiday mode. Jai seemed to relax for the first couple of days, becoming the carefree, affectionate man I'd fallen in love with. Then, by day three, his mood had changed again and he began to feel guilty for being there. There were things to do and he had no business lying on a beach whilst the work was piling up! I couldn't win. It was no surprise really. I realize now it was all part of the same low self-esteem pattern, Jai didn't actually believe he *deserved* a holiday.

While we waited for the plane to take off for the journey home, I was blissfully unaware that my life was about to alter dramatically from this moment on. The flight attendant handed us a Sunday gossip newspaper as we boarded. The front-page news featured a picture of a radiant looking Madonna (my icon) with her husband Guy Ritchie, and the words 'It's a Boy!' leapt out from the page. The article was confirming that she and her husband were expecting their second child, a son, who was to be called Rocco.

I hadn't done the maths, but I knew my menstrual cycle ran like clockwork. I was ten days late and, in that moment, a thought of absolute certainty came over me, 'I'm pregnant … *and it's going to be a boy…'*

One week later I sat on the bathroom floor for over an hour, motionless except for a trembling hand that cupped the pregnancy testing kit with the clear blue line that now stared up at me. A mixed medley of thoughts ran through my mind: 'How would I cope?'; 'At forty-five wasn't I too old to have a baby?'; 'How would Jess take the news?'; 'What about the workshops?'; and then, 'Wow' it hit me … 'How wonderful, I'm going to have a baby!' … One emotion after another crashed through the core of my being like waves across a tempestuous sea … *gut-wrenching fear, panic, exhilaration … and perfect joy.*

Tracking Jai down to tell him the news turned out to be a far trickier job than delivering the news itself. I didn't know when I would next see him and he hardly ever answered his mobile telephone. For weeks now a pattern had developed: three or four nights away working and sleeping at his 'offices', then coming home for three or four nights, then disappearing again. I noticed his eyes always seemed bloodshot and his usual healthy complexion had begun to take on a grey and dull pallor.

I knew he was spending long periods in deep silence and

prayer, often during the late evening before midnight, because he would ring me excitedly to tell me what new insight or inspirational thoughts he'd just had during his meditation. He'd also increased the frequency and duration of his fasts, sometimes not eating and drinking for two or three days at a time. Add to that a new found compulsion for rhythmic drumming, day and night for hours on end, and it was little wonder that on the occasions I saw him he seemed to have difficulty functioning normally, as though he were in some kind of strange, sleep-like torpor.

I often cautioned Jai about the perils of journeying into the mind too deeply through meditation, without first protecting the aura or subtler energy bodies. It was a discipline I'd learned the hard way, having come under psychic attack on more than one occasion. When a person meditates, chants, fasts, or practises any other spiritual discipline for prolonged periods of time, they must also adopt a sense of spiritual responsibility.

"I don't need all that stuff, God protects me," he would say dismissively.

"Yes, but God also gave us free will," was my response, "and it's up to us to psychically protect ourselves."

This nonchalant attitude towards any form of energetic protection both worried and annoyed me. I could see that the prolonged fasting was draining him and I wondered whether the 'visions' he began to tell me he was having were not actually mild hallucinations. But he wouldn't stop and listen to me, not for a single second. My knowledge, he said scornfully, was 'head knowledge', stuff I had read in books ... and he already *had* all the answers.

Book knowledge I may well have had, but I also practised regularly, having been first trained in the principles of meditation by an Ayurvedic Master. I *knew* its immense power *... and I wondered what 'other worldly realities' Jai was opening himself up to.*

I was getting anxious to deliver the news that he was to become a father and was mildly stunned when he actually answered the telephone. Apparently I'd caught him at a rare moment during the day when he was watching television. *'Relief'*, I remember thinking, he's doing something normal for a change.

"Are you coming home?" I enquired. "There's something really important I need to tell you."

"Can't you tell me on the phone?" he replied. His casual tone was upsetting. He *knew* I wasn't in the habit of wasting his time. Seconds later I just blurted it out.

"Really?" he answered.

There was a pronounced silence that seemed to go on forever. "That's good," he said finally, with not a shred of emotion in his voice. I wanted him at that moment to rush home to my loving arms and tell me his heart was bursting with joy. But he didn't.

It would be another twenty-four hours before he finally came home and took in the news. I returned to my bathroom floor and quietly wept.

The man I knew and had grown to love so deeply ... was silently slipping away from me.

For the next few weeks, I masked the growing fears I had about our relationship and instead threw myself into the preparations for the opening of Sai Workshops. I could barely think about my joyous news for concentrating on the immense project that lay ahead of me. I shared it only with my sister, Jayne, who was entirely supportive and has since been a tower of strength to me in my darkest moments.

By early May we had the keys to the premises and I was busy with organizing furnishings, flyers, decorations and putting the final preparations into an 'opening day' that I'd planned for June 7th. I was exhausted. Where the strength came from to cope with those early months I've no idea, but it came.

Jai was noticeable only by his absence. I managed on one occasion to enlist his help to choose the floor covering to be laid in the thirty-foot room that was to host the talks and workshops I'd spent months planning for. I remember we bumped into one of his many business contacts in the carpet shop and the gentleman asked what we were doing there. "I've opened a spiritual centre close to the town," Jai claimed enthusiastically. "Here's my card. Come and see what we can do for you."

I was incensed, as I was to be on many occasions from that day, when he claimed the workshops to be a result of his own efforts. Nonetheless, I let it go despite feeling a growing repulsion at a sense of self-importance that seemed to creep into every conversation and with every person he encountered.

By late May he was spending practically all of his time at his 'offices'. Yet when I reflect on those months, very little was actually being achieved. He jumped erratically from one activity to another whilst he engaged me for hours in endless conversations and the promises of great things to come … all of which seemed to dissolve like sugar into a vast sea of nothingness.

The constant 'meetings' with significant others and the anticipation of the launch of this new business idea or that new project failed to bear any real fruit. He began to blame everyone he'd gathered around him for his own lack of progress. Initially they were of use to him, then something would sour early on in the relationship, and eventually it would be severed … long before any real work got started.

I began to feel an ever-increasing resentment towards his lack of practical help in the workshops. I was up to my neck with laying carpets and refurbishment as well as devising a talks programme for the launch. I didn't even have time to visit a doctor. Here I was, at a rough guess, eleven weeks pregnant and I was up a ten-foot ladder at midnight painting the walls!

"You need to understand the principle of leadership, Jacky," he protested. "A commander of his own vessel doesn't wash down the decks."

Of course not! The new role he'd carved out for himself was of far greater importance. Anyone who was prepared to listen became an audience for his deep philosophy and a new found 'godliness' which he rammed down their throats at every opportunity. Ironically, the more he tried to convince everyone around him that he alone had discovered God on the planet, the more he drove them away, especially those closest to him.

And I had become his nearest target.

The communications between us grew increasingly intense. Jai's compulsive demands for me to "shut my mouth and listen" seemed to dominate every conversation and understandably created in me the opposite effect. Little by little, I could feel myself withdrawing, confused and overwhelmed by his seemingly untamed and erratic outbursts that appeared to make very little sense.

He was, he told me, the keeper of 'secret' and 'sacred' knowledge and it was his role to make all humanity understand. How could the world embrace him and believe his claims, when his own partner, the woman he loved above all things, seemed to reject what he was saying?

The powerful drive to *make me understand* became almost a mission in itself. When I listened and *tried* to understand, I was 'the most magnificent woman on the planet', his 'twin soul' and together we would change the world. When I challenged him or reacted defensively to his often cruel and injurious remarks, I became a woman of 'limited understanding' and … 'not fit even to sit at his table'.

I was struggling to reconcile his demands for closeness and utmost respect with the compulsion to push me further and further away. It was as though, in distancing himself from me, he was in some way sadistically withholding his love. The more he withheld, the more I tried in my love for him to keep him close. Slowly, little by little, I watched our relationship degenerate into a web of warped, destructive power games...

Nothing could have prepared me for that fateful telephone call which woke me just after midnight on Friday, 2nd June 2000, a day that will be imprinted on my mind forever. All the irrational ramblings that had gone before I could have dismissed as mild insanity, put down to lack of sleep, irregular eating patterns, stress, anxiety or any other easily observed behaviour, but this was coming from a place far more sinister.

"Are you with me, baby?" he began, pacing his words to the slow, rhythmic beat of a drum. "SAY IT, I NEED TO HEAR YOU SAY IT ... ARE YOU WITH ME, BABY?" he thundered. The question hung in the air with an ear-piercing shriek that caused me to wrench the telephone about a foot away from my ears. There was something dark and almost mocking in his tone.

"Don't you know that the **greatest** man **ever** to live has been in *your* bed ... and he can still stay in your bed if you let him. But if you **push** him, then he'll be gone, and that's what makes him **that** great. You with me now, baby? **ARE YOU WITH ME NOW?**"

I began stammering through muffled sobs. "I'm ... I'm ...frightened by what's happening to you," I answered thinly.

A bizarre torrent of words followed, one moment high-pitched and deafening, the next, feverish and whispered.

"My momentum's building every day now..." he went on. "Every day it's building and you can see it, you can see it, and you *really* want to come with me, but the darkness is holding you back! Giving you excuses to stay back, yeah? I'm the light, I want you to come with me, **so** bad, but you can *only* come with me if you're true. True from the heart, no pretending, 'cause I can pick everything up.

"You know how much power I've got, don't you? I'm figuring things out at such a rate … and I'm going to tell you something, Jacky. *They will* try and blow my house up: they *will* try and *blow* me up, but you know something else? They won't do it. Why? … 'cause I'm the **only** man who's **right**! And they're all going to make me out to be the bad guy … 666 is his birthday they'll say, right? Satan's number - 666 they'll say … you with me? **He's** the Satan, the sign is there! I told you a long time ago, remember? My birthday is 6.4.66 … and I'm telling you now so you can go and tell the world … that I'm 666 … that's if you wanna work for them. But the minute you break the **code**, then *you* broke the code, **not** me.

"The dark forces are working, Jacky … You know that same day that Nostradamus said that the world would blow up, **I'm** the man who's **blowing it up** and June 7th is the day that Nostradamus said the *world* would blow up, as you know it. Upside down, 'cause I'm gonna turn it around!"

'June 7th,' I repeated in my mind, the day of the workshop's opening! A cold chill ran up my spine. "Where does it say June 7th ?" I asked feebly.

"You check it out, baby, you check it out, because as I am talking it's coming from **top,** not from him, yeah. You check it out! 2000 June 7th, check it out! Nostradamus said it… but if he got it *wrong* three or four days then forgive him! Because the Aries bit is right, and the descendant of an Aryan is right … you with me, baby? … 'Cause this is the **main** man. You know the same man, Jesus says in the Bible … will turn up like a thief in the night and no one will see him coming?

"Do you know where that thief was on Sunday? He was at the Swaminarayan Mandir (*temple*) knocking down the door at 11:30, with my shades on. Garry was with me who's a black guy and they look at black people as thieves, yeah? And they thought I was pretending to be a *good* guy? And I'm really a thief, that's what they were thinking, do you understand?

"The world will know that he comes like a thief in the

night – that's **me,** baby, that's **me** that Jesus Christ wrote in the bible about. You Christian guys are confused. But I will straighten you guys out, but first I'm going to sort the Swaminarayans out. Because they are the biggest bullshitters and I'll tell you … you know how **powerful** I am, Jack? It's taken them three hundred years to build that temple, yeah? To build their movement? They've got sixteen *million* people in the movement who are so disciplined and if you multiply all that money they've got, they must be into the *billionaire league*! You with me? But do you know something? Their main guy is coming this week … and he's shaking, 'cause he knows I'm standing. And I'll look at that guy and I'll say to him, *'I'm not the man you **think** I am'*. He'll be **shocked**! Do you understand? Then I'll look at his public and say, *'You **guys** don't know who **I** am, but I **know** who **you** are!'*

"Got it? *'Pieces of shit!'* Who the fuck is this, they'll say? Then I'll drop in some lyrics and say, *'You know something, my man? I can show you **God!** How about that?'* That's my first line that would destroy him, *you know why?* 'Cause he'd have to answer, cause that's a challenge now … you with me? And what can he say to me? … **One lyric and what can he say to me, Jacko?** 'Cause there's only **one person on this planet,** you know? **Only one person on this planet** who has … **really** … **seen** …**God!**

"Do you know who that is … do you know who that is?
"*Me!*

"'Cause I'm a serious master, you know … and a serious master will do **anything** … every single *fun* thing; every single *sad* thing; every single *easy* thing; every single *hard* thing; and every single *bad* thing … doesn't matter what he has to do … he wants it **so bad** … that even when a person he **knows** is lying to him, lies to him, he will still do it *faster* … 'Cause I **know** God's power. That's how powerful **I** am …

"'Cause I'm the **baddest** motherfucker with the **most** power, remember?

"The dark forces may be working, Jacky, but shall I tell you who works for me! Bill Gates works for me; Robin Sieger works for me; Richard Branson works for me; President Clinton works for me! But do you know what else? ...The Lord said to **me** that, because I am the **man** I am, then *He* works for *me! I've had to earn the right ...but the Lord works for me now!"*

To this day I cannot fathom what possessed me to reach for the tape in the bedside drawer. Ironically it was a karaoke tape of Jess's on which she had recorded herself singing her favorite pop tunes. I rewound to a blank space on the tape and then almost robotic-like pressed the PLAY and RECORD button. Something in the dark recesses of my mind knew that one day this tape would find itself in the hands of someone, *anyone,* who would make some sense of it ... and rid us once and for all from the madness that had contaminated our lives.

The energy in his voice subsided. It was eleven minutes past two in the morning. I was exhausted. It had been a ninety-minute monologue, the entire content of which he believed fervently. No, there was no doubt in Jai's mind ... 'The Vision' had confirmed it... GOD WORKED FOR *HIM* NOW!

Jaya Kham Daridra was The Saviour, 'The Chosen One' our planet had been waiting for. The man that Nostradamus had predicted would come like a thief in the night, the King of Terrors, King of all Kings, whose prime mission and Divine destiny was to shake up all of humankind ... and take each and every one of us ... back to God.

I placed the receiver down and sobbed. Sleep would be a long time coming that night. The thought of his key turning in the lock filled me with terror. I checked on Jess, she was sleeping like a baby ... Thank God for small mercies, I thought.

Tomorrow was another day.

CHAPTER THREE: 'THE ROAD TO HELL'

'Why this is hell, nor am I out of it. Thinkst thou that I who saw the face of God.
And tasted the eternal joys of Heaven, Am tormented with ten thousand hells.
In being deprived of everlasting bliss?'

(Doctor Faustus I)
Christopher Marlowe 1564 – 1593

When I look back at those crucial thirty days that preceded 'The Vision' and the weeks that followed, I am haunted by a hideous kaleidoscope of unfathomable outbursts, wild fanciful claims and twisted rages … that lurk in the shadows of my memory … and wait to engulf me.

From that point on I began to watch the man I loved hover on the brink of insanity and it was the most traumatic experience of my life. Like a ship marooned in the vast ocean, my life took on a turbulence I could barely master. Tossed between the currents of his daily verbal onslaughts and irrational ramblings I found myself constantly praying for calmer waters. Occasionally they came.

I had no idea at this point in my life that I would spend the next two years riding out the waves.

The week prior to the opening of the workshops, I spent clinging tenaciously to every ounce of normality and routine I could muster. Jai in the meantime had slipped into a strange world of spontaneous visions and dramatic spiritual insights leaving him see-sawing between states of acute anxiety on the one hand and overwhelming euphoria on the other. He took to wearing dark glasses *all of the time*, because he explained, "These eyes have seen God and no one is worthy to look into them."

I noticed a marked obsession with his body image and

cleanliness. The mirror became his best friend. He would catch his own reflection and contort and twist his face until he was content with the image staring back at him. "I've been called the Buddhist Marlon Brando, you know," he would say to me quite seriously. Many times I caught him sitting in front of the dressing table mirror studying his own face with the same intensity an art student studies a great work of art. I found it odd, but I rationalized it as him accepting his own attractiveness perhaps for the first time in his life. He often confided in me that he always *felt* ugly as a child.

On top of that he was taking four or five freezing cold showers a day. Cold showers are the fastest spiritual accelerator and psychic cleanser known to man and, even though they'd always been part of his routine, now, as this high voltage energy literally blasted through his system, he seemed never to be out of the shower. Whether they were intended to cool his body from a heat so intense it was palpable, or whether his obsession with bodily cleanliness had simply escalated, I'm not sure. Perhaps it was both. I can vividly recall seeing the steam literally pouring from his body as he showered.

Rather than being perturbed at finding himself in such treacherous and uncharted waters, Jai positively thrived on his new found cosmic status. After all, God worked for *him* now. What could there possibly be to worry about! Though he barely slept and talked incessantly, his energy levels seemed at an all time high. He became increasingly hypersensitive and hypervigilant, seeing meaning and 'signs' in everything and identifying with every heroic character ever written about, whether real or imagined.

For months I'd noticed an increasing obsession with 'The Mahabharata', the monumental epic of Hindu literature, containing all of India's myths, fables and fairy tales. Now, as he sat glued to volume after volume on video over and over again, he took in its entire contents as 'literal truths' and persistently urged me to do the same. Not only did Jai identify with Arjuna, the central character in the Bhagavad-Gita, the sixth book of The Mahabharata, but he also firmly believed he *was* Arjuna.

The energy it took for me to handle his daily emotional demands was overwhelming. I'd been blessed with a robust and resilient nature and an ability to handle stress and pressure, but this was something entirely different. The strain of watching him disengage from ordinary reality into a mysterious world of deities and divine beings almost tore me apart. Jai's cosmic line to the heavens had connected him to the great wars of every century passed as he witnessed scenes of death and destruction and watched the ultimate dissolution of the entire cosmos ... and yet it seemed the deeper he journeyed ... the more elated he grew.

The bizarre swings in mood were the hardest to bear. There were times when he was perfectly rational, attentive and incredibly loving. Then, in an instant, he would switch into a rage that seemed to come from nowhere. Even more worrying was that his frustration at not being able to control everyone and everything in his environment had now given way to bouts of physical violence.

For several months Jai had become inseparable from a friend whom I shall refer to as Garry. I'd met Garry on numerous occasions, a small-framed, black man with a pronounced 'stoop' that he explained away as the result of lifelong back pain. He was of average intelligence with a seemingly gentle nature. Yet it was Garry who accompanied Jai when he was 'knocking down the doors of the Swaminarayan Mandir' at 11:30 p.m. on the previous Sunday. They went everywhere together. Garry believed everything Jai told him and was now, according to Jai, his number one soldier in the God's army he was building.

It was Monday, 5th June and Jess and I had been out until quite late visiting relatives. Any excuse to escape and 'do normal things' drove me through those last few weeks and I'm sure kept me sane. This particular night, as I put the key in the door, I found it had been locked from the inside. I knew Jai was in because his car was in the drive and all the lights were on. We knocked loudly … nothing. Then again, still nothing. It took him a good ten minutes to come down the stairs and he was talking so loudly to Garry on the telephone we could hear him through the front door. "Here they come," he jeered, "the dirty liars, the little pair of witches."

Jess flashed me a look of worried concern. I urged her to go straight to bed and not say a word to him but, from the moment we walked in, he began tormenting both of us, particularly Jess. Irked that his jibes were failing to induce the required reaction, he followed her into the bedroom, throwing his fifteen-stone bulk on to her top bunk bed. She made a polite request for him to move. "Make me!" he said.

I was tired and I had no time for his games. "Off the bloody bed, Jai!" I yelled.

With wild eyes flashing, he was off the bed in an instant and squaring up to Jess, poking his finger in the middle of her chest and calling her the most disgusting names. I began pleading with him to leave her alone, but my concern at that moment for Jess's feelings over his was just the right ammunition to feed his frenzy.

He started to back me into a corner of the room and, towering over me, a stream of vile insults fell so fast and furious I could barely catch my breath, never mind respond. "What the hell's wrong with you?" I demanded. "Calm down or I'm calling the police."

"Call the whole damn force," he stormed with a challenging air. "They *all* work for me."

He grabbed the telephone and redialled the last number. Garry answered. He began telling Garry how I didn't respect him; how I'd failed to *recognize* who he was; that I was enmeshed in my 'bullshit world' and refused to acknowledge that he was the saviour of mankind, the man God had put all His faith in. "Tell her what happened at the temple last

Sunday, Garry," he commanded. "How I had to dismantle all their bullshit … how I *killed* five people … how in the end the truth *always* wins."

A sickly knot rose up in my stomach. He handed the telephone to me as a macabre expression passed over his face.

"What does he mean, Garry?" I stammered

There was a long pause, then, "Jacky … if Jai *says* he killed five people last Sunday … then he *did*."

"You're as deluded as he is!" I stormed, cutting the call off and throwing the telephone on the bed in disgust.

I knew Jess couldn't possibly fall asleep amidst the melee and I was terrified he would start on her again. But Jai was like a dog with a bone and proving his claims to me was of paramount importance. He wasn't going to give up easily. Apart from that, I'd now become the disobedient child and he saw it as his role to *make* me understand.

"Why don't you believe I'm enlightened?" he persisted.

"Because your words and actions aren't coming from a place of love," I stated, "and enlightened people are *loving* people."

With Jai I always seemed to fail in my attempts to diffuse the situation and he took my getting ready for bed to mean that I was ignoring him. Now he was on my heels following me into every room, persistent, going over and over it all again … the 'vision' and the mission God had given him. It was impossible to 'tune him out' as hard as I tried. The more he sensed I wasn't listening, the more vehement his tone grew. Had I not remembered that God had chosen him to do his *dirtiest* work? Did I not *know* what that meant? Did I not realize that he had been given unlimited power? Or that he was invincible and could not be killed? *I felt as though my head would explode.*

Jess appeared at the doorway, I knew, out of concern for me. She was eight years old … and yet in that moment her face wore the tired and worn expression of an adult who'd been to hell and back.

"Jess, go and get a chopping board and a knife from the kitchen!" Jai ordered her.

Oh please, God, what now? I remember thinking. Jess knew better than to argue with him and, before I had time to fathom what was on his mind, she was back up the stairs, handing him the items.

He set down the chopping board and knife on the desk in the study, placing his hand palm downwards firmly in the centre of the board.

"Chop my little finger off!" he commanded. My head began to swim.

"Don't be ridiculous, Jai," I retorted, pushing Jess back into her bedroom, her face ashen.

"Do it!" he stormed. "I can't bleed and I won't feel pain!"

I began to sob; he was scaring the hell out of me now. I grabbed the telephone and frantically dialled my brother's number amid his accusing screams. "Yeah! That's right, go crying to your family. You're weak, you're nothing, you're just like the rest of them … You don't know my power, you don't know who I am …" On and on and on he went.

My brother was at the door within five minutes. To Jai that was a bonus … he now had an audience! But Colin's aim to calm everything down and take the intensity out of the situation was no challenge for Jai; he would rather 'sport' with him for a while.

They sat facing each other, whilst I sat on the floor with my back propped against the wall. "You see, Colin," Jai began, "that's where a woman should be, sitting at her man's feet … that's if she *truly* respects him."

I could see my brother's hackles rise and it took all his resolve not to rise to the bait. "Let's leave Jacky out of this for the moment, shall we?" he said, a marked tension in his voice. "I'm more interested in these superhuman powers you've got."

Jai sneered at him, "What would you have me do … levitate off the chair?"

"That would be a start," replied Colin coolly. "I'd like to see that."

The gauntlet was down.

"Do you know you're sitting in the presence of a Master?" Jai's reply came swift as an arrow. "I *know* who I am, but do you know who *you* are?" There was a contemptible sneer in the way he asked the question. "I can take *any* challenge as long as you respect me enough … and you don't. You're not freshly showered and you're not even worthy to be in my aura. I won't waste my energy."

It was to become Jai's standard answer whenever his new found powers came under scrutiny. He was unable to demonstrate them because his challenger was either unclean, unworthy or disbelieving. *It was a neat cop-out.*

By two o'clock in the morning, Jai had grown bored with his numerous failed attempts to stir things up and with Colin's steadfast refusal to play the game. Slowly, like a balloon deflating, his energy levels subsided and his mood grew quieter. One way or another he'd been 'cornered' and, predictably, whenever that happened, he always seemed to have a neat explanation up his sleeve to excuse his behaviour. "It's just my passionate nature," he argued. Surely anyone could see that it was only in his love for me and his desperation to make me understand that his words and actions sometimes came across as overly harsh? *Overly harsh?!*

Somehow, despite his reluctance, I managed to persuade Colin that night that it was safe for him to leave. I will always be grateful for the protection his mere presence brought to me. Later, as I lay awake in the darkness, I was struck not by the remembrance of the evening's events, but by the sudden realization that I'd failed to keep my appointment that afternoon at the hospital for my first scan. It should have been a date that I was eagerly looking forward to.

Instead I could barely bring myself to think of my unborn

baby, real and growing inside me, with all the madness that was going on around…

The following night, on the eve of the opening, Jai arrived home unusually early, at a little after eleven. He rang the doorbell having apparently mislaid his keys. I wasn't prepared for the half distraught, crumpled vision that greeted me on the doorstep that night and his mood could not have been more different from the night before. There was an almost bewildered, faraway look in his eyes.

He walked in without saying anything and immediately reached for a loaf of bread, buttering about six rounds of jam sandwiches and eating half of them. I noticed his craving for sugar had practically quadrupled. In a single sitting he would consume an entire home-made treacle sponge pudding, normally enough for four or five portions. I could only rationalize this as his body's way of replacing the energy he was burning. On this particular night I could see his body was wracked with exhaustion. Gently, without pressing any conversation and with an arm protectively around him, I led him like a small child up the stairs to the bedroom. "Even superheroes have to sleep sometimes," I remember saying to him softly.

He climbed into bed and curled himself up into a little ball. I remember staring at him for ages. These sudden shifts in his moods from one day to another were the hardest to fathom and the most stressful to bear. I had no idea what was going on inside the tortured complexities of his mind and yet that night he looked so vulnerable. All I could feel was a rush of overwhelming love towards him. So many times I tried so hard … to reach him. Then came the words that I shall never forget as he quietly slipped into sleep. *"I'm terrified, Jacky…"* he said in a half whisper. *"I'm terrified of my own power..."*

I pushed those nights out of my mind … just as I did with much of Jai's irrational and disturbing behaviour at the beginning. I'd only confided in the two people closest to me about what was happening to him: Kate, my dearest friend and co-researcher for this book, and Jayne, my sister. Who would believe such a fantastical story anyway? I could barely believe it myself. It's painful enough to watch a loved one struggling with some emotionally charged crisis, like a marriage break-up or life-threatening illness. But this? I had no experience of dealing with something so bizarre and extraordinary.

Now Kate and Jayne were urging me to keep Jai away from the opening day I'd spent months preparing for. Why I was so hell-bent on him being there, I've no idea, other than I'd so wanted this to be a shared experience and a spiritual enterprise of which we were both a part. Yet what the hell was I thinking? It wasn't as if he'd contributed *anything* and how could I possibly anticipate his mood given all that had gone before.

"For heaven's sake, Jacky, think about what he's said to you!" Kate pleaded. "He said the world will blow up on June 7th and *he's* the man blowing it up. You've no idea what he is capable of!"

She was right of course but, for whatever reason unconscious to me at the time, I thought it wiser not to exclude him. "I think he's calming down," I maintained, only half believing what I said. God knows, I'd prayed long and hard over the preceding weeks for him to return to normal. I suppose, when I look back in hindsight, a huge part of me was in denial, a little like the way someone reacts to alcoholism or drug addiction by a family member … it can't really be happening, surely? … Or maybe if I ignore it for a while, it will go away.

Mercifully, the following morning I left Jai sleeping like a baby, whilst I was up and out of the doors early, putting the finishing touches of fresh flowers, candles and incense to the centre. The room looked spectacular and the caterers had produced a buffet fit for a king. Wednesday, June 7th 2000 was a warm and sunny day and I wore a golden yellow shift dress, flatteringly cut, yet hinting at my slightly protruding belly and the early signs of my pregnancy. Cleverly applied make-up did nothing to hide my tired and anxious expression.

I had no idea if Jai would show at all. Despite what else was going on, he had always displayed a considerable lack of ease in social settings, especially those involving large numbers. I even half suspected the date, although important to me, would pass by him unnoticed. He'd seemingly lost the ability of late for any kind of forward planning, choosing instead to create his daily reality, anew, in every waking moment.

How wrong could I be? The only thing predictable about Jai … was his unpredictability! He arrived about half an hour before the buffet was due to be unveiled, immaculately dressed as had become his recent trademark. I saw he had on his dark glasses and my stomach did a nervous flip. Martin, my brother, who had been filming the whole proceedings, had the video camera turned on me as I was poised, ready to start my presentation. I aimed to keep it brief, mainly because I didn't want to detract from the intention of the day. This was, after all, a social gathering of forty or so like-minded individuals linked by a common aim... the pursuit of spiritual growth. Apart from that, I was dreadfully camera shy.

"We don't profess to have all the answers here," I began nervously, "but we are truth seekers and this centre should be viewed as a spiritual haven, a sanctuary where we can meet, discuss and debate those deeper questions from the wellspring of all life's mysteries …" I outlined the forthcoming programme. Then, inviting him to come forward and say a few words, I tentatively handed the microphone over to Jai. "Please keep it light," I murmured, squeezing his hand lovingly.

He began to pace the room in slow, deliberate movements as though forming an invisible circle. With his head tilted downwards, his eyes, though behind blackened glasses, seemed to bore a hole in the floor. At first he began to reiterate more or less what I'd said, but then added that 'I had *made a mistake*'. "This woman before you is being modest," he observed. "She failed to tell you that we *do* have all the answers here ... to every life question you will *ever* ask ..." There was a mild shuffling in the room as he went on, "That is because this magnificent woman you see before you has no idea of her true power..."

The momentum in his voice began to gain pace. No one dared interrupt as he broke into a speech of how I was the best friend a person could have, the best sister a sibling could have, the best mother a child could have, the best lover a man could have, the best wife a husband could have ... the list of qualities idealizing me went on and on. It was so embarrassingly over the top I just wanted the floor to open up and swallow me. Finally he ended with a statement that I was the most *powerful* woman on the planet but I just didn't know it yet... "She has to be," he exclaimed, "because she is with *the* most powerful man."

A kind of stunned silence fell about the room. Kate threw me a look that said, 'please, *please* stop him now'. I realized I'd been holding my breath and, quickly overcoming a feeling of dizziness, I made a faint attempt at interrupting him. But as swiftly as Jai sensed my lack of overwhelming joy at his public display of adoration, his mood changed, becoming sombre, almost bitter. Even behind the dark glasses, his audience seemed to shrink from his gaze as his voice then broke into a 'holier than thou' tone. "How dare they call themselves Christians," he scorned, "when they ate meat and shunned Jesus's message. Thou shalt not kill... *Thou shalt not kill* ...THOU SHALT NOT KILL," he commanded, his voice rising, until the last repetition hung ...tenuously in the air.

He was in his element. This was the floor show he'd been craving and now, under the scrutiny of the camera lens, no one was going to escape his biting criticism. He had 'the Truth' after all; *his* was a message of cosmic importance and they, like the rest of mankind, were just hypocrites ... fearfully hiding in the shadows of their dull and pathetic lives.

I'd heard enough. I managed to use the excuse of lunch needing to be served to stop him from completely sabotaging the day. The simple truth was that several people at the back of the room had already begun putting on their shoes and were making for the exit. I suspected they'd decided we were some kind of religious nuts. His explanation later for this, of course, was that they, like the rest of humanity, were not ready to hear his message. It wasn't their fault naturally, just that they had 'limited understanding'. That was an expression I was to hear about a thousand times in the coming months ... *fuelled by an air of arrogance and inflated sense of ego that was to reach monumental proportions.*

The only good that came out of it was that, at least with the workshops officially opened now, I had a place to escape to where I could be still, meditate and regain my sense of balance. God knows I needed to! Despite the long hours, daytime and evening that I put in regularly, I began to view my time there as much more than a full-time occupation. For me, the place became ... a kind of sanctuary.

I tried not to reflect on how much damage Jai might have done the day before. Frankly, I only had myself to blame. Whatever happened now, I was certainly not going to let him destroy what I'd spent nine months and a great deal of hard work putting together. The day after the opening I'd arranged for my healing group to meet at the workshops, in order to discuss the programme and throw around a few ideas. I was no businesswoman, but I knew that I needed a great deal of activity in the centre from the outset if I were to start clawing back the initial capital expenditure.

Halfway through the meeting the doorbell rang and, for a few brief seconds, I became excited thinking it might be a potential enquiry. Instead, I opened the door to Jai. He seemed irritated. "You need to get me a key cut for this place," he said, marching authoritatively into the main room and setting down his briefcase. He ordered me to make him some herbal tea.

I asked him what he was doing there. It was a valid question considering over the last six months or so I'd barely seen anything of him in the daytime.

"I'm working here today," came the brusque reply. "Wherever *I* am is my office and today *this* is my office." With that he began spreading out his papers, bills, invoices and a pile of unopened mail all over the floor.

"No, Jai," I began firmly. "This is not Dove St or your office. This is a healing centre and I'd really like to keep it that way."

That was all that was needed to ignite the spark. It didn't take much, it never did. The experience of being with Jai was a bit like wading through a minefield and never quite knowing which slight twist or turn would be enough to set off an explosion. In the next breath I was accused of being manipulative, controlling, shallow-minded and a liar and, of course, I was only with him for financial security. The endless accusations of things I'd never said or done … the distortions of the truth … the exaggerations.

He began demanding the keys from me. I told him I didn't understand why he needed a set; that on occasions I would be hiring the centre out to other workshop leaders and I needed to preserve their privacy. But the one thing I was beginning to learn about Jai of late was that he didn't take too kindly to being refused *anything* and in the coming weeks the keys were to become a *major* issue between us.

It would have been impossible not to hear the fight on the floor above and, within minutes, Kate and Diane, another member of the healing group, stood in the doorway asking if I was okay. Another audience and Jai loved nothing better than when others got caught in the crossfire. Swiftly his attentions turned to Kate. Something else I'd only recently begun to notice about Jai was that he had a way of twisting personal information that he'd gathered about other people, data that he'd innocently and unwittingly solicited from me. He would store it, waiting for the right moment to use it callously against his target. Now his target was Kate and he aimed right at the jugular … personal remarks meant to cause her embarrassment and injury.

The problem was Jai was never any match for Kate. She was by far his intellectual superior and our friendship was so solid she was usually able to see through his insults. I think he actually envied our relationship. Kate knew the meaning of true friendship and Jai hated it that she was so special to me. He seemed determined to break the closeness.

But it was like he was playing some twisted game and the rules went like this: ignite the spark and quickly 'dismantle' the person. Watch them squirm and fall apart before your eyes and, once the sweet satisfaction of pain was sensed, back off … victory accomplished! In the next breath, he was asking to kiss her feet …

Another part of the all too familiar pattern. With Jai, one minute you were being insulted and viciously reviled … and the next you were an object of worship.

I hastily suggested we abandon the meeting for another day. Jai had given me no alternative having become of late a master at wasting other people's time. In a vain attempt to provoke a reaction he shot a question to Diane as they prepared to leave. "Do any of you know how powerful this man is who stands before you?" he asked.

Diane considered his question for a few moments, and then in a quiet and sympathetic tone, answered, "What I see before me, Jai … *is a terrified … six-year-old boy.*"

It was probably the most insightful comment he would ever hear and I knew it to be so close to the truth. But it was a truth upon which he'd woven a defence mechanism so tight it was impossible to penetrate …

It wasn't enough that he'd broken up the meeting that day. The issue of the keys wasn't going to go away … and, once on our own again, he began demanding them from me. Although I was furious with him, it wasn't the reason for withholding them. I was beginning to realize that Jai's energy was so disruptive he was more likely to repel than attract light workers to share the space with us. In hindsight though, my timing was all wrong. The last thing I needed to do in this situation was to fuel his anger. His mood grew more and more intense. He began accusing me of a deplorable lack of respect for him. Did I not understand that my happiness was linked to him, that my way to God was *through* him, and it was only in showing him the respect he deserved and believing in him, that my life would be filled with blessings? "Without me you are *nothing*," he said. It was a line he used on me over and over.

Swiftly his focus moved to my own upbringing and, not for the first time, my father came under scrutiny. Now he'd hit a raw nerve and I was livid.

"It's not your fault of course," he stated in a patronizing tone. "Clearly you were not disciplined properly as a child … if only your father had punished you correctly…"

Within seconds I was seeing red! "How dare you profess to know what my childhood was like," I was screaming in my defence. "I *was* punished and I had enough discipline to last me a lifetime!"

But Jai knew which buttons to press. He always had a way of neatly calculating his attack. He would strike like a cobra … spitting abuse, controlled, venomous, leaving his victim crushed, helpless under the sting of his powerful words. I always failed miserably in any kind of articulate response and, thus trapped in his predator's grasp, I would end up muttering a string of meaningless gibberish and obscenities under my breath as I slowly crumpled … piece by piece into an emotional and physical wreck…

This occasion was no exception. One minute I was defending myself poorly against his vicious, calculated verbal attack; the next I was at the mercy of his ferocious strength … as his fifteen stone bulk had me pinned helplessly against the wall by the throat. Slowly he drew back his arm, clenching the fist of his right hand, poised and aimed at my face. Tears burst forth from tightly closed eyes and rolled down my cheeks. I uttered a silent prayer in my head to whoever might be listening.

From that day to this, I cannot fathom exactly what happened, but in that instant an energetic presence of such heavenly magnitude passed invisibly between us, stopping his fist dead … a millimetre away from my face.

I slumped to the floor, gasping for breath, but the oxygen didn't seem to fill my lungs. I'd never experienced a panic attack in my life before, but I knew I was having one then. "Oh, look at what a good actress you are!" he jeered as he watched me writhe on the floor for air. My heart was pumping furiously and I felt the nausea rise in the pit of my stomach. All I could think about was the baby I was carrying and the damage I was doing. "*Enough*, Jai," I gasped, slowly regaining my breath. "Enough!"

"Do you see now," he sneered, "do you see how much control God has given me? If I'd *wanted* to kill you … I could have done it with one blow."

I have very little recollection of the remainder of that day, other than at some point Jai left the workshops and didn't return to our home that night. I'd fallen asleep on the sofa and awoken about four o'clock in the morning, cold and fretful. 'I *have* to get out of here … *I have to leave him*'… came the waking thoughts, clear and resolute.

The first thing I did that Friday morning was telephone Jai's brother, Nara, to let him know what was going on. It was obvious he was reluctant to discuss Jai with me and, keeping the conversation brief, he simply said, "I've been on the case for a couple of weeks now." He told me he'd involved a highly respected psychiatrist friend of his to see Jai. To some extent I was relieved, although something deep down inside suspected that that meeting would never take place.

Then, as soon as the surgery opened, I booked an appointment to see my doctor for later that day. I will not name her so as to preserve her professional identity. What I will say is that she was marvellous, not only in lending a sympathetic ear but also in giving me the short sharp reality check I needed.

Walking into her surgery with my brother, Martin, whose support I'd enlisted, all the emotions of the last six months, the anger, the confusion, and the fear seemed to just hit me in one gut-wrenching pain. I collapsed in a heap of uncontrollable tears, unable to speak for ten minutes.

"When you're ready ..." she said softly, with a faint, sympathetic smile.

I took a deep breath and began to pour the whole story out, *everything*, disjointed, chaotic, but nonetheless every unbelievable detail. She listened to the taped conversation of 'The Vision' and Jai's belief that now God worked for *him*.

There was a tense silence; then she quietly turned to me and looked me straight in the eyes. "Is he taking drugs?" she asked, almost clinically.

The thought hadn't crossed my mind before. "I ...I don't think so," I stammered, letting the question sink in. I knew Jai drank very little alcohol in my presence and I'd never known him to smoke, but drugs? But then, what the hell did I know? Everything I thought I knew about this man was just a sham now ... or so it seemed.

I was still throwing the question around in my head when she announced, "You're fourteen and a half weeks pregnant, Jacky" speaking the words slowly and clearly, as if to spell them out and giving me a due date of December 6th. I was far more advanced than I'd thought and, although the idea of a termination was utterly unthinkable to me, my emotions were a jumbled mess. Even worse, now I was plagued with the thought that all the stress had caused irreversible damage to my unborn baby. I couldn't think straight. I just sat there and cried and cried.

"You have to take yourself and Jessica out of the situation," she advised me, "out of the energy. Go to relatives, anyone, *anywhere,* just as long as you are well out of it."

Outside, in the coolness of the early afternoon, Martin and I stood in the car park, not speaking. Tears streamed down my face. Here I was barely past my first trimester and being forced for my own safety and sanity to walk out on the father of my unborn child and a man I'd fallen passionately in love with.

Do you walk out on someone because they're having some sort of psycho/spiritual crisis? Jai's intense mystical revelation was playing out in his life in a way I was struggling to comprehend and evoking within me a myriad of conflicting reactions. Frankly it felt like I'd jumped on a roller-coaster ride to hell and there was no exit platform in sight …

I found myself thinking that if being on the receiving end felt this overwhelming and turbulent, then what on earth must *he* be going through? My heart was urging me to stay and remain a stable loving focus for Jai but my head was telling me I also had a right to protect myself and my unborn child from the violent backlash of his crisis.

Whatever internal struggles were going on for him, I knew the man I loved was still in there *somewhere* and somehow I had to help him. It felt like my world was crashing down around me. "I'll come back with you," Martin offered. He knew on a practical level I was virtually incapable of the step I was about to take.

Jai walked in whilst I was haphazardly throwing things into a suitcase. Garry was with him. I had an odd feeling, as though he'd somehow sensed that I was planning to leave. This uncanny knack of second guessing what I was doing, even thinking sometimes, was something else I'd noticed recently.

"What's wrong, baby?" he shot the question almost in a lighthearted tone. "Can't handle the competition … can't handle being with the most powerful man on the planet?" It was aimed at Martin; he so wanted him to bite and yet there was a part of Jai that would have shrunk from my brother's challenge. He despised the fact that I held Martin in such high esteem and that, as one of the top martial arts instructors in his field, I knew my brother's steely calm would not waver an inch.

Fixing his eyes on Jai, Martin said something along the lines of "Drop it, she's out of here, you've pushed her too far this time." He realized I was serious and, in that instant, a look of genuine panic flashed across his eyes. Suddenly he began pleading with me not to go, telling me he realized he'd been scaring people, that the energy in him had subsided and he planned to "calm everything down."

His ability to switch in an instant from abusive and controlling to rational and understanding staggered me. In the next moment he was grabbing my feet and kissing them, amid outrageous and overwhelming declarations of undying, eternal love…

I think the only outcome that would have brought Martin any sense of relief was to see me walk out then and there. The problem was I wasn't ready to give up on Jai … not just yet. I don't think I ever had any intention of leaving, not permanently. I just needed to gain his attention, to let him know that neither of us could carry on any longer in this emotional chaos. Whatever was happening to him I truly believed it was just a temporary crisis and that with my love and support, he would somehow come through it.

That day I made him promise me two things: that he would spend a whole weekend in our home doing 'normal things' and that he would talk to the psychiatrist whose help his brother had enlisted. He agreed … *and I thought the worst was over.*

Over the next twenty-four hours his mood grew more rational, almost cheerful. We avoided any discussion about his visions, the mission, any matters of a spiritual nature and, with Jessica safely packed off to my sister's for the weekend, the time was spent engaged in practical things around the house. He'd ignored the lawn for weeks and, as tenants, we were responsible for maintaining the tidiness in the garden. That afternoon he mowed the grass for hours … barefoot. A wave of relief washed through me. I knew connecting to the earth in this way would be very grounding for him. We watched videos, shared a carpet picnic, listened to music, drank a little wine … and made love. As I held on to him tightly in the darkness that night, I felt like I had him back, for a little while … from wherever he had been. *Moments of normality, like these, however brief, I learned to cherish.*

Late that Sunday evening, Jai telephoned me from his 'offices', asking me to send some faxes. "I need you to set up some meetings as fast as possible, Jacky," he said.

"Who with?" I enquired, wondering what was so urgent.

"Bill Gates, Richard Branson and … Tony Blair," the response came, clear and direct.

Oh God, the madness was back already.

The reason for these meetings, Jai explained, was simple… He now had all the answers to *all* the world's problems and it was imperative he conveyed this information to the people to whom it mattered. He'd also set up a meeting that week, he told me, to see Robin Sieger, the author of 'Natural Born Winners' and the speaker at the Westway's awards ceremony.

"Robin's on my wavelength," Jai declared. It was Robin after all, he claimed, who'd 'recognized' him as the top business brain in the country … *a gross distortion of the truth I remembered thinking at the time; all Robin had actually done was comment on his sound business sense!* Despite the mind-blowing nature of his 'God-given revelations', Jai was confident Robin was "on a level to accept them."

Meetings of such high profile required of course a new wardrobe of clothes and, by the following afternoon, he had one: all designer, right down to his underwear and socks. I estimated he had spent over a thousand pounds. He purchased not just one but several jackets, short, long, light, heavy, leather, fabric. Trousers, sweaters and T-shirts in an array of different styles; expensive leather shoes, leather belts ... and every single item was without exception ... *black*.

"Only black clothes from now on. It's the colour of protection," he explained. "I *need* to wear black ... to deflect the poisonous arrows."

Oh God ...and I need a second opinion, I thought ... badly.

I *did* send a fax that day. But it wasn't to Bill Gates or Richard Branson or Tony Blair. It was to an award-winning health journalist called Hazel Courteney, author of the book 'Divine Intervention'.

I'd read Hazel's book whilst on holiday that year in Fuerteventura. In it she recounts her own near death experience which results in her receiving and channelling messages from Diana, Princess of Wales. The book, a phenomenal account of her journey into the realms of spirit and, ultimately, her own spiritual transformation both fascinated and inspired me. I never doubted for a single second whilst reading it that Hazel's experience was real. I resolved to contact her via her publishers.

It took less than twenty-four hours for Hazel to respond. Although a busy lady, she said my fax 'struck a chord'. It was as though she instinctively knew the experience I'd described was genuine.

It was an enormous relief to tell my story and I filled her in briefly on what was happening to Jai. "Without doubt he's going through some kind of 'spiritual emergency'," she explained. "This is when a spiritual awakening becomes a physical and also a mental crisis." *She wasn't kidding, I thought.*

"If he allows the ego to take over, he will believe himself to be God; this is the most dangerous part of the experience."

"He already does," I sighed. "Worse, he says God works for him now."

"Oh dear," she said, sounding concerned. "He needs to come down to earth."

"Basically, Jacky," she continued, "if he doesn't get grounded and quickly, the energy will literally *cook his brain* and the whole experience can spiral out of control."

I was trying to take in her words whilst at the same time wondering what the average family doctor might make of such a surreal conversation.

"Feed him grounding foods such as porridge and root vegetables. Give him sweet puddings, bread and jam, anything with sugar as his brain needs more glucose for fuel," she stressed, "and when the symptoms are at their worst, get him to lie on the ground and hold on to trees. This will all help to ground him."

I could hardly believe what I was hearing. Had I somehow unconsciously 'tuned in' to what he needed?

She told me about her own experience; how she thought she had become like some kind of enlightened Master and at one point had literally started to dematerialize. She had finally consulted a truly enlightened Indian guru who confirmed for her that many people who undergo these types of spiritual emergency believe themselves to be 'totally enlightened' or 'spiritual masters'. But that's a bit like saying you're a doctor simply because you have passed the entrance exam into medical school! she told me.

"Remember, Jacky," she said, "the training to hold this Divine energy and integrate it into one's everyday life can span years." Frankly, she hadn't had that … and neither had Jai.

In her case, the experience had triggered deeply passionate

and compassionate feelings. "If the ego gets out of control," she reiterated, "it can become very dangerous." I had an inkling of what she meant. Suddenly I felt very nauseous.

I confessed to her that I was struggling with his aggressiveness, although I didn't spell out the details. She confided how she had seen her most evil and her most beautiful sides, how she'd faced demons and angels. "He will face multiple realities," she said. I hurriedly made notes, desperately trying to let it all sink in.

She instructed me to sit him down that night and say the following words to him, slowly and authoritatively, "You are Jai Kham Daridra. You are part of God in a physical body – *we all are* and what you are going through has happened to others."

"I'll try," I replied feebly, knowing just how *that* would be received by him.

Finally, she gave me the name of a respected healer in Islington, London, who specialized with such 'emergencies'. The problem now, she told me, was that a chemical imbalance can easily occur in the brain. He would need to be fed a high dosage of B complex plus multi vitamins and essential fats to support the nervous system. She strongly advised me to get him to the healer as soon as possible, where she told me, "He will be stood on tectonic plates to help ground the energies."

I thanked her, several times. She added that she would like to meet with Jai and interview him about his experience. She was planning to write a 'Divine Intervention II' that explored the myriad effects of 'spiritual emergency' and the science of miracles.

"I hope he comes through this," she added sympathetically, "for your sake, Jacky." I remembered reading that her experience had lasted several months and I wondered how much more I could cope with. She gave me her mobile number and we left it that I would contact her again very soon.

The information had unsettled me; there was no doubt about

that. *But for the first time in six months, I felt there was a light at the end of the tunnel…*

Jai answered his mobile in the car. "Hazel Courteney wants to set up a meeting with you. I thought Thursday as you are going to be in London anyway … she has filled me in on what …" my voice trailed off as he abruptly cut in. I didn't get a chance to say anything else, before he was shouting to Garry in the passenger seat, "See, I told you she'd recognize me … she knows, she *knows* who I am. All of these people are going to have to sit at *my* table soon … okay, babes, Thursday sounds fine … give me the details later."

"B..but …" He was gone and I was left speaking to a ringing tone.

Later on that evening he dismissed the entire contents of Hazel's telephone call, even accusing me of 'conspiring with her' to concoct the whole conversation. "She doesn't know anything, she's not even on the same level. It's *her* that needs help," he said scathingly. "She hasn't even grabbed him." By that he meant Sai Baba.

It was another meeting doomed never to take place. She would have to come and see *him* were his final words. There was no way he was ever going to London to see *her*.

The light at the end of my tunnel quickly turned … to a faint and distant glimmer.

The more Jai became filled with a sense of his own importance, the more impatience he displayed with the humdrum daily life. He didn't want to hear about any theories that might steer him through his mind-blowing experience or 'ground' him back in the real world. His experience had been unique, exclusive, awe-inspiring and no one, not even Hazel, was going to take *that* away from him.

Life was far too mundane for him now and two days later, as we sat in the pre-natal ward awaiting my scan, his whole body language conveyed to the outside world that he had more important things to do and more important places to be.

The consultant asked to see us beforehand and I still cringe with embarrassment at the memory of that meeting. To be informed of the various tests available to check for abnormalities was standard practice, but I knew it wasn't necessary. Despite everything that was going on, deep down my intuition was telling me that all was well. Nevertheless, I listened to what he had to say attentively.

Jai interrupted with an arrogant and inappropriate remark. "How can there be risks? My sperm is perfect!" he exclaimed indignantly, leaving me wanting to kick him under the table! Thankfully, the consultant appeared to pay no attention to it.

Then he cut in again, saying that there couldn't possibly be anything wrong with his son because, "This is Daridra sperm we're talking about!" At this point the consultant gave an irritated sigh and continued to address his remarks only to me. Once again, Jai butted in, the hostility at having been ignored rising in his voice. "Why are you scaring her with all this?" he protested. "I'm telling you it's impossible for there to be anything wrong with my sperm!"

Finally the consultant, who had had enough by this time, swung his chair round to face him and yelled, "And I'm telling you, Mr Daridra, that this has *nothing* to do with *your sperm* and *everything* to do with *her age!*"

Under any other circumstances, it might have been hilarious and, even though it shut him up, I was beginning to deeply regret having him there. I couldn't believe how he'd even managed to make a routine check-up all about *him*.

Half an hour later the scan revealed that my pregnancy was even more advanced than my GP had led me to believe. I was sixteen and a half weeks and now being given a due date of 23rd November. As I lay there staring up at the ceiling, my head began to spin. The date struck a chord with me immediately. I threw Jai a quizzical look.

"What?" he asked, bemused.

"Don't tell me you don't know whose birthday it is?" I stammered. Still it didn't register. I couldn't believe after everything that had gone before, he hadn't instantly recognized the date ... "It's Sai Baba's, Jai," I groaned finally.

He took it as an instant sign from the heavens. Surely if his son shared his birthday with Sai Baba, the physical incarnation of God on the planet, then all of the visions *must* be true?

I'd walked *into* that hospital that morning with one firm and desperate hope. If I involved Jai as much as possible with the pregnancy and made him hang on to what was 'real', eventually he would emerge from this bewildering episode ... and in time, be able to integrate the whole experience into his daily life. I would have the man back that I loved and whom I still believed had the makings of a wonderful father.

I couldn't have been more misguided. I walked *out* of the hospital that morning in a daze ... and wondered if this latest revelation wasn't the universe playing some sick and twisted joke on me! I couldn't make sense of anything anymore, no longer clear in what I believed or disbelieved.

Worse still, I was even beginning to doubt my own sanity.

CHAPTER FOUR: 'INSANITY OR INFAMY'

'Show me a sane man and I will cure him for you'
Jung, Carl (1875-1961)

'Fame is like a river that beareth up things light and swollen, and drowns things weighty and solid'
Sir Frances Bacon (1561-1626)

I needed a breakthrough and all my hopes were pinned now on Jai's meeting with Robin, scheduled for the next day. *'He will listen to Robin,' I thought, 'he respects him.'* Even though we'd only met briefly, I trusted Robin's wisdom and I knew him instinctively to be a deeply spiritual man. I wondered what he would make of Jai's so called 'enlightened status'. Surely enlightenment brings bliss and a surrender of personal will. And for the fortunate recipient who finds himself in the presence of an enlightened being, they should feel bathed in a wave of peace and joy. Whatever else transpired in the meeting, I knew Robin would give him some sound advice.

At the awards ceremony the previous October, Robin had generously given Jai a personally signed copy of his book, 'Natural Born Winners'. It is one of the most inspirational books I have ever read, loaded with personal experiences, both touching and humorous, and packed with the tools and techniques for accessing the unlimited field of potential within every human being. If Jai could have read past the first chapter, he would have gained much from Robin's wisdom, but he didn't. In fact he passed it on to an acquaintance of his and the book I thought he would cherish always has to this day never been returned.

The whole meeting on Thursday, 15th June 2000 was

recorded. *In fact Jai had taken to recording every conversation of late.* In the writing of this book, I forced myself to listen to the hour-long tape many times, for the essence of that meeting and the verbal exchange that took place between them is a hugely important and intrinsic part of my story.

Robin's opening remark was engagingly frank as he confessed to having been "professionally cynical" about the spiritual revelations Jai had to tell him.

"I'm a little sceptical of people who claim they want to change the world," he told Jai. Believing however that there are no accidental encounters in the universe, and with his curiosity somewhat aroused, Robin had agreed to the meeting.

As they began to share information about their respective upbringings I noticed some interesting parallels. Like Jai, Robin confessed to having very little confidence as a young man and he had gone through school, university and his work experience expecting failure. He'd lost his father whom he "loved dearly" at the age of twenty and his worst fear as a young man, he told Jai, "was of dying alone and dying poor." At some point in his life he developed a faith in what he called a "universal God ... a universal intelligence."

"Life is a wonderful school," said Robin. "It will teach you lessons. If you do not learn the lessons, it will re-teach the lessons but only more painfully." *If only Jai had listened to that piece of advice, I remember thinking.*

Jai went on to outline his own upbringing, telling Robin how he'd "really suffered as a child" and how throughout his life people had always put him down. "I must have had about a million knock-downs," he said. His parents' volatile relationship had only added to his problems. "But I realize why they had those burdens now," Jai added. "It was to carry me ... because of the individual I was to become..."

When the conversation moved to the subject of God, Robin disclosed that he'd been diagnosed with cancer at a very early age and had attributed his recovery to full health to his underlying faith and a lifelong belief in God. He remarked, "I think it's the Hindus who say the guide to God is God himself. God will find you and bring you in; if you seek God you will find Him."

But that was a statement of course that didn't conform to Jai's new found truth *and only he had the truth.* "No, Robin, you are going to have to cry for Him like a child does for its mother ... you're going to have to search for Him. But if I tell you where He is, you are going to have to make an effort to go and see Him ..."

At a certain point on the tape it becomes obvious that Jai's energy levels are building as the passion in his voice becomes more detectable and his speech gains pace. Up until this point, the tone of the conversation is one of marked politeness, an agreeable exchange of spiritual truths, but Jai's excitement was building and he was keen to reveal the purpose of the meeting ... *his awesome revelation ... his trump card.*

"Robin ... *you're sitting in front of a master here,*" said Jai. "Krishna's right-hand man in the Bhagavad-Gita ... was me. My name in that life was Arjuna. That Arjuna is also this same Jai..."

He told Robin how, four months earlier, he'd stayed up for four days with just two hours sleep a night, reading The Gita and ..."It was almost like my Lord was speaking to *me.*" Then he added, "But I sit here today *knowing* he was speaking to me. My Lord, Sri Sathya Sai Baba, was also Krishna back then and because as Arjuna I was so close to him in that lifetime, I have been the first to recognize him in this one."

He didn't leave any room for Robin to respond to that statement before continuing, "And Arjuna had to stand up five thousand years ago and kill his own family; he had to kill his own gurus, he had to kill his own friends because they were all wrong and Lord Krishna told him, 'you've got to clear the ground'. Back then it was a righteous period and there were only 283,000 people who were wrong and so he could clear it. But today God has said to me, *everyone's* wrong, the whole world is wrong and so He's given me 'the power to do whatever I want'."

I suspect at this stage Robin was wincing at the sheer arrogance that had begun to punctuate every sentence. It was a far cry from 'the man of immense humility' that he'd met several months earlier at the Westway's awards ceremony, the man on whose 'sound business wisdom' he'd been moved to comment.

What follows next is a ten-minute monologue in which Jai recounts his 'vision' and the mission he'd been given by God. It was the second recording of his 'vision' on tape. The first formulates the prologue to this book and is a transcript of Jai's mind-blowing telephone call to me on 2nd June when the energy first hit. He was unaware at the time that I'd recorded it. In that recording, the tone was jarring and the words disjointed and there was an irreverent, almost sinister quality in its delivery.

In the meeting with Robin, some two weeks after the initial influx of energy, the forceful quality is still detectable but the message is clearer. By the time he saw Robin, Jai had his claims well formulated and I have reproduced them here. For to understand Jai's vision, the signs from heaven, his divine role, and the mission God planned for him … are central to this story.

"I had an influx of energy on 17th May 2000," he began, "and the rest of the world just looked at me and thought '*wow!* he's out of control', because I had to go through so many tests for my Lord in my head, some of which are still outstanding. I was prepared to die for Him; I was prepared to kill for Him; I was prepared to lose my arm for Him; I was prepared to cut off someone else's arm for Him; I was prepared to lie for Him; I was prepared to tell the truth for Him and not care what other people think for Him. If you truly want the Lord, Robin, then you've got to be prepared to do *anything* for Him."

In 'The Vision' bestowed on him by God, Jai offered to do His 'dirtiest work' and it was this work that now formed the basis for his mission. These are Jai's words verbatim from the meeting with Robin in which he describes 'the vision':

"We all sat around the table in the grand halls of the kingdom of heaven. Krishna Bhagwan, my Lord, asked 'Who wants to go down and do the mission?' and all the masters, Jesus, Buddha, Mohammed and Hitler, put their hands up, except me (Jaya). Then the Lord said what needed to be done: you have to be prepared to lie, prepared to die, prepared to kill, you have to do everything and anything, break any discipline and live every discipline.

"Jesus was given the option to come down and take this mission on originally but he was not prepared to be anything other than compassionate. But God said, 'It's gone so bad, that if you stand by compassion, people will beat you up.' So Hitler said, 'I'll go down and sort it out.' He's a master, you know; he sits in the same halls as Jesus Christ, but Hitler said, 'I've got no patience, I'll just go and kill them all and sort it out in a day.' Then Buddha said, 'I can't go down, I won't break a discipline.' Mohammed was not prepared to grow up. Then all the masters put their hands down, because none of them were prepared to do it.

"Then this guy (meaning himself) who came down and did what I did five thousand years ago and who now sits at His feet, I put my hand up. So then God looked at me and said, 'Why didn't you put your hand up first?' And I replied, 'Because, Lord, there's no place I'd rather be than at your feet.' Then He asked me why I was putting my hand up now and I said, 'Lord, there's nothing more important to me than doing your work.' And He got really happy and He started clapping and I said, 'Stop' because I hadn't finished. I like to impress Him though, I like to do that extra bit, you know, like we all like to do, as a student does for a teacher.

"So He stopped in his tracks and said 'Yes?' And I said, 'More than do your work, Lord, I'd rather do your dirtiest

work, that no one else wants to do.' And He said, 'Today, Jaya, you've overtaken me.'

"I said, 'What does that mean, Lord?' and He said, 'Today I'll grant you all the powers these masters have, to go and do the job and, on top of that, I'll grant you the unlimited life you need.' Then He said, 'I'll give you one more power on top,' and I said, 'But what's that, God?' and He said, 'I'll give you My power.'

"And I got scared and I said, 'What does that mean, Lord?' He said, 'It means today you are on top of me.' And I got scared more and I started crying and I said, 'No, I can't, I'm so scared I can't do that,' because I know being in that position I could fall. Then He just shouted and He said, 'Today, Jaya, I'm telling you not to defy me, because today if you don't take this opportunity, the universes will collapse, not just this one, but all the universes will collapse because the law is no longer standing.'

"And I got scared and I was crying and He was crying and got angry as if 'You've got to do the job now, you've deserved it, you've earned it, you've got it.' So I dug deep and, realizing the seriousness of the situation, I said, 'Okay, God, I'll take it on one basis, that you do one thing for me,' and He said, 'What's that?' and I said, 'Put me in your lap and then put me on your head.' Do you understand the meaning of that? Like a child is protected in its mother's lap, and then put me on your head, because I haven't got what it takes, but if I'm in your lap, then you're protecting me and I'll be safe.

"In the Krishna period I worked behind Him and He worked in front giving me orders. In this period He's saying to me, 'You make the moves, Jai, and I will listen to you,' because God likes to experience things just like we do and He's never had the opportunity until now to be a back runner …"

So God had given him the reins and the work had now started, he told Robin. I can only *imagine* what must have been going through Robin's mind.

"I know who the Lord is; I know who I am; I know who I was and I know what my mission is." It was a fourfold enlightenment as he called it and the mission was to convince the whole of mankind that Sri Sathya Sai Baba was the living God on the planet.

Whatever thoughts Robin might have been entertaining, he certainly didn't voice them. His responses were direct, sensitive and yet laced with caution. Here was this man he'd met only once, sitting in front of him and telling him that *'God worked for him now'*; a man he instinctively *knew* was deadly serious about everything he was saying. Having the wisdom not to ridicule Jai nor make light of his claims was a testament to Robin's character and the sensitivity with which he handled him.

"We all have our own belief systems, Jai," remarked Robin, "and we can't force the world to fit our belief. The Aborigines have never heard of Krishna; they'll live and die without ever hearing of Sai Baba …"

"They *will* hear," Jai said in a self-assured tone, "because I'm going to get the message there."

"And I think your gift, your challenge," said Robin, "is to get it there in a way that they'll accept it. I'm a great believer in allowing people to find their own truth. It's like when Mohammed and Christ came to give the good news and the world turned their backs on them …"

But Jai didn't want to hear about the world turning its back on him or words of warning that conflicted with his new found cosmic status. In any event, he told Robin, he was ready for *any* challenge. He'd proved that when he broke into London's Swaminarayan Mandir 'like a thief in the night' a couple of weeks earlier. He related to Robin how he'd 'dismantled' ten security staff who'd tried to block his way and how he'd demanded an interview with the head devotee at eleven thirty at night.

His aim was to tell them his 'news', that he was the soul of Arjuna, and that he was the only mortal in existence who had recognized Sai Baba as the living God on the planet, knowledge he assumed that would blow apart their belief systems. "Your whole system is full of bullshit," he'd told them aggressively. "Either admit your guru's not God or I'll destroy you …"

It was the type of disturbing behaviour that resulted in his access being blocked but Jai failed to recognize it as in any way threatening. "You've got to understand how this sounds to them, Jai," said Robin cautiously. "Frankly, I think you're scaring people. This energy is coming across to me as aggression… Do what you have to do, but do it with compassion and peace and love in your heart."

But Jai had 'The Truth' and if the truth scared people then that was their issue, not his. He told Robin how he had to raise his energy levels by demanding an apology for their discourteous treatment towards him. "Say sorry; say sorry or I'm going to dismantle you in less than two seconds, so fast, you won't know what hit you … and each time I said 'say sorry', Robin, I raised my energy. It got to the stage where I just shook all the negativity up. I just broke them down, dismantled them, fearful that I was right."

I don't doubt for a second that there were alarm bells going off *loudly* in Robin's head as he listened to Jai's intense account of how he had to "destroy all their foolishness" at the mandir. This was, after all, a man who was claiming to be 'enlightened', a man who was supposedly in a perpetual state of bliss and yet his words were punctuated with aggression, threats and foul language.

"You don't need to be in conflict," Robin warned him. "You don't have to discredit other people. You don't have to say 'your guru's not God'. What you have to understand is the truth exists."

But Jai disagreed; only *he* had 'The Truth', his information was coming from the highest dimension, "because I sit in the same halls as Jesus Christ."

Faced with Jai's challenging and threatening energy that day, Robin must surely have struggled to equate the man sitting in front of him with the man he'd encountered at the Westway's awards ceremony. Back then he'd seen in Jai a man with seemingly no trace of ego.

"You weren't sitting there giving it large. You weren't saying 'I'm going to do this and I'm going to do that' and you weren't chasing money," he told Jai. In fact, Robin was so impressed that day by Jai's quiet confidence and humility that he'd resolved to comment on it and had publicly delivered those words … "I've heard more business wisdom from this man in the last ten minutes … than I have from the experts in the past ten years."

How could Robin have possibly known how Jai was to take that sincere and well meaning remark in the months that followed? Just as I had fuelled his self-belief *often* with words of praise, admiration and encouragement, Robin had no inkling of the ego that lay beneath the surface, craving to be fed.

Ironically, it was the accolade that Jai had been searching for all his life…

I'm sure Robin couldn't wait to terminate the meeting and after an hour or so he politely reminded Jai that he needed to take his other appointments and enquired what it was he wanted from him. Jai told him that he needed Robin's expertise on how to go about a book *he* intended to write, a recording of his heavenly visions and the mission he'd been given by God. A book in which he planned to tell the world that in the year 2020, at the age of fifty-five, when Sai Baba passes, he would be taking over "the whole mantle" and Sai Baba would be working with him "in the higher dimensions."

Tactfully Robin told him that he couldn't be personally involved, but offered him some practical advice. Then he added, "You must allow me to challenge you, Jai. I'm not saying I'm going to challenge your sanity, but what I am going to challenge is your behaviour. I will say to you, look, I think this behaviour is going to send the wrong signals. It's not a war, but I think you're going to go through a testing time…"

But it was a war in Jai's mind, a war which had only just begun and one in which God had given him unlimited power…

It was nearly two years after the event when I finally had the chance to listen to that hour-long tape in full. At the time, Jai had cast it to one side and not placed any degree of significance on it, although he was swift to assure me that the meeting had been a great success. I didn't buy it at all. It was obvious that, like Hazel, Robin had known instantly that there was something desperately wrong, as indeed any rational person would!

I often wondered what Robin's assessment was of Jai at the time and it wasn't until the early part of 2006 in the research for this book that I finally got the chance to ask him that question personally.

"I knew he was having some kind of psychotic episode," Robin confided to me, "but all my instincts told me that his mental state was so fragile that he needed to be handled with kid gloves." He said that he'd often wondered why Jai had selected him to be the recipient of his 'mind-blowing' news, when all he'd done was made a complimentary remark about his business acumen. He'd also found it curious that, having gone to all that trouble to initiate the meeting in the first place, Jai had made no effort to contact him ever again.

Of course he hadn't, because Jai didn't get from Robin what he needed and that was the recognition and total acceptance of his claims. Neither of course in the coming months did he take on board any of Robin's cautionary words. I don't know why at the time I thought he would. If God was taking orders from *him* now, why on earth would he respect the advice of us mere mortals?

Since the day the 'emergency' hit, he hadn't stopped for a single second to listen to how irrational his claims sounded to the outside observer. I felt I'd lived every minute of his experience with him and yet to Jai only *his* view mattered and the rest of us were misguided.

The day after his meeting, Jai asked me to book him a three-week trip to India for as soon as possible. He'd told Robin that he believed Sai Baba was going to hand over to him a million pounds and it was the exact sum of money he needed to cement his status in the business world ... And even if he didn't, he told Robin, Baba at the very least would give him a plausible reason for not blessing him with the money. The main object of his trip was to have his visions confirmed and for the Indian Avatar to point him on the next step of his journey.

Frankly, India couldn't come quickly enough and I was relieved to some extent that he would at least be out of my energy for a while. I hoped and prayed that during the next three weeks, he would find the answers we *both* needed, that somehow by experiencing the 'silence' of the ashram and finding himself in such deeply reverent surroundings, his vibration would be lifted.

The night before his trip, Wednesday, 21st June, he returned home in the early hours of the morning, quieter and more thoughtful than normal. I was curled up in the armchair, unable to sleep, as had been the pattern for weeks now, often waking hourly in a fretful and anxious state. He sat down opposite me, just staring at the floor. I just *knew* he'd been to the casino and probably lost an enormous amount of money.

I sat and looked at him, looking 'beyond his physical body with lazy eyes', a technique I'd developed to read people's auras and I was suddenly struck by the 'blackness' of his aura. So much so that I had the instinctive urge to move my chair further away from him.

"What's the matter?" he asked in a mocking tone.

"You look ... dirty," I said.

"How can I be dirty, babes? I've had at least four showers today," he replied.

"I don't mean unclean, Jai," I responded thoughtfully. "I mean … your aura looks *dirty.*"

The following day I packed his suitcase. "You can't wear black in the ashram," I told him, ironing as many white shirts and light-coloured trousers that I could find. That evening, a couple of hours before he was due to be taken to the airport, I held a farewell dinner for him, inviting his brother, Nara. There was a strained silence throughout the meal, although I knew his brother and I had the shared unspoken thought that 'this trip somehow *had* to work'. Halfway through dinner, Jai asked us if we thought Sai Baba would instantly recognize him as the soul of Arjuna and kiss his feet to welcome him into the ashram. "I think he'll roll the red carpet out for me, you know, especially as he knows I'm coming."

How on earth do you respond to a statement like that?

"I don't know what he has planned for you, Jai," I said. "All I know is that I think you are *meant* to go."

He said something else that evening that defied an answer "There's only seven people on the planet that can do what I can do, do you know that?"

As his car sped off into the blackness of the night, I cried like a baby. I was deeply in love with a man whom I'd seemingly lost to an 'unseen world', a man whose mind appeared to be fragmenting into a million pieces before my very eyes and a man I was terrified of labelling crazy or insane. I couldn't tell anyone what I was going through because they simply wouldn't understand; worse, they might not even believe me.

I felt as though I were in possession of an appalling secret that was draining the very life force out of me … *and for the first time in my life, I felt truly helpless and desperately alone.*

On the Friday evening around 10 p.m., Jai telephoned me to

say that he'd arrived in Delhi and all was well. He'd taken a hotel room for the night and planned to fly out to Bangalore in the morning. That was all.

Earlier that day, badly in need of some company, I'd asked Kate to come round to the house for a few hours. She had begun to avoid visits when Jai was there. I can't say that I blame her. His ability to make incongruous statements, mostly of a sexual nature when she was around, staggered me. Whether it was to shock or embarrass us, or both, we could never really fathom his motivation.

One particular time, a couple of months earlier, I remember Kate and I had spent an evening together talking. Jai joined us later. Within minutes he'd turned the conversation round to sex and implied that Kate and I were having a clandestine lesbian relationship. "C'mon, just admit it the pair of you," he said teasingly, but deadly serious. This was followed by a remark so profane in its content that it was worthy of a porn magazine and certainly not one that I could include in the pages of this book. My mouth gaped open. "What?" he asked, shrugging his shoulders and donning the innocent expression of a six-year-old who'd just been falsely accused of something by his teacher. "Oh, sorry," he laughed, "is that bad?"

With Jai now in India and having the security of knowing that he wasn't going to intrude on our conversation, Kate and I sat watching a video documentary on Sai Baba. I don't know what we were looking for really; clues, signs, confirmation … *anything*. "I so want to believe, Jacky," said Kate, "but I see more love coming from the faces of the people in the crowds than from him." It was genuinely how she felt.

Jai telephoned again on the Sunday, this time for a full half-hour. He told me that he'd had a visitation from Sai Baba. The Indian Avatar had come to his room, sat at the end of his bed and delivered this message personally to him. "Jaya, how can you possibly expect them (*meaning mankind*) to understand, when they can't even remember what happened to them last year … what you have been given is for you and you alone."

"He's confirmed *everything,* Jacky," he added excitedly. "I may as well come back now." *What? All that build-up and you're only going to stay two days!*

I pressed him a little; had Sai Baba appeared in living flesh or had Jai sensed him to be there? Had Jai been awake or sleeping? Did he tape any of it? He scolded me for asking him 'stupid' questions. "It's hard to stay rational, when you're in the presence of the Divine," he retorted.

I asked him *where* he was sleeping and he told me that he had a room to himself although at first he'd shared a dormitory. "Are you managing to sleep?" I enquired, fearing that just the opposite was the case. He was almost irritated by the question. "I haven't slept for three days now; I don't need food or water, I'm just filled up on his energy." I knew the effects that fasting and not sleeping had on Jai … *here we go again, I remember thinking.*

I was keen to know whether he'd received darshan yet. Darshan is when you sit and pay respects to the holy person in order to receive blessings and purification from him. From the many videos I'd watched, I knew that, during darshan, the Indian mystic was in the habit of taking letters from devotees, conveying questions of a spiritual nature they wanted answered. I'd given Jai a brief letter in which I'd appealed for Sai Baba's guidance, but he hadn't been able to get a front row position he told me, even after waiting in line for two days. "So have you managed to give him my letter yet?" I asked him.

"No, it wasn't important," he replied dismissively.

"It was to *me,* Jai," I sighed.

He told me he had to end the call as there was too much going on around him to miss a single moment. Just before he put the telephone down, he made me promise not to tell a single soul what he'd shared with me. "It's too mind-blowing, Jacky, and it just creates jealousy," he said.

I sat there for a while thinking about the conversation. There had been no red carpet, no kissing of the feet, no special treatment, no darshan, *nothing* and yet, to Jai, the whole experience had been 'mind-blowing'. I remembered Hazel telling me how in the state of 'emergency' he will believe his insights and realities one hundred per cent, when the problem is of course they are mostly only real in *his* reality.

Jai may well have tapped into some potent archetypal imagery and accessed some universal 'spiritual truths' in his visionary dialogue to the heavens, but I was now expected to believe that Sai Baba had confirmed *everything* to him. I was expected to believe that all the visions were true, that Jai was the saviour of the planet sent to take all of mankind back to God, whether by fair means or foul ... and I was expected to believe it all ... simply because he was telling me so.

Ten minutes later the telephone went again. I thought it was Jai back. Instead it was an old friend of mine whom I hadn't spoken to for over a year.

"I can't believe I'm ringing you, Jacky," she began, her voice sounding deeply troubled. "I've had a dream and it's really upset me. I know you are good at interpreting things like that. Please, I just want you to put my mind at rest."

She began to relate her dream to me:

"I dreamed we'd gone to look round a flat to see if it was suitable for rental. It was completely empty, devoid of all furniture. Suddenly I found myself on another floor and my baby (who's eight months old) had disappeared. I started frantically looking for him, only to find him in a cot in a far corner of the room on the floor below. A woman I recognized to be a 'vampire' was gnawing away at the cot with her fanged teeth. "Get away from my baby, get away from him," I screamed. "You are not having his blood." She just looked at me. "I don't want his blood," she answered. "I want ...his soul.""

A cold chill ran up my spine and my eyes started to fill up with tears. I composed myself quickly and began asking her questions like had she been forcibly separated recently from the baby and maybe this had subconsciously fed her fears? She told me she was thinking of putting the baby into nursery care, simply because she *had* to work.

"It's an anxiety dream, Pam," I told her. "It will be fine. Seek out a good day care centre where he will be happy and the fears will subside." She seemed relaxed with that explanation and we chatted about other things for a while.

As I put down the telephone, I just *knew* that the dream was a message for me. *A message that had dark and sinister connotations and one that would unfold in the course of time …*

I had only one other call from Jai the following Tuesday at eight o'clock in the morning. He sounded manic. "He's confirming everything for me as Arjuna, which he did when I was in heaven," he said. "If you like, he's giving me an apprenticeship on earth as he did in heaven. He's confirmed my mission …"

"Which is?" I cut in.

"To take the rest of mankind back to God … I've told you this already," his tone became impatient, "and he's told me loads about you."

"Like what?" I answered.

"That you're more in tune with him than you even realize. You really are connected to God as you keep saying. And you've done loads for me, you know…" His voice trailed off a bit and then he added, "I've been thinking a lot about you while I've been here. How hard I've been on you. I'm sorry … I'm really sorry." He sounded genuinely remorseful.

I didn't say anything, responding only with a deep sigh.

"You're leaving me, aren't you?" he stuttered after a long pause.

"It's not that simple, Jai, is it … it's just not that simple."

I didn't hear from him again until he'd landed back in England ten days later. I had no idea what to expect on his homecoming. My life was fast turning into one of those psychological thriller movies where the plot twists and turns each time you least expect it. Although I'd sat every day glued to my computer screen at the workshops, my mind for those ten days remained firmly in India, with Jai.

In a way I was desperate to see him, despite being apprehensive about what startling new revelations he had to tell me. *I'll deal with it, I thought, it can't get any worse surely.* When he exited the taxi as it pulled up outside our house late on the day of his arrival back in England, the physical sight of him took my breath away. He'd lost over two stone in weight. He looked dishevelled and positively ill and his eyes had taken on that vacant, staring expression when, as a result of drastic weight loss in the face, the eyeballs just seem to hang loosely in the sockets.

"What a journey, Jacky, what a journey!" was all he said before stripping off his clothes and heading for the shower less than five minutes later and I suspected he wasn't just referring to the physical 'journey' either. I'd never seen him look so dreadful.

In the days that followed, little by little, the full extent of Jai's 'journey' began to unfold. Rather than being afforded the special treatment he'd anticipated and *expected*, the opposite had become his reality. There had been no private room and he'd been forced to share his space with other devotees in a sparse and cramped dormitory.

There are 'rules' in the ashram that visitors are respectfully reminded to follow. One is the adherence to a strict code of peace and silence. Security guards known as sevadahls stand by at various locations, protecting the grounds and quietly enforcing the rules. This gave Jai an obvious problem. In his new role as 'supreme commander of the universe', he'd dispensed with the rule book a long time ago and, despite frequent, polite requests by the sevadahls asking him not to use his tape recorder, he'd insisted on turning it on at every opportunity and, as I've said before, Jai didn't take kindly to being refused *anything*.

On the eighth day he somehow landed himself in jail. What actually happened for him to be forcibly removed from the ashram and incarcerated for the night, I've no clear idea. I suspect he lost control at some minor polite request by one of the guards. I was fast learning with Jai that it didn't matter whether you used low arousal techniques or if you played him at his own game and fought fire with fire. If he didn't get his own way, he simply flipped out.

But there's an old saying that negative attention is better than no attention at all! In just the same way that a child reacts, caught out by their own bad behaviour, Jai thrived on the attention this opportunity afforded him. He had a captive audience after all, one to whom he could reveal the details of his heavenly visions and lay bare his claims and he wasn't going to waste a single second of it. "If you are the soul of Arjuna," the guards challenged him, "show us how you can meditate for several hours standing on your big toe!" It was a ridiculous challenge of course and one that he was physically incapable of meeting, despite his numerous attempts.

The only thing Jai succeeded at that night was in creating an unnecessary disturbance and wasting a great deal of everyone's time and energy. As for his claims and his heavenly mission, his shameful display had destroyed any chance of credibility and succeeded only in evoking … their mockery.

I can only assume that he threw one temper tantrum too many because Jai's planned stay in India was cut short by three days. Not because he was homesick but for the simple reason that he was ordered to leave. He was actually manhandled off the premises and thrown into the last carriage of a filthy cargo train headed back to Bangalore. "People were going to the toilet on the train right there in front of me, Jacky," he told me, a look of disgust crossing his face at the memory. It was the final humiliation.

Rather than gaining the respect and adoration of the people he'd gone there to befriend, he had attracted instead their loathing and ridicule ... and in the process made them his enemies.

The next seven days he spent huddled under the duvet cover, emerging occasionally only to shower and to eat. He said he needed time for reflection and a period of rest to organize his thoughts. The security staff's treatment of him had been so far removed from his own expectations, he could only attribute it to their 'limited understanding' and, despite everything that had happened, he concluded the trip had overall been a positive one. It never occurred to him for a single second that Sai Baba had drawn him there to 'break down' the ego and to teach him humility and compassion.

Jai viewed it that God was simply testing his levels of endurance to see whether he was worthy of the mission and of the mammoth task that lay ahead of him. He convinced himself that the visions and the signs were accurate and that no change needed to take place in his way of thinking. It was just going to be a much harder job than he anticipated ... convincing everyone else around him.

Something did change for a brief time, however, and I wasn't sure that it was a wholly positive change. For a while, Jai retreated into a world of silence.

He'd been moved to bring back a picture of Sai Baba, dressed in white as opposed to his customary orange. In the picture, Sai Baba is depicted holding his index finger to his lips, as though suggesting an action of not speaking. Jai took it as a sign.

I didn't know what was worse, him telling me as he had done for the last several months, the deepest darkest secrets that lurked in the shadowy recesses of his mind ... or him retreating into a silent world ... *of unspoken visions and untold horrors that threatened the very fabric of his rationale.*

Despite my fears, for the next few weeks an element of peace prevailed. Sometimes I would forget my pregnant state completely, pushing my body to the limits with the daily demands of running a home and the workshops. Occasionally when I stole a few quiet moments to sit in silence and meditate, a kick or jerk from deep down in my tummy would remind me of the growing child inside me.

These brief moments should have been times when I 'gave' to myself, but they were often spent in prayer and distant healing and always with Jai as the focal point. I tried not to speculate on where it would all end. In a way I think I was gathering coping mechanisms that somehow kept me sane and got me safely through each day.

A great deal of my emotional solace came from being of service and I submerged myself more and more into my work. The weekly talks-based group that I called Q.E.D (which stood for Question... Enquire ... and Discover) had attracted a membership into the workshops that was slowly but steadily increasing. I wasn't covering the overheads, not by a long chalk, but I knew I was on the right track.

I also knew that Jai ... was in deep trouble. Rather than alleviating his crisis, his trip to India appeared to have forced the powerful spiritual energies deeper within. Jai's inner world was not a happy one. The angrier and more frustrated he grew, the more he used those around him as an outlet for his pain. The period of silence was short-lived; he had knowledge of cosmic importance and no one, absolutely *no one* was listening. It led to dissatisfaction with everyone around him and with everything he saw.

To Jai, the outside world was a world full of twisted paradoxes inhabited by a misguided populous, lost in their materialistic and empty existence. It made him even more determined that, as the man God had sent down to change the world, he was going to make one huge and dramatic mark on it.

Somehow in early September of that year, I managed to persuade him that we all needed a break and I booked four nights away at a family-run guest house in Torquay. I suppose in hindsight it was an attempt on my part to create a diversion and one that I thought would serve as a 'temporary vacation' from the madness that had come to dominate our lives.

I'd be kidding myself if I looked back and saw *every* moment of that time away as wonderful. There were moments of deep tenderness between us. There were even moments of side splitting laughter and then there were times when Jai, for absolutely no reason at all, would make some callous and contemptuous remark and go and spoil everything.

Staying at the guest house at the same time was a young man in his early twenties whom I shall call Dan. Jai asked him to accompany us to a water park for the day. Afterwards I realized he had just used him, to sport with, to taunt and tease, as he bragged excessively, exaggeratedly, even to the point of lies, about businesses we didn't own, famous people he hadn't met, accomplishments he hadn't achieved.

He had got into the habit of introducing me as his wife, a psychologist with ten degrees and a phenomenal woman! Jaya and I were never married and I am a psychotherapist without a degree to my name. But this was the same phenomenal woman who at one point during the day, he found it hilarious to squeeze a cold, soaking wet T-shirt all over, as I relaxed on a sunlounger quietly reading my book. Naturally I was upset and when Dan commented that he thought his actions cruel and childish, Jai swiftly turned on him, 'dismantling' him in seconds as had become his latest and greatest skill. Dan was just another pawn in his perverse game and when, at the end of the day, he grew tired of him, he dumped him without so much as a backward glance.

I was finding this desperate need of Jai's to be seen as utterly superior to everyone he met thoroughly bizarre and utterly repugnant. Did he really believe the things he was saying? Was his self-esteem so low that he had to continually make things up, create a web of lies and a fantasy world that made him look more exciting and interesting than he really was?

I was no expert, but I could only rationalize at this point that the 'spiritual emergency' he was going through had dredged up deep-seated inadequacies, fears and anxieties to the surface. Hazel had warned me that the crisis would make him 'face his darker side'. I was desperate for him to undergo psychotherapy because I'd convinced myself that he would benefit from it, but I also knew that I was far too emotionally involved to work with him personally.

A few times I tried to engage Jai in hypnotherapy, working with 'goal-focused' trance scripts which I thought might help him stay motivated and improve his business aims. Every single time he would bring himself back out of the trance early, thereby sabotaging any hope of success, claiming he hadn't got time for it and he had other places to be. I avoided any attempt to penetrate his childhood experiences, believing that he was neither prepared for, nor capable of dealing with whatever lay deep within the psyche.

I remember early on in our relationship, Jai relating this observation about his childhood. He told me that his happiest moments as a child came at the exact halfway point as he walked between home and school. The family home to Jai represented constant tension and violent arguments, resulting from his parents' volatile relationship and school was a cold and unfriendly place where he felt 'different', foolish and gravely misunderstood.

It was the fifteen minutes between home and school, this small window of time where Jai felt truly safe and free. It was there that he had created his own place of perfection, *his little oasis of Nirvana...*

I recall my eyes filled up with tears at the time. I stored away the memory labelling it 'Jaya's fifteen minutes of happiness'.

I think it gave me one tiny glimpse into his early experiences and the enormous pain he'd spent a lifetime masking. Frankly, I knew it would take a very skilled therapist to help Jai lay the 'ghosts of his past' to rest and for any therapy to succeed at all, he had to acknowledge that he had a problem in the first place *… and, to Jai, it was everyone else who had the problem.*

Nothing changed by us taking the break away. These short periods when we escaped our daily routine only served to alleviate Jai's boredom for a brief while and failed to have any lasting effect. Dove St News was no longer any challenge for him and he was spending more and more time away from the shop, oblivious to the impact this was having on the business.

He spent all of his time at his 'offices', alone, engaged in philosophical writings, formulating business ideas, none of which gathered energy or amounted to anything but just remained there on the paper … endless lists and ideas that came to naught. Not surprisingly he'd taken to signing his name on every piece of paper as 'Krishna' or 'Arjuna'.

It was impossible to talk to him without the conversation turning around to his daily 'visions', his mission and his God-given role that was of supreme importance. When I look back I don't know what was worse. If I 'bought into' the visions and believed everything he told me, it meant I respected him, I was his best friend, but I also became part of the madness.

If I challenged or rejected what he was saying, I was his arch-enemy and I risked his terrifying wrath. I was in a no-win situation and my days were spent as though picking my way through a minefield *…and, like an animal in captivity, I was thoroughly and helplessly under his control.*

Jai found a new weapon up his sleeve as a means of controlling me … money. By early November it had begun to run out. Whilst out shopping for baby clothes, I'd had the embarrassment of my Switch card being rejected because I'd exceeded my overdraft limits. It was a shopping trip Jai and I should have done together but he arrived four hours after the arranged time and I was forced to postpone it until the following day taking Jayne with me instead. Shopping for essentials for the baby like a lot of other things ... it just wasn't on his list of priorities.

Whether he was intentionally withholding money, or he genuinely didn't have it, or whether he was gambling it away, I simply didn't know. I knew Jai's brother had made the decision to tighten the purse strings and, although I don't want to speculate on their relationship in the pages of this book, especially where money is concerned, I suspected Nara was far from happy with Jai's operational handling of the business.

I tried many times to draw Nara out on what had caused the deep and unforgiving rift between them, but he was a man who kept things very close to his chest. I was fed Jai's version ... and there are two sides to every story. I suspected the feud had a history that went back years.

Early in November in the final month of my pregnancy I booked a stand at the Complementary Health Exhibition for later that month where I planned to promote the workshops. I was also booked to do a talk on stage on the subject of 'Mind Power'. Everyone thought I was crazy taking on something so demanding four days before my due date, but I badly needed the marketing and saw it as a great opportunity. All my daily efforts were being geared up to this point, producing endless flyers, posters and promotional material. Frankly, looking back, I don't know how I kept going.

Something that had become my practice at every talks evening in the workshops was to place a message in the form of a spiritual quote or inspired piece of writing on each seat. It had become a kind of trademark of mine. People would take their seat and find the message placed there to have some personal importance or specific meaning to them. Many would approach me afterwards and say, "Jacky, it was as though you *knew* I needed to hear this."

Jai liked what I was doing. "Run off a load of these for me, will you? I need to give them out to my customers." There were seven particular readings that he was especially drawn to. I said I would when I had a few minutes' spare time.

On the morning of Monday, 13th November 2000, after several days had passed, Jai reminded me that I hadn't produced the copies he'd asked for. I replied that I simply hadn't had time and handed him instead another paper I'd written entitled 'Twelve Spiritual Disciplines for Contented Living'. I thought it would appeal to him and suggested he photocopied it for his staff. I knew he liked it, but he seemed determined to hide his appreciation. It wasn't after all what he'd asked for and he took it that I'd ignored his original request … and, to Jai, that meant I had no respect for him. He began getting ready for work but I could detect from his shift in mood that the oversight had really irked him.

It didn't take much to light the touchpaper. With Jai, fury and rage were always lurking just below the surface. A split second later all hell broke loose and I was subjected to the most scathing and hateful verbal attack, so intense and so utterly out of proportion to the complaint, it rendered me speechless. He allowed me no let up for a full half-hour. And although Jess was doing her level best to keep out of the way, she couldn't fail to hear every word.

"Shut up! Just shut up," I was screaming at him whilst holding my fingers in my ears, anything to block out his vile and ugly words. The more I did this, the more he raised the volume, following me around from room to room, giving me no respite from the tirade of abuse that so readily spilled from his mouth. I kept begging him to leave me alone but he was relentless, seemingly gaining some warped pleasure from it. Powerless to respond, I finally sat down at my desk in the study, put my head in my hands and wept. Once again he'd reduced me to an emotional wreck and I felt *pathetic*.

Several minutes passed and then something stirred deep inside me. All the confusion and hurt suddenly gave way to a wave of anger. I was utterly sick of his punishing behaviour. Fearing that I was about to explode, I picked up the telephone and rang Kate, desperately needing to hear a rational voice. I spoke to her for less than two minutes but she could detect from my tone that something really bad was happening. Jai, dressed and ready to leave, walked back into the study where I was sitting.

"I need some money from you before you go," I said. There was an undeniable hardness in my voice that was impossible to mask.

Jess was behind him. "Mum's only got ninety pence in her purse," she butted in. It was the absolute truth; I had no money at all for food. Reaching into his pocket, he offhandedly threw her a twenty-pound note.

I guess it was something in her response; I suspect all she did was raise her eyebrows, but he took it instantly to mean that she wasn't grateful.

"Give it back. You don't deserve it," he demanded, lurching towards her in an action of snatching back the money.

"Mum needs it," she replied, hastily screwing it up and concealing it in her hand behind her back.

"Give it back now," he bellowed "or I'll *make* you."

Within seconds I was between them, fearing the outcome of his rage would be visited on Jess. "Before you lay a finger on *her,*" I retorted defiantly … "*you go through me first.*"

The slap came from nowhere … but it wasn't the sharp stinging sensation that caused me to catch my breath. It was the shock that he'd hit me at all. Finally it had happened, what everyone close to me had predicted all along … *that one day our relationship would turn violent.*

For a few brief seconds I was frozen to the spot, unable to move. The telephone rang and jolted me back. It was Kate; we had a brief exchange of words.

"He's hit you, hasn't he?" she questioned.

I was still in a daze. "Yes," I murmured.

"Right, that's it, Jacky … I'm calling the police," she said and put down the telephone.

I walked back towards the bedroom. Of course now was not the time, but I needed to make sense of what had just happened. "Why couldn't you just leave me alone?" I asked. "All I wanted was for you to stop going on at me." Then I added something about the money, how I was tired of begging him for every penny.

"You can have all the money you need when you respect me enough," he said, with a marked contempt in his voice.

"Do you call *that* respect?" I flared. "Find me a woman who would respect you after what you just did!"

"There are plenty of women out there." His response was so arrogant. "Why do I need to be stuck with a forty-five year old dog like you … when I can have *any* woman I want?" It was perfectly aimed and timed and like a poisoned arrow when it struck… wickedly hurtful.

He made to go down the stairs and I ran faster to get ahead of him. I knew Kate would have made a call to Martin or the police, or both. I wasn't thinking rationally, but I was desperate for it all to stop.

I stood in front of the door refusing to let him leave. Martin was on his way, I told him, to talk some sense into him. "*Bring* your brother here," he sneered. "I'll fight *him* and his top men … I'll destroy all of them."

"You're no match for my brother," I shrieked. "You only pick on weak people …" It was a cheap shot and one which, in hindsight, I bitterly regret, but there is a limit to how much one person can endure … and that morning I'd reached it!

I'd relit the fuse. As he made for the front door, I stood spreadeagled, blocking his way. Another slap to my cheek and this time it knocked me sideways.

"Out of my way," he roared, "or I'll knock you out of my way!"

'Oh, please God, end this madness!' I repeated over and over in my head.

"You're not leaving... you're not leaving!" I screamed at him. A hard slap struck me on my other cheek. I stumbled ... and got up again.

Another slap aimed at my face somehow caught my lip and I felt a sharp sting. I grabbed the sleeve of his T-shirt, ripping it clean off.

"Look what you've done!" he shouted, appalled at the sight of his damaged clothing.

Still I didn't move. His finale was precisely aimed, a kick to my upper thigh which, as it made contact, brought with it the full force of his fifteen-stone frame.

It disabled me completely and I folded in a crumpled heap on the hallway floor as three police officers, swiftly followed by my brother, burst in through the door.

It all happened so fast.

A plaque, knocked from the wall in the fight lay broken beside me. It read ... *'Happiness is not a state to arrive at, but a manner of travelling'*. I began to sob uncontrollably... tears of relief ... and disbelief.

CHAPTER FIVE: 'NO WAY OUT'

> 'The pain of loving you is almost more than I can bear.
> I walk in fear of you.
> The darkness starts up where
> you stand, and the night comes through
> your eyes when you look at me'
>
> D.H.Lawrence (1885 – 1930)

Several hours later, as I stood in the garage of my dad's house, dressed only in my night clothes, I viewed the entire contents of my life, all my treasured possessions, discarded haphazardly into a scruffy trailer … and I wondered how on earth it had happened? How had my life been so ripped apart? The tears fell again.

My dad was mystified at my reaction; why on earth was I crying now that I was out of there! But he, along with everyone else, was incapable of comprehending the mixed medley of emotions I felt in that moment. The last nine months had been a living hell. I was ten days away from giving birth and the man I loved and the father of my unborn child had spun wildly into orbit. …

Jai told the police officers that 'he'd hit me in places where he knew it wouldn't hurt the baby'. The fault was entirely mine because I'd blocked his way. What's a man to do, he asked them, when he's prevented from leaving his own house? It was an explanation he believed excused *him* and laid the blame squarely at my feet. It only served to evoke their sickening disgust.

I spent the remainder of the day in hospital, strapped to a monitor that was checking the baby's heartbeat and watching my blood pressure rise and fall at an alarming rate. Kate stayed with me for the whole time.

My dad, who up until that day had only an inkling of what was going on, became acquainted with all the painful details. He was livid with me, understandably. Why had I kept it all so closely locked inside? What was I thinking of? What about Jess?

At some point in the melee, I'd seen my eight-year-old daughter huddled at the top of the stairs, clutching the banister. I just remember her anguished cries, "Stop hitting my mummy … stop hitting my mummy." Now I was wracked with guilt at what trauma, having witnessed everything, I'd locked deeply inside her.

It had taken my brother and his friend less than two hours to empty the house of everything they believed to be mine. I knew they were acting out of my own best interests but now it felt as though a year of my life, the most confusing and extraordinary year of my life, had been erased … just like that, in a heartbeat.

Jayne, my sister, took us in. "Stay here until at least after the baby is born," she urged me. "We'll take it a day at a time." Jayne allowed me to deal with my pain in my own way and in my own time; she is the most empathic person I know. Sometimes I could barely bring myself to speak; other times I felt crazy with rage; and most of the time I just sat and cried my eyes out.

My statement to the police, the day after the assault, took six hours to make with me sobbing frequently throughout its duration. I found myself intellectualizing, rationalizing and even excusing Jai's behaviour many times. I blamed myself. Had my angry reaction to his hateful words caused him to lose control? Had I provoked him? Should I have just taken the insults and let him walk out of the door? The only thing I wanted that morning was for the 'madness' to stop. The *last* thing I needed was police involvement.

Automatically and understandably, Jai was painted as the

criminal and I was the victim of domestic violence. They were labels I refused to accept. "He needs help," I repeatedly told the female police officer. "He needs a psychiatric assessment; he's not a wife beater … *he's ill*." Sympathetic she might have been, but she wasn't really concerned with any theories I had about Jai's supposed mental state. If that was in question when the case came to court, then a psychiatric assessment would be ordered. Jai, she reminded me, had been found to be perfectly lucid, rational and extremely articulate during questioning and there was no doubt in their minds that he'd been in full control of his actions.

"What made it kick off in the first place?" she asked me. I remember the vacant expression on her face when I replied, … *"Seven sheets of paper."*

Some help of sorts came during that week at my sister's. Ram was a friend of my brother, Martin, and a highly trained psychiatric nurse with a good long-standing reputation. Their relationship had developed over the years that Ram had become a student of Martin's in the practice of martial arts. At Martin's request, Ram listened sympathetically to my story and my descriptions of Jai's sudden mood changes, the impulsivity and the aggression. He said that, without a face to face consultation, it was virtually impossible to diagnose any underlying mental health issues Jai might have but, from what I'd described, it sounded very similar to the classic symptoms of manic depression.

"There may well be other more complicated issues," Ram said, including the possibility of 'deep-seated feelings of inadequacy'.

"Why did he react with such rage to something I thought he would be pleased with?" I asked Ram.

"Can't you see what happened, Jacky?" he responded. "You displayed your effectiveness to him and in that moment he was confronted by his own … ineffectiveness." I thought back to how many times my creative efforts had been met with indifference or even annoyance, but hardly ever commended. In fact, the more I thought about it, the more I realized that Jai seemed to get irked by many of the things that I did *well*.

All of this conflicting behaviour was to make perfect sense in the course of time … but back then I could hardly make sense of any of it.

Ram went on to explain that he may well have a brain enzyme dysfunction which would account for his 'calmer' moods in the winter time when there was less serotonin from the sun available. He pointed out that his brain was 'burning up vital calories' and I thought of Hazel's words back in June. Treatment, he suggested, might involve the use of mild, low dosage drugs to help counteract his mood instability.

"What of all the visions and prophesies?" I asked him. "Is the God madness all part of the condition?"

"No," he answered quite firmly. "If you take God and spirituality out of the equation, this would be a far easier problem to deal with."

It was information which at the time gave me more insight and a smattering of hope that whatever was wrong with Jai was in some way treatable. Ram suggested that, if I could set up a meeting with Jai, he would talk to him, simply talk. He wouldn't be acting in his professional capacity and he wasn't asking to be paid for his services; it would just be an observation based on his experience. I thought it was a generous and unconditional offer of his time and replied that I'd do my best to arrange a meeting between them.

"People do heal from this, Jacky," he reassured me, "but he has to *want* to, from the very depths of his soul."

Loving someone gripped in the terrifying throes of a 'spiritual emergency' is not something you can just run away from. Not only was it impossible to 'turn off' the love and concern I had for Jai, it was inconceivable.

On the third day, Jai telephoned Jayne's house. I wasn't surprised; I knew it wouldn't take long for him to find me and make contact. As intense as the assault itself had been … now the remorse was overwhelming.

'How could he have possibly let things get so out of hand? Why hadn't he been able to control his temper that day? How did he end up hurting the one person he loved most in the whole world? How could he contemplate life without me? Was there any way I could possibly forgive him? If only he could turn the clock back … he deeply regretted what had happened … he was truly sorry … he would seek help …and he would never hurt me *ever* again …'

I believed it all because I *wanted* to believe it. My entire pregnancy had been far from the wonderfully nurturing experience I had hoped but now I clung *desperately* to the tenuous belief that fatherhood would change him. I rationalized to myself that if he witnessed the impending birth of his son, the most real and most awesome experience of his life, surely he would come to his senses? My emotions were raw but I knew I didn't want to go through this experience alone; I wanted him at the birth. Five days after my family had moved me out, I convinced them, albeit reluctantly, to move me back in.

I can't blame you, dear reader, for thinking at this point in my story *'Is this woman mad?'* and *'What on earth was she thinking?'* I can only ask you to bear with me and remember that the awareness and the understanding of Jai's *true* condition came much later in my relationship with him and as a result of much gathered knowledge and research. On top of that, as any woman who is about to give birth knows, my emotions were all over the place and I wasn't thinking straight. If I knew back then what I learned later, maybe things might have played out differently between us.

Or maybe they played out exactly as they were supposed to…

Jai didn't show up at all that first weekend; I suspect he wanted to avoid any members of my family at all costs. The only tangible sign of him having stayed there that week was the strange sight of the duvet and pillows on the living room floor. He was never able to sleep in the bedroom if I wasn't there, he once confided to me; the darkness held untold terrors for Jai…

On the dining room table stood an unopened bottle of champagne with two glasses next to it. I walked into the kitchen and a karaoke machine, brand new and in the box, sat on the work surface. There was a note pinned to it which simply read 'Jess, I am so sorry, love, dad'.

I spent my time on Saturday, 18th November getting the house back to normal and preparing for the Health Exhibition I'd planned to attend the next day. I had no intention of cancelling as it was always my work and being of service that drove me through my darkest times.

How on that Sunday I masked the trauma of the week before, I've no idea. The only visible sign of my injuries was a sustained limp caused by a severe and painful bruise to my right thigh that had begun to blacken as the days wore on. The event was a huge success, although the result of standing up all day so close to my due date left me exhausted. Despite that I left on a high, having attracted some much needed clients and putting Sai Workshops firmly on the map.

It was Wednesday, November 22nd, and about ten in the evening Kate rang. "Any twinges or pains yet?" she asked. She'd been checking on me every few hours for the last two days.

"Nothing," I responded. It was true; I hadn't even felt any mild backache, normally an indicator of things starting to happen. I knew I needed an early night, but felt restless; all the emotional turmoil of the last few weeks had left my sleep patterns erratic, to say the least.

It was just before midnight and I was resting on the settee when Jai walked in. It was only the second time I'd set eyes on him in nine days. He had an anguished look on his face and, sitting down beside me, said, "Why don't you believe my visions, Jacky?"

"I do," I answered quietly. "I've never doubted for a second that you *had* the visions; it's how you've used the information since that concerns me." I couldn't believe I was having this conversation on the eve of my due date but it was probably the calmest and most rational discussion about his experience we'd had so far. I told him what I believed had happened, that when we open ourselves up to altered states of consciousness sometimes repressed material from our past can rise to the surface and cause our emotions to be disturbed.

"Occasionally, the psychic energy that is released can be so powerful we can be confused by it, thinking *we* are all powerful," I commented. I knew his first impulse was to reject anything he perceived as criticism. He was still firmly holding onto the belief that only he had The Truth and his message for mankind was of cosmic significance.

"I'm walking the path of righteousness," he said, as a look of deep consternation swept across his face, "and it's a path I'm being urged to walk alone."

What on earth did that mean? *Oh God, Jai, you certainly pick your moments, I remember thinking.*

"You mean like Buddha just got up and left his family, you think God is asking that of you now?" I stammered, feeling a wave of emotion rise to the surface. I knew I couldn't have this conversation there and then; it was far too heavy. All I wanted was some normality. "This isn't the time, Jai," I said. "I have to try and sleep ..."

As I stood up to go to bed, I felt a sudden gush and right there at that moment my waters broke, all over the living room carpet. I could barely take it in. Jai gave out a nervous laugh, followed by the words, "Does this mean my son is coming?"

It would be hours yet, but I knew without doubt that our baby would be born later that day and as the news he'd longed to hear began to sink in, his face lit up with ecstasy.

Unable to rest, I spent the next few hours preparing myself for my hospital admission, whilst all the time Jai lay sleeping soundly in the next room. I'd not experienced my waters breaking with my first labour and at 4 a.m. it occurred to me to call the midwife out, just in case I was running the risk of infection. She checked me, saying everything was fine and urged me to get some sleep. She didn't expect much to happen until later that afternoon …

By 9:30 a.m. I was having rapid and painful contractions. With Jess safely packed off to school, I spent the next hour and a half sitting on the toilet; it was the only way I could relieve the pressure! The midwife finally arrived at quarter past eleven, declaring I was eight centimetres dilated and needed to get to hospital quickly.

As Jai dropped me off at the emergency exit, then disappeared to park the car, hundreds of people were exiting the building. It was a 'routine' fire evacuation! The midwife began pushing her way through the crowds exclaiming, "Out of the way please, this lady's in hard labour!" I remember being hit by a mild wave of hysteria at the absurdity of it all.

But then everything about my life at this time was tinged with the surreal.

As none of the lifts were operational, I was forced to walk the two flights of stairs to the delivery ward, just managing to get on the delivery table when the nurse declared I was in the final stages of labour. Jai spent the whole time fiddling with the video camera and I couldn't believe it when he announced he was going out for new batteries!

There was no time for pain relief and, even though I insisted on gas and air, he repeatedly told the midwife to take it away from me. Just as I was yelling, "I can't do this" and feeling like my spine was about to snap in two, the strangest thing happened.

"Look there's a light!" I exclaimed. "A blue light." In the corner of the room, a thin stream of the brightest azure blue light 'hovered', just like a magic carpet.

"She's probably seeing her mother," Jai offered. "She sees spirit sometimes …"

"No, no …it's there, a light … blue … shimmering … beautiful," I protested. Then it was gone.

Minutes later, as I twisted the sleeve of Jai's T-shirt into a tightly wound tourniquet, Temujin Daridra, our son, made his way into the world. It was 1:37 p.m. on Thursday, 23rd November 2000.

I guess it's the most natural thing in the world for any mother to gaze down at her newborn and feel overwhelmed with love but, when I looked at Temujin in those first few moments, his eyes shone with the depth and mystery of moonlight over a blackened ocean … and I was in awe, swept away. He was the most gorgeous baby I'd ever seen. His olive-brown complexion glowed, flawless and bearing none of the marks that accompany a protracted labour. Here was this tiny person, exquisite, perfect. I felt a wave of blessed tranquility wash through me. After stealing an hour or so to study his new parents, my newborn son promptly fell into a deep and peaceful sleep that lasted for twenty-six hours.

Even though the nurses were relentless in their attempts to wake him and get him to feed, no amount of coaxing would disturb him from his slumbers and at about four o'clock in the morning I was awoken, not by him, but by the cries of the other babies on the ward. I glanced across at my tiny bundle and surrounding him and his little plastic cot as he slept was the shimmering blue light again, now tinged with opaque iridescent hues.

At that moment I had the answer to a question I'd been asking in my head for a long time, 'At what point does the soul enter the physical body?' This light, which now radiated from him as the energy of his aura, was the same light I had seen in the delivery room several minutes before he was born. I realized I had watched the soul; the subtle energy bodies of my son enter his physical body … and I was touched by a sense of awe and privilege.

Jai was either so overwhelmed by his newborn son or he'd gone into some mild form of shock but, for once in his life, he was speechless! In those first few hours, he just stared down at him in disbelief, oddly balancing his tiny six-pound frame on his outstretched arm, cradled in his forearm. I prayed he was feeling the same sudden rush of love that I had felt …

Just after the birth I wanted what every woman wants her man to say, like 'well done' or 'I'm proud of you' or 'you did great' or words to that effect. What I got was, "Gosh, Jacky, have you any idea how much energy that took from me. I thought I was going to have a bowel movement right there on the spot!"

I'd come the closest to a natural labour without actually opting for one that a woman could get! The stitches that followed were hellish and I'd endured the indignity of giving birth with a saucer-shaped bruise on my right thigh. *I think if I'd had any energy left in that moment … I'd have punched him…*

Thankfully, even though my family visited one by one on that first day in hospital, their paths did not cross with Jai … except for my brother. It was almost inevitable that Martin would arrive whilst Jai was there. Martin congratulated me and then, turning to Jai, offered to shake his hand. "Be good to them," was all that my brother said.

Considering what had gone before, it was a gallant gesture on Martin's part but the spirit of which Jai chose in that moment to ignore. He was more concerned with reminding everyone of the significance of Temujin's birthday. "The doubters have been proved wrong today," he announced smugly. "My son shares his birthday with the living God on this planet. Surely proof that all my visions are right?"

Martin didn't retaliate. Whatever response he gave would

not have been met with acceptance. The seeds of jealousy on Jai's part had long been sown in their relationship and Martin was always going to be a target for Jai's hostility.

I arrived home from hospital two days later to find the house bedecked with flowers; it was typical of Jai. From the start of our relationship he often expressed in gifts and flowers the sentiments he found impossible to express in words. He also used flowers as a way of saying *sorry.*

There was little to be gained by looking back and I clung now to the desperate hope that the future would bring with it the peace and normality that had eluded us for the past twelve months. With Jess besotted with her new brother, it felt for the first time like we were a proper family.

Jess was only too willing to help with Temujin's daily needs; she had a real live doll after all! It was every little girl's dream. I wondered how much help Jai would be. Nara had warned me that, in Hindu culture, the father tends not to get involved at the baby stage, preferring to pay more attention to the child when they were about two or three.

I knew I needed his help and all the bed rest I could get if I was to recover quickly and be back at work within a week as I'd planned. But as any woman knows, the first few days after the birth are the worst; my body ached and the stitches were painful. On top of that, I was breastfeeding which tends to burn up more calories and so led to needing regular nourishment.

It was the fourth day since giving birth and I had been awake most of the night feeding Temujin. I asked Jai, who was dozing beside me, if he would make me some tea and toast. "I will in half an hour," he answered. I let ten minutes pass then gently reminded him again "Please, Jai, I can't wait. I feel so tired and hungry." He told me to ask Jess to do it. It was early Sunday morning and I knew she would still be sleeping. I pressed him again and still he refused to budge. As I physically dragged myself out of bed to make my own breakfast, I burst into tears … as he just lay there.

I remember afterwards desperately trying to work out what could possibly have been going through his mind. Was he so lacking in empathy that he genuinely couldn't comprehend how my body must be feeling? Did he blatantly not care? Was there a part of Jai that was so sadistic and twisted, a part of him that surfaced every so often and from which he gained some warped pleasure? None of it made sense. On the one hand, he seemed capable of extreme and genuine declarations of love and, on the other, a chilling withholding of any loving feelings at all. The pain of that memory stayed with me for a long time. *I think it was the one moment in our entire relationship that I felt a deep and genuine loathing towards him.*

It dawned on me that I was going to have to get through those first few weeks alone and, six days after giving birth, I was not only back in the workshops, with Temujin strapped to my back in a little papoose, but I was also back in my size ten jeans! The ladies who ran the sandwich bar at the back of the workshops simply gaped in astonishment when they saw me. I'd never weighed much more than eight stone, but the post pregnancy pounds just dropped off me. I put it down to all the stress of the last twelve months and to my punishing schedule.

I had no idea of the toll on my health all of that would take in the months to come. Just soldiering on without complaint was an endurance pattern I knew wasn't serving me and one that before long I would be forced to address. One thing was for certain: I couldn't ignore the running costs the workshops were incurring and I busied myself with identifying marketing strategies to attract new members.

The run-up to Christmas 2000 with a newborn was hectic but joyous. Temujin was the easiest, least demanding baby a mother could wish for, a pure delight to be around. His temperament was so incredibly peaceful that Jai decided he couldn't possibly be spending his days on earth but was obviously slipping back to heaven without us noticing! Sometimes when I held him, he would just stare up at me with those intense black eyes that seemed to carry the depth and understanding of a wise old sage. It was as if he knew *everything*.

We still had the business of formally registering his birth and it took three attempts and practically seven weeks after he was born to do it! Although Jai agreed to Temujin as his first name, the name that had been 'given to me' whilst he was still in the womb, neither of us could agree on his middle names.

I had wanted to give him the second name of Nicholas. It was the name of my brother who died at the age of six and a half in 1979. He was killed crossing the road for an ice cream by an over zealous seventeen-year-old motorcyclist. Nicholas's birthday, December 6th, was also the first expectancy date my doctor had given me. I was once told by a clairvoyant several years after his death that I would see the soul of my late brother reflected back to me through the eyes of a child born into the family. I wondered if this was her prophesy returned to me. But it wasn't to be. Jai fought me on it, wanting to give Temujin 'traditional' Indian names and, as I've said, he mostly got his own way.

Diana Cooper in her book 'A New Light on Ascension' writes that every person's name is telepathically communicated to them via their parents before they are born. Each name is carefully chosen to carry the correct 'vibration' and "When it is thought or spoken," she says, "it contains your lessons, your mission and the essence of your destiny."

Eventually our baby was registered on 15th January 2001 as Temujin Sathya Narayana Jaya Kham Daridra … His full name wouldn't even fit on his passport. The origins of the name, Temujin, belonged to one of the greatest tyrants in living history; it was the birth name of Ghengis Khan which in his native language means 'iron man' or 'man of iron'. Story has it that when Temujin was born, his fist was found to be clutching a clot of blood, an omen, it was declared, that meant he was destined to become a heroic warrior.

I wondered with such a name as this what weighty karma my son would have to carry.

Temujin certainly looked more like an 'angel' than a warrior and Jai himself attributed his own calmer mood during December and January to being in his son's peaceful energy; perhaps it played a part. He certainly *appeared* to be besotted with his son and whatever practical skills he lacked, he made up for in the attention he gave him. Sometimes he would just sit holding him for hours in his arms whilst singing a beautiful Indian lullaby to him until he dropped peacefully to sleep. We gave him the affectionate nickname of 'Bobo', I don't know where it came from but it stuck for a couple of years.

Oddly, Jaya and I spent more time together in those first few weeks when Temujin was born than we had for a very long time. Sometimes I would forget the mind altering event that had happened the previous June and, from time to time during this period, I saw the 'old Jai' resurface, reminding me of all the things about him that I'd fallen in love with…

These moments of 'normality', however, rarely lasted for long and by this time, after nearly two years together, I'd begun to notice a definite cyclical pattern developing in Jai's emotional ups and downs. Ram had mentioned the neurotransmitters, the many complex chemicals in the brain that control our moods and emotions as well as memory and learning. Impulsivity and aggression are associated with serotonin and I had noticed that there was a heightened upsurge in Jai's temperament during the spring and the summer when more sunlight is available.

Now, as he approached the winter months, he appeared to be entering the 'passive' phase when his days were filled once again with inertia and inactivity. In the weeks that followed he became the closest in all the time I'd known him to appearing genuinely depressed.

It didn't stop him, however, consorting with Garry who was still joined to Jai at the hip and seemed to hang onto his every word. It irritated me that Jai would decide to 'go to work' at eleven o'clock at night when he'd been lying in bed all day. I knew where they were going; it was all part of his 'mission' he told me … that he had to wipe the planet clean of all negativity … and, in order to do that, he needed to spend all night every night in the casino, working out a 'system' that would beat the tables and bleed the place dry.

Frankly it sickened me; I didn't buy his explanation for a single moment. But with Jai any perceived criticism, particularly if it was aimed at his God-given mission, was simply met with outrage and hostility. He was after all only doing what he had promised, a clean-up campaign and … "God's dirtiest work."

So for a period of six weeks, from mid-January through to the end of February, Jai played the tables, every single night, in one casino after another claiming that he had discovered some bizarre mathematical calculation that worked in his favour. Whenever I challenged him on why he needed to do this, the answer was always that he needed the money to 'build up his power base'; only then would people take him seriously … only then could he help the starving millions.

I hated his nocturnal wanderings. I knew that being up all night and half asleep all day was undoubtedly contributing to the chemical disruptions in his brain. Apart from that, he had taken to prowling around the house in the middle of the night. Sometimes I would wake to find him looming over me, just staring down at me whilst I slept. It would freak me out. At other times I caught him gazing into the cot at Temujin with an almost puzzled expression on his face. It gave me the strangest feeling, as though he was somehow reminding himself that he had a son and a family, that all of it was real and not just some figment of his imagination.

As if to prove this somehow, he would study his reflection in the mirror whilst cradling Temujin in his arms, as though affirming, 'Look at me, I have a son and look how perfect he is!' The new image that stared back at him now, the one of himself … as a father … was one he was struggling to identify with. I was finding it increasingly more difficult to differentiate between what appeared to be a genuine display of love for his son or what was simply pride and a need in Jai to show him off like some trophy or prized possession to everyone he met.

Whether it was because I'd simply been around him more I don't know, but, by late March, I noticed the mirror obsession and other bizarre behaviour resurfacing but with new and added twists. Flexing his muscles in the mirror, he would ask me, "Where do you think all this strength comes from? I don't even work out." That aspect *did* worry me because it seemed as though Jai's brute strength had quadrupled since the 'emergency' had hit him.

This 'super-strength' and almost visible increase in his physical stature didn't seem to fit however with him developing what I can only describe as a mild obsession towards minor health ailments. "What do you think this is?" he would ask me whilst analyzing a blemish on his skin or a white spot under his nail as though it were some developing, rare disease. I found it irritating that he would ask me the same things over and over that I'd several weeks earlier gone into a lengthy discussion about, only to find myself repeating the information. They were questions only and ever about *him*, his health, his nutritional habits, his bodily functions, his daily disciplines. I found his utter self-absorption nauseating at times.

Something else was bothering me. Jai had started to take risks with our safety in the car, claiming that Temujin didn't need his baby seat strapped in by the seat belt because he was protected by God. His driving habits grew more and more erratic; he was constantly pushing the speed limits and parking in restricted areas. Several times when I challenged him after crossing a red light, white-knuckled and with my stomach in a knot, he would flippantly say, "There's nothing to worry about ... the car becomes invisible!" The debt he had accumulated in unpaid parking fines was enough to pay a month's rent on our three bedroom house, but he simply didn't care. Jai truly believed he was untouchable and completely above the law...

Feeling himself above the law didn't quite fit, however, with his obvious anxieties about the impending court hearing. I knew this was something that had been niggling away at the back of his mind since Christmas and I tried not to contemplate how much anger towards me he was secretly concealing. I suppose when I look back at that period, both of us were treading on eggshells with each other. Jai was expending all of his energy trying to suppress and control his temper and I was expending mine watching my every word and action to avoid arousing it. Frankly, it was like living in a pressure cooker.

Several times he asked me to write to his solicitor and drop the charges. I refused, explaining that everything I had said in my statement was the truth and my only motivation that day had been to get him some professional help, not send him to jail. I thoroughly believed anyway that when it came to court there would be no case to answer. It would clearly be obvious to the judge that we were back living together and that Jai was making every effort for the sake of his son.

I'd been advised that the charge of common assault was considerably minor, added to which it was a first offence and there had been no previous history of violence. Taking all of that into account ...there was no way he was facing a prison term. It was something I tried to tell him many times.

I had a bigger problem to think about by late March. We were already two months behind with the rent and it didn't seem to worry Jai one bit. I was barely covering about twenty-five per cent of my overheads in the workshops. Every source of income I gained whether through Q.E.D or my own private hypnotherapy sessions, I was putting back in to cover my costs. I'd exhausted all my savings and it meant I had to ask Jai for money for our day-to-day living costs and for the rent on our property. The more pressure I put on him, the more resentful he became, accusing me of making a shambles of the workshops and viciously arguing, "If you'd let me take over I'd turn it into a million pound company overnight!"

By late April I could feel Jai's energy levels rising again. The passivity was now giving way to the familiar aggressiveness and the rapid, ever-changing moods. I didn't want to be on the receiving end of any of it and, as I've said often enough, it didn't take much for him to flip. On top of that he'd finally received notification to appear in court on Friday, 27th April for sentencing, more than six months after the original offence.

I thought it wise to escape for a while and so, taking the children with me, I headed off to my sister's in Cornwall for a long weekend. Whilst in Cornwall I used the time to write Jai a very lengthy letter. I knew I needed to find a better way of handling our problems and I thought by writing everything down, all my frustrations and concerns, but at the same time emphasizing my love and support for him, that the communication between us might improve.

It was to be the first of many letters I would write to him in the course of our relationship…

On Thursday, 26th April, the night before the court case, I asked Jai to come home for four o'clock because I had two appointments booked at the workshops that evening and I needed him to babysit. He promised he would. My first client, due at five thirty was an extremely punctual lady and, as she didn't use a mobile, I had no way of contacting her if I was going to be late.

I waited … and waited until, eventually, Jai's car screeched into the drive at twenty minutes past five. Seething though I was I kept quiet so as to avoid a row, but I suppose it was something in the way I snatched the keys from him and hastily relayed the instructions about Temujin…

Arriving home at ten o'clock that evening I was greeted by an odd scene. Jessica, my then nine-year-old, was struggling awkwardly to give Temujin, dressed only in his vest and nappy, his bottle. I asked where Jai was and she told me that he'd been in the bathroom for an hour and a half. I took the baby from her and fed him, dressed him and settled him down for the night. As I tucked Jess into bed half an hour later I asked her if Jai's behaviour had been strange that evening. "I've looked after Tem, Mum," she told me. "He's spent all night on the phone and in the bathroom."

I was at the kitchen sink washing up a pile of dishes from that evening when Jai eventually showed his face and walked up behind me. "Leave all of that," he instructed me. "We've more important things to discuss." Initially I protested, saying I needed to eat. I'd skipped tea owing to my commitments and, on top of that, I had to make the whole night's bottle feeds.

He became more insistent. "This is exactly what I mean about you disrespecting me," he said in a tone of voice that became more demanding and aggressive. He took my arm and pulled me away from the sink. I had no option but to follow him where he led me into the lounge and ordered me to sit down on the sofa next to him.

Utterly convinced that he was going to prison the next day, he told me he wanted the two of us to work out the payment arrangements for the household bills. It was ironic really, considering he'd never taken any responsibility for the rent, never mind the bills. Just the day before when I'd asked him what we were going to do when the landlord called, his answer had been, "Fuck him! The landlord will have to kneel at my feet before he gets any money from me."

I told him he was worrying unnecessarily; that he *would* be returning home from the courts, and that we should *then* sort out our financial problems. I went to get up from the sofa. "I really have to make Tem's bottles," I said. Apart from that I was hungry and tired and frankly just wanted to go to bed. Jai could never comprehend how draining my work was sometimes.

"I'm not finished with you," he said, pulling me back down on the sofa and, this time, straddling me so that I was unable to move. "Look into my eyes when I'm talking to you," he persisted. "Look into my eyes because you don't know what you're dealing with, you don't know my power. Don't mess with me. You see *him*?" He swung his arm out and pointed at a picture of Sai Baba above the fireplace. "He now works for *me*!"

My legs were feeling numb as his weight pressed down on me. I didn't say anything but struggled to move my body. Every time I tried to release myself from his grip he pushed me back down again. "You're hurting me!" I screamed at him finally. "Let me go!"

Grabbing the handset of the telephone as it lay next to me, I threatened him with calling the police. "Go on, see how far you get," he snarled, seizing the telephone off me. "If you move towards the phone, I'll break your wrist. If you move towards the door, I'll grab your legs, and if you don't sit still, I'll head butt you till your teeth fall out!" Then, as if to reinforce the threat, he slammed his clenched fist containing the handset of the telephone down, hard on my upper thigh … again. *Goddam it, the same leg, I remember thinking.*

The look I gave him in that instant translated to mean *'I despise you'* causing him to follow the first thump by three more in exactly the same place. *My thigh ached.*

Suddenly the telephone rang. It was Garry. Jai calmly held a conversation with him as though nothing untoward was happening and told him that he was just 'teaching me about respect'. Garry must have asked, "Have you hit her?" because Jai's response was, "Only once, is that bad?"

Choking back the tears I yelled in the background, "He's a

liar, Garry. He's hurting me… please stop him!" Garry asked for the telephone to be passed to me. Tearfully I told him Jai had hit me for no real reason. "Surely that's not right?" I appealed to him.

There was a brief silence and then he said, "Jacky … he's your *husband*."

I couldn't believe what I was hearing. "You're saying that gives him the right …"

He cut in again, "*Jacky …he's your husband.*"

I passed the telephone back feeling sick with disgust … and fell quiet. Jai ended the conversation. Then, putting aside the telephone, he remarked, "You see that's better; *now* you're starting to respect me."

I looked hard into his eyes and answered, "Of course I am, Jai. Look at the size of you to me … I'm in *fear* of you."

"Do you want to know what real fear is?" he thundered. "What does this feel like?" and, in that instant, he grabbed both my hands behind my back and began twisting my right wrist hard round. At the same time he forced me off the sofa and I collapsed to my knees on the floor. A knife-like pain shot through my wrist and arm. "I'm going to break this wrist before the night's out," he vowed, "because I need to teach you about submission."

I pleaded with him to stop … but he'd restrained me by my hair with his one hand and both my wrists with the other. There was an excruciating pain coupled with a burning sensation, I thought both my wrists would snap. "Please, don't do it, Jai, *please* don't…"

"Now you're learning," he breathed with an air of satisfaction. Releasing my wrists and still holding onto my hair, he forced me to turn and look at him. "This is because you weren't correctly punished by your father. He was weak and your mother was in control!" I didn't dare move my eyes as they held fast to his. There was a glazed, almost robotic look about them.

"But you see *this* guy," he stormed beating his chest with his fist. "I'm Ghengis Khan, king of terror, he who Nostradamus predicted would come like a thief in the night ... you need to read more, you need to read The Bible, The Gita, The Mahabharata, you disrespect me by not going through them page by page and asking me any questions because I can answer them ... all of them ...*that's my power.*"

...And in that moment whatever malevolent, uncontrollable force had gripped him ...just seemed to expire with those words ... as the energy subsided ... and he let go, leaving me in a helpless, trembling heap on the floor.

"You really shouldn't mess with me, Jacky," he said, calmly getting up and making his way up the stairs to bed.

The evening did not end in that way, but the events of the next few hours, until five o'clock in the morning, are committed to a confidential police statement and will never find their way onto the pages of this or any other book ... primarily out of protection for my children's feelings.

As I limped towards the school gates with Jessica that morning, I burst into tears in front of the head teacher and she gently led me by the arm into her office with the words, "Jessica has told us more than you realize." Taking one look at the distraught state of me she added firmly, "If you don't call the police, then I'm afraid *we* will."

Jai left the house for court that morning acting as though nothing had happened. As he got into the car, he beeped the horn several times until the noise forced me to go to the window and watch him ... blowing kisses and giving me the tenderest of smiles ... as he drove away...

As the reader, you must now be thinking 'surely after *this* she'll leave him!' It would be the reaction I'd expect from any normal person of sound mind as they digest the details of these events through the pages of my book. It would be *my* reaction, had these events not *happened to me*, had I been the one *listening* to my story ... and not *telling* it.

It's almost impossible to explain in words the power Jai held over me, but what I can tell you is this: back then, my relationship with Jai had been like walking into a field of poppies, dazzling ... wonderful ... and then suddenly looking down only to see the spikes protruding from beneath the earth ... and knowing that what you had really entered ... was a minefield.

And once trapped in that minefield, I could never have imagined that it would take me the next three years to pick my way out...

The disturbing truth was that I'd become so 'exposed' to his psychosis, at times I could barely differentiate between what I instinctively knew to be normal, rational behaviour and what, on the other hand, had become downright insanity. Kate was to tell me months down the line how she often remembered listening to me reciting an occurrence so extreme and bizarre in nature in exactly the same way and in the same tone as though I were reciting a recipe from a cookery book. It was as if I'd crossed the line somehow or that the line distinguishing between rationale and bizarre had ceased to exist. Just as if I'd unconsciously slipped into Jai's world ... *and in the process become 'numbed' to the potential dangers of his temporary madness.*

Within half an hour of him leaving the house that day, I fled to my friend, Anita's. I didn't plan my exit; I just reacted in that moment, knowing that for the time being all that was important was a place of safety. Anita allowed me to talk in my own time ... and to cry. She is a sensitive and skilled therapist and I will always be grateful for her support that day.

Jayne came to pick me up and, later that same evening, the police took my statement. They assured me that Jai would be called in for questioning as soon as they could track him down. I was advised to stay away from the house, at least until after the weekend, just in case they had a problem finding him.

Ram telephoned. He was sorry to hear what had happened. "Regrettably, Jacky, these types of conditions tend to be progressive if left untreated," he said.

A meeting of sorts had taken place between himself and Jai sometime in December. I realized afterwards that Jai only agreed to it to appease me and not because he thought for a second that he needed help. It hadn't gone well. Ram had listened to him recounting his 'visions' and his 'mission' without challenging him, even though Jai had been extremely confrontational and responded to most of his questions with contempt. He even questioned the motive behind Ram's offer of help, accusing him of having romantic inclinations towards me.

"He is suffering from delusions," Ram concluded, "and without doubt there are chemical disturbances in his brain."

"Surely he won't return to the house knowing that I will probably have alerted the police?" I asked him.

"Oh yes, he will, Jacky," he replied quite chillingly, "… *a dog always returns to smell its own shit …"*

My life was becoming more bizarre by the day. The day after the assault Jayne and I sat watching the lunchtime news on television. A live report about the forthcoming census was being conducted and members of the public from some of the major cities up and down the country were being asked their opinions as to its value.

The news camera panned to a busy shopping street in Birmingham city centre and, right there in front of the camera lens, … Jai's face loomed up …dressed from head to foot in black and with the trademark dark sunglasses, confidently and impressively airing his views. I just stared at the screen in disbelief not knowing whether to laugh or cry… *There were moments during this period of time when my life felt utterly surreal.*

Somehow I got through the weekend, although I just remember a prolonged feeling of numbness. I suppose looking back I must have been in some sort of shock.

It was Monday morning, 30th April, and I felt sure the police would have called him in for questioning by now. I drove Jess the five miles from my sister's house to school and, because I had to practically pass by the bottom of our road leading to our house, I dropped Jess off and then drove past our home.

Jai's car was parked in the drive … and a police car next to it. I drove straight back to Jayne's. "It looks like they're interviewing him right now," I told her. They'd assured me I'd be informed if and when he was charged, but I heard nothing for the rest of the day.

Mid-morning the following day I got a call from the police station requesting that I go to the house to meet with two police sergeants who needed to obtain photographic evidence and go over my statement with me. I asked how the interview went with Jai and whether he'd been charged.

"Oh, he's still being interviewed," they said.

I was confused. "*Still?*" I asked incredulously. Well, he *had* only been brought in that morning, they replied.

"Why were the police at the house yesterday then?" I asked.

It transpired, they told me later, that the previous morning Jai had been arrested and called in for questioning at a different police station altogether, on a completely unrelated charge. There had been a serious complaint against him for threatening behaviour and harassment to someone who apparently owed him money!

I remembered how Hazel had warned me that the 'emergency' left untreated would cause him to spiral out of control.

Oh God, I wondered how many others he'd affected on his rampage of rage...

Walking into the house an hour before the police arrived, I felt an odd mix of emotions: repulsion on the one hand and acute sadness on the other. In several vases around the room and in one large bucket in the middle of the floor, there were at least two hundred roses, in every possible hue, leaning over and wilting. Photos of the two of us together and of Temujin as a tiny baby lay in piles around the room.

Less than an hour later, as our home was invaded by police and viewed only as a crime scene, it all began to sink in … the overwhelming hopelessness of it all.

Two of the officers completed their photographic work and left, leaving me with the two main police sergeants in charge of the case. Choking back the tears, I watched as they photographed the numerous pictures of Sai Baba all over the house and discussed between them Jai's weird obsession with the Indian avatar.

I was made to stand against a blank wall while they took close up pictures of my wrists and the bruising that had started to appear. The endless questions … *it was all so cold and clinical, I couldn't bear it…*

The police sergeants were desperate to keep him in custody but they needed more evidence to support that he was a danger to me and, probably with the latest turn of events, a menace to others. The only leverage they had was the fact that he had reoffended during the period between the first assault and the time it had taken to come to court. Despite being charged with common assault *and* indecent assault, they suspected that even the gravity of the attack itself might not be sufficient enough to detain him.

Jai banged up in jail didn't bear thinking about; I knew it wouldn't help his mental state. "If he is kept in, will he undergo a psychiatric assessment?" I asked tearfully.

"Possibly … it's not automatic … you have to remember that in the interviews he has always come across as completely rational, very articulate … he's given us no reason to suspect his mental state."

Kate's words to me that morning kept playing over and over in my head "You must let them hear the tape, Jacky ... you must let them hear the tape."

"I think there's something you need to hear." ... The sinking realization of what I was about to do gave way to a torrent of tears. "I should have given this to you six months ago," I stammered.

My heart pounded violently as I pressed play on the tape recorder. There was a tense silence between the two police officers as Jai's chilling words filled the room.

I played only fifteen minutes of the whole ninety-minute monologue ... and then that deafening crescendo ...

"But if anybody ever *fucks* **with** *me!* **...***This* **motherfucker is the** *baddest* **motherfucker that God has** *ever* **sent down to sort out** *all* **the motherfuckers; the motherfucker of motherfuckers ...** for pretending they're good guys ... do you understand? 'Cause *I'm* the *man,* baby! You better *believe* it – *I'm* the **man!** You were right, Jacky, you've unleashed a **monster** ..."

I watched the colour drain from the officers' faces.

"We've heard enough," one of them said starkly. "That's all we need to convince the CPS to keep him in custody."

He paused and then, in a loathsome tone, added, *"That is one twisted fuck."*

I didn't want to hand over the tape. For a while I sat there holding it in my hands, playing the repercussions over in my mind, knowing that by releasing it Jai would be labelled 'crazy', a 'madman'.

"Do I *have* to give it you?" I asked weakly.

One of them cautioned me that they would exercise their right to confiscate it.

"Please ... *please* then, let this get him the help he needs," I implored.

It was Tuesday, 1st May 2001 and the day that I'd finally realized this situation was way out of my control. As the officers left and I closed the front door behind them, I walked into the downstairs bathroom … and vomited.

An hour or so later I was driving back to Jayne's feeling as though my whole world was collapsing around me and agonizing if I'd done the right thing handing over the tape recording. I kept telling myself that now Jai would *have* to accept help and if getting the treatment he needed meant a brief spell in custody, it *had* to be the right course of action.

I switched on the radio to drown my thoughts. It was playing the last minute or so of 'Every Breath You Take' by The Police and when it had finished the presenter said, "That song was for Julie, from her husband Keith, who says that he may not be the best nappy changer in the world, but wants her to know how much their new baby has changed their lives and how much he loves them both …" *I pulled the car over into a lay-by and cried my eyes out.*

That same night I dreamed a dream:

'I was in a derelict building and I was frantically looking for my daughter, Jessica. She wasn't there. In the corner, amongst the piles of bricks and rubble stood a toilet. It was filthy…disgusting. I turned to my baby, Temujin, who was then five months old and told him, "We've got no choice, sweetheart; we've got to use this toilet." Both of us sat on the toilet crying and surrounded by the ruins of what was once a house. As I looked up, the roof was open and I could see out skywards … to the heavens.'

Once again my subconscious was speaking to me in my dreams. Buildings can represent the 'body' which I'd seen as empty and derelict. Faeces or excrement is usually an indicator of 'dirt from the past'. I realized the dream meant that I was 'cleansing' myself of something distasteful in my life and, on a conscious level, the emptiness represented a moving away from the home environment.

As for the view of the heavens through an 'open roof', I took this to mean the 'higher mind'. Whatever tests and trials I'd somehow chosen, I knew my spiritual faith would remain steadfast.

I think I moved through the events of the next few days as though in a dream. Even though I was exhausted, I couldn't sleep for recounting over and over in my mind the events of the past few days. All the hideous details pervaded my sleep and fed my nightmares. I was plagued with obsessive thinking, analyzing, playing over and over alternative scenarios in my head in a desperate attempt to understand what had happened.

The guilt was overwhelming; the man I loved was in jail. Did I somehow cause this to happen? Was all of it *my* fault?

Women who've been in abusive relationships will tell you these feelings are normal; that *every* woman at some stage blames herself. They will also tell you that at some point in the course of the relationship, they believe that there is no escape, no possible way out of their situation. Even though Jai was in prison and I was physically removed from the situation, I *knew* that that wasn't it … it could never be that easy … he wasn't just going to let me walk away.

The suicide threat came on the third day that he was in prison. That Friday morning I'd returned to work; I knew I had no option but to just get on with life and somehow my work instilled in me a sense of normality.

Then the telephone rang … I didn't want to answer … but I couldn't avoid answering the telephone forever … and then I heard his voice, tormented, anguished. "I'm going crazy in here, Jacky. They've asked me if it was my daughter … how old she is. They all think I'm a child molester. You *have* to get me out, you *have* to. If you don't, I'll kill myself. The only way to go is the same way as my dad. Please don't leave me.

Don't desert me, Jacky, don't let go. I'm so sorry, I'll have the therapy, I promise this time … anything but this … but please, no drugs … no straitjackets."

Goddamn it, Jai, don't lay this one on me, please …

CHAPTER SIX: 'BEHIND CLOSED DOORS'

'Freedom is always and exclusively freedom for the one who thinks differently'
Luxemburg, Rosa (1870-1919)

Now Jaya's daily life was running parallel with a story that was written five thousand years ago. He had gone in search of enlightenment and, on his journey into the mind, his blinding vision had told him that he was the mythical hero, Arjuna. As Arjuna, God had granted him a mission to perform here on earth … a dark and dangerous mission … and one that was accompanied by unlimited power. As Jai began to act under the influence of these powerful and unconscious forces, he drew havoc and devastation into every area of his life … and his actions had now landed him in prison.

I thought back to the taped conversation with Robin Sieger almost a year before, when Jai described the feelings that accompanied his so-called enlightenment, "I could be happy anywhere now. You could put me in jail and I'd have a great laugh with the prison wardens. You could put me in the gutter and I'd still be happy…"

Right now Jai was *anything* but happy. For months he'd been telling me he was invincible and above the law and now, ironically, here he was in jail, his liberty removed and undoubtedly not feeling so powerful. I sat with the knowledge of that telephone call and the suicide threat for nearly an hour before I rang the prison. In the end, it felt like I had no choice and I hated that feeling. A part of me cared so much that to ignore it would have left me panic-stricken and plagued by the thought that he might actually *do* something. But it felt like I had no option but to give way. 'Get me out of here … *or I'll kill myself*' was a threat, direct in its intent and one that I dared not ignore. As usual with Jai it was a no-win situation.

Much later I learned that the wardens moved him to an isolation unit where he was put on twenty-four hour watch. *At some point in the future he was even to hold that against me.*

Later that day I sat at my desk in the workshops and posted this brief note to him in prison.

Jaya,

These are the only words I have right now. I am not in a good space. This feels worse than bereavement. Please face up to your actions and, more importantly, get the help that you desperately need, if for no one else's sake but your son's. He needs a father who is healthy in body and also in mind. In my heart I have not deserted you, Jacky.

I had to let him know that I still cared *deeply* and I suppose I knew it would prompt the start of an exchange of numerous letters between us over the months to come. Even though I kept telling myself that Jai had put himself in prison as a result of his own actions, I couldn't seem to shake off the guilt … and the thought of him being there in his current unbalanced state was killing me.

Unable to relax or switch off my thoughts, everywhere I turned something seemed to remind me of my situation, either in the words of a book I picked up, the lyrics of a song, or a line from a film. That same night Les Miserables appeared on TV and the central character, for whom the audience feels a great deal of sympathy, finds himself in jail declaring, "They took my dignity … they took everything from me…"

My thoughts were consumed by Jai; how was he feeling right now? Would he survive the experience of jail? Would he emerge suddenly transformed or would his imprisonment just serve to fuel his anger? Someone once said to me 'anger is one letter short of *danger*' and the longer his state of 'spiritual emergency' went untreated, the more dangerous a threat Jai posed to me. I knew that no matter how much energy and effort it took, I simply *had* to get him professional help.

Right now though I was struggling; my energy levels were at an all-time low and I was hurting, *emotionally hurting* from what had happened. I'd given my heart to this man; how could he abuse it in this way? I knew it would take months, even years to erase the pain. A line in Melody Beattie's book 'Codependent No More' struck to the core: 'the pain that comes from loving someone who's in trouble can be profound' …

The pain *was* profound. Healing from that second attack took many forms and unfolded like a list of symptoms from the post-traumatic stress disorder checklist. I was gripped by acute anxiety and the fear of where it would all lead. What of the future now? Everything seemed so uncertain. Over the weeks that followed, people around me were to comment on my subdued behaviour; that I'd changed somehow from my normal outgoing self and become more introverted. I went out of my way to avoid speaking to people. How do you begin to communicate all of what happened? How could anyone understand? What would they think?

Even my normally sharp thinking seemed to erode away and my usual keen memory had now been replaced by muddled thinking. Yellow Post-it notes adorned every surface of my kitchen and became a lifeline and yet still I forgot things, everyday things that had been part of my normal routine.

A week after the assault, I forgot to pick Jessica up from school in the afternoon, leaving her sitting in reception for a full hour until it suddenly dawned on me where I should be. I'll never forget her panic-stricken expression when I finally walked in. With all that had happened I could only imagine what was going through her mind.

Quite frankly what *was* going on in Jess's mind was worrying me sick. She had become withdrawn since the assault and had taken to retreating to the silence of her bedroom where she scribbled endless entries in a diary that she kept safely locked away from me. I knew I had to find her a counsellor, or at least someone not emotionally involved with the situation to whom she could talk.

Thankfully that help came quite quickly. As part of the follow-up routine by the police it meant that I had now been referred to the Child Protection Officer and a lady whom I shall call Jean.

Jean acted on behalf of the victim and their families in conjunction with the Domestic Violence Unit. She was brilliant in her approach, able to combine the sensitivity and compassion of a counsellor with a sound working knowledge of the law. In my appointment with her a few days after the incident, I talked to her about Jessica and my concerns that, having heard and witnessed things 'so out of the norm', she may well have difficulty comprehending it all. I also suspected Jess was holding on to a great deal of anger towards Jai and I felt she needed a safe and supportive outlet to release it. Jean recommended the Children's Society to me, a voluntary organization that specifically helps children to deal with the accompanying emotions surrounding domestic violence situations. For Jess it prompted a year, off and on, in which she engaged in the therapeutic process.

I switched the conversation around to Jai, how I believed that he was suffering from a spiritual emergency that had gone untreated and that a custodial sentence would only serve to exacerbate the problem. "He needs a psychiatric referral ..." I began to say. She stopped me. "And what about you, Jacky?" she said quietly. "You've been the victim of domestic violence. How are you feeling about it all?"

I gave her a bewildered look as though she had said something completely off track. "Oh no, you don't understand, it's not like that at all. It wasn't his fault, he's not in control of his actions ..." She cut in again and repeated slowly but firmly, "Jacky ... you have been the victim of domestic violence."

Three times she repeated it while I sat there biting my bottom lip waiting for the words to somehow be absorbed.

It was the first time I'd really thought about it in those terms. Whatever underlying force was driving Jai, I *had* been the victim of domestic violence and there was no getting away from that. It was still to take me a long while before I accepted that all the accompanying emotions I went through during that period, the guilt, the denial, the shame, were all normal and part and parcel of the process. It was to take me even longer to realize that the assault was not my fault. Slowly, over the weeks that followed, the impact of the last twelve months began to sink in. I'd minimized all of it and, what was worse, I'd negated my and my children's feelings completely … in a desperate attempt to find solutions to Jai's crisis.

The first weekend Jai was in prison, following the suicide threat, I dreamed a dream:

Jai's mother came to me in the dream. I recognized her from the photo Jai kept on his bedside table. We were sitting around a large table; myself, her and a boy aged about six or seven. She had papers in front of her and was trying to write something down, but it was in a language that I didn't understand. We were both getting frustrated that we couldn't communicate with each other and I had the feeling that she was conveying 'alarm' to me.

The dream bothered me. I realized that whatever it was that was so important, Jai's mother had come to me in 'spirit' in my dream to tell me. I think the boy was Jai at the age of six or seven. Interestingly, the age of six is the time when Jai's life was beset with difficulties; when in 1972 he and his family, along with thousands of other Asians, had fled Uganda as a result of the Amin exodus.

I remember when I told Jai about this dream weeks later, he initially felt that it represented his mother's anguish over signing the papers that meant his father, under the Mental Health Act, would be sectioned. Later he changed that story, saying that it attested to his mission and that his mother was confirming that he would one day write a book.

I somehow felt that that first initial instinct was right ... with the little that Jai had told me about his father's suicide and the circumstances surrounding it, Jai had *every* reason to be terrified of the mental health scheme.

After they had fled from Uganda, Jai's family had originally settled in a small Lancashire town and his father had been forced to accept a menial factory job. A move to the outskirts of Birmingham led to a job working on the underground railways. It was low-paid work but work nonetheless and meant that he could put food on the table for his family. In the early seventies, with very little command of the English language, it was the only work on offer to him.

It was a far cry however from the great outdoors and the warmth of Africa, where Jai's father had supervised a huge outdoor leisure complex and been a keen, strong swimmer. He didn't care much for his work in a dingy, dark underground railway station; starved of daylight and over a period of several years, he began to suffer frequent bouts of depression. Jai told me very little about his father's recurrent difficulties, emphasizing only his admirable qualities and that he was a proud man with firm principles.

I learned from Jai's brother once that their father had been clinically labelled schizophrenic and as such was treated with suppressive medication and ECT (electric convulsive treatment). Schizophrenia is one of the more serious mental disorders and, from the research I did, sufferers seem inclined to be emotionally intense with distinctive personalities. Often fear is at the root. Jai refused to acknowledge his father however within the framework of any such disease, claiming that he suffered dreadfully at the hands of 'outside influences' and other people's misguided perceptions of him.

According to Jai, there was a simple and rational explanation for his father's difficulties; he was 'grossly misunderstood'. That aside, clearly there was something terribly wrong as his emotional fragility gave way to dark depressive moods, confused thinking and occasional displays of violence. On one occasion, Jai told me, it took several ambulance men to physically restrain his father and transfer him from his home to a waiting ambulance. Jai talked proudly about this episode, seeing it as a testament to his father's physical strength.

I cannot speculate in the pages of this book what ultimately drove Jai's father to suicide, but I can only imagine the devastating effect that that action had on his family. The *way* his father took his own life was simply horrendous; ... *he burnt himself to death in the family home ...*

Despite the horrific nature of his burns, his father lived for several hours or so in hospital before he died. To wish himself off the planet in such a way can only serve as a testament to the fragmented state of his mind at the time and the despair he must have been going through. Jai told me that he was the last person to see his father alive. As he stood at the bottom of the hospital bed he asked him, "Why, Dad?" A single tear sprung from the corner of his father's eye ... and sealed his passing.

Apart from the obvious trauma of losing his father in this way, growing up in such an environment *had* to have had a negative effect on him. He was barely twenty when his father took his own life after several years of mental illness and I suspect that Jai suffered extreme emotional neglect during all of his growing up years. When one parent's attention is clearly so diverted towards the other's difficulties, where does that leave the needs of their own children?

I remember asking Jai the first time he ever spoke to me about his father if he felt that he'd fully grieved for him. He was most emphatic that it was a part of his life he'd dealt with and yet later, on the same night his father died, Jai told me he went to the casino. The one feeling he admitted to 'owning' was one of immense distrust and anger towards the mental health profession. As a young teenager, Jai had endured the agony of seeing his father emotionally numbed on suppressive medication and he had witnessed electrical charges coursing through his father's physical system in order to alleviate the depression. Imagine the emotional impact all of this had on Jai. Was it any wonder he'd sought to defend against it? From his prison cell, he'd said to me, "I'll have the therapy, Jack… but *please*, no drugs, no straitjackets."

I realized that it was a secret underlying terror of being labelled insane that blocked Jai from seeking help. "They broke his *spirit*, Jacky," he once told me whilst relating what his father went through, an anguished look on his face. Now, from his prison walls, I sensed his fear acutely. It was fear that was now blocking him from moving forward and unconsciously motivating him to walk in his father's footsteps.

Sometimes there is an unconscious drive to play out in our own lives the unhealed trauma in an effort to heal it and, of course, pain of this nature can *never* be healed in this way. In one of his letters from prison, Jai opened up to me about his childhood. He told me how unhappy his parents were and how, as a child, all he remembered was the fighting and the endless rows. He had no one to talk to and not being conversant with the language meant that he could not even open up to his classmates, his teachers, strangers or the authorities.

By the age of seven he had developed 'coping mechanisms' which helped him to deal with the fear and the loneliness. He wrote, *'So I just kept everything to myself and suffered by myself, stealing happiness by counting pavement slabs to school, then counting the road edges to school, by jumping puddles or playing make-believe games or dreaming in my head about wanting to be a sports superstar.'*

Jai referred to his only friend back then as *'my companion, hardship'.* As a small child, he'd learnt to accept pain and suffering as normal; it became his learned behaviour and a way of being that he'd carried through to adulthood. I was beginning to understand that Jai had unconsciously shunned my love for him in the belief that he didn't deserve any happiness in his life, *only hardship*. More importantly, he was terrified of *loving* for fear that the bubble would burst, as this had always been his expectation.

Sadly, I also knew only too well that what we *expect* in life... becomes our reality. I so desperately wanted to help him, but I was also realistic enough to know that Jai's problems were complex and they were not going to go away in a few short hours of psychotherapy. Neither did I realize how much courage it took to admit the depth of his fears and insecurities to me. In one of his letters he wrote, *'I was so scared to be honest with you for fear that you would abuse my love or I would lose you because you thought I was weak and you would look for a stronger man ...'*

I knew some form of healing needed to take place if Jai was ever going to have a place in our lives and somehow he had to find a way to work through his fear.

Even though I had no way of knowing exactly *how* he would be treated by the mental health experts, I tried many times to reassure him that the methods of treatment had changed dramatically over the fifteen years or so since his father's death and that there were kinder, more humane ways to deal with this type of crisis.

But, as much as he heard those words, he didn't truly believe them. During the first few days in prison, he bombarded me with letters. In one he wrote,

'I am putting my destiny in your hands, Jacky. Will you promise to care, nurture and protect me from what they did to my dad? Or do you just want to shut me away, let me be your servant and not grow to my full potential. I was born to grow and you have stunted me. I am feeling so low and broken. Don't send other people to talk to me as I need to talk to you. Up until today I've tried to hold out and stay positive and protect my pride and now I realize pride has no value. Nothing has any value except pure love. If you even have one per cent

of pure love in your heart for me, then you will dispel any doubts of not wanting to help me ... and you will rush to my aid and make me whole again.'

In many ways Jai *made* me feel responsible for him and I had somehow unconsciously slipped into the role of caretaker. It was a role I felt overwhelmed by and uncomfortable with. How could I or anyone make him 'whole?' That was down to him. But as much as I kept telling myself that it was his own actions that had put him in prison, unconsciously I took on board the guilt.

Behind his prison bars, I knew Jai's fears and insecurities could only grow, and imprisonment would only serve to magnify his despair. He'd learned to cope so well that his apparent rationality to the prison authorities would only act as a block to any psychiatric referral. To the outside world, Jai was anything but a 'crazy' man. He was lucid, coherent and extremely articulate ... and yet I knew, deep down inside, he felt like he was drowning in quicksand ... and spent his daily energies ... *managing an underlying terror of life itself.*

I didn't really know at this stage who to turn to for help. Kate was a constant tower of strength to me, but I was consciously aware of the effect that living this daily nightmare might be having on her.

Most of my family had understandably written Jai off as a 'bad man', happy in the knowledge that he was out of my life and locked away. As far as they were concerned the prison authorities could throw away the key! I realized if I was going to get Jai the help he needed I would have to turn to those people around me who would view the situation from a higher perspective.

This change in thinking led me to Sid Wieghall, a well respected healer and Sai Baba devotee in Hall Green, Birmingham. Jai, Kate and I had all at one stage or another visited Sid for healing over the previous two years. Sid was a gentle man in his late fifties who had long been awakened to the power of his own healing ability and had put it to good use in his lifetime. I rang him during the first week that Jai was in prison and, after telling him what had happened, asked him if he would include Jai in his prayers.

"You know it's not him, don't you, Jacky," he said to me with a pronounced sensitivity. "Trust that spirit knows what he's going through and will sort it out for the highest good of all concerned. We all *choose* our experiences and, on some level, Jai has chosen this. I will put it up to God … know that we are here for you."

I was deeply grateful to Sid for those comforting words at the time and for the help, albeit distantly, that he offered … I knew Jai was going to need all the healing he could get.

On the 8th May 2001, one week after his imprisonment, Jai's bail was refused and set for a future date of June 5th. The mounting grief I felt over his imprisonment was overwhelming. That same night a programme came on television called 'Brian's Story'. It was about a tortured, albeit talented writer named Brian who was suffering from bouts of 'hyper-mania' interspersed with long periods of depression. There were constant references to house fires occurring, for which the police suspected he might have been responsible. Eventually, after years of suffering, Brian drank a bottle of martini one night and threw himself off the roof of a building, killing himself. Everywhere I turned there seemed to be signs giving me the message: *Jai is ill … and no one is listening!*

The following day I wrote a letter to him in prison. I tried to write it from a higher perspective, avoiding any blame or accusations and trying to appeal to the rational, balanced part of him. In the course of writing it, I sat still and steadied my thoughts and, in an action of prayer, asked God to tell me what was happening to Jai.

In that moment I was guided to open a phenomenal book by Neale Donald Walsch, entitled 'Conversations with God: Book 3'. It is the last of a trilogy of books in which the author is engaged in a private and awe-inspiring dialogue with God. It was to page 132 that I turned ... and this is what God said in answer to my question about Jai:

'Paramahansa Yogananda is an example of a person who was very close to "perfect" as an out-picturing of what he thought of himself. He had a very clear idea about himself, and about his relationship to Me, and he used his life to "out-picture" that. He wanted to experience his idea about himself in his own reality; to know himself as that, experientially.

Babe Ruth did the same thing. He had a very clear idea about himself, and his relationship to Me, and he used his life to out-picture that; to know himself in his own experience.

Not many people live that level. Now granted, the Master and the Babe had two entirely different ideas about themselves, yet they both played them out magnificently.

They also both had different ideas about Me, that's for sure, and were coming from different levels of consciousness about Who I Am, and about their true relationship to Me. And those levels of consciousness were reflected in their thoughts, words and actions.

One was in a place of peace and serenity most of his life, and brought deep peace and serenity to others. The other was in a place of anxiousness, turmoil and occasional anger (particularly when he couldn't get his way), and brought turmoil to the lives of those around him.

Both were good-hearted, however – there was never a softer touch than the Babe – and the difference between the two is that one had virtually nothing in terms of physical acquisitions, but never wanted more than what he got, while the other "had everything" and never got what he really wanted.'

Babe Ruth was a world-famous baseball player in the 1950s, who gained his place in the history books as the man who made the most strikes for his country in the game. I remembered once, as a teenager, watching a film made of him in which he was depicted as colossal, both in physical stature and in personality. 'The Babe' attributed his ability to overcome the many obstacles and difficulties in his life to an abiding faith in God.

So wherein lay the answer to my question in those pages? In my letter to Jai I wrote,

Is there a Babe inside you, Jaya? What is it that you are searching for? Is it wealth and success on the material plane or a craving for the buzz and excitement gained from living life on the edge? The inner peace within your heart cannot be found in any of these things. It can only be found in watching a child laugh and play and seeing the unconditional love in their eyes staring back at you. It can only be found in the waves of the ocean, watching the sun rise over a vast canyon, or the warmth of your lover's embrace as you drift into sleep. I believe, Jaya, that you are getting to know yourself, 'experiencing yourself' through your relationship with God. When you emerge from the shadows – then I know you will become the Master you truly are inside …

It was a letter that turned into several pages and was full of supportive words. Even though I reassured him that I hadn't deserted him, I urged him to question the path he was now walking. It was also a letter that made absolutely clear that I could no longer endure the destructive dynamics of our relationship and that he *must* accept help.

Jai wrote back to me almost *daily*. His letters, sometimes ten or fifteen pages long, were full of declarations of love, loaded with his philosophical beliefs, his claims, his visions, his mission … and, at the same time punctuated, albeit briefly, with words of blame, hostility and anger. Sometimes they were too painful to read. This is what he wrote to me on the 11th day of his imprisonment,

I feel like a tiger who's been caged, so desperate for your help and healing that I'm now begging on my knees with tears in my eyes and my hands folded, looking up at you as I'm crying. Please, please, please, please help me. I'm trying to

stay positive, but keep getting the mood swings. I keep reading The Gita, chanting, meditating, thinking of God and pulling out all the positive techniques I know but to no avail. I still keep coming round to feeling desperate again. It seems forever that I'm caged, in fact worse than forever. Please get me out or come and kill me as death would be easier to face than this...

I've said before in the pages of this book that the pain that comes from watching someone you love 'fall apart' before your eyes is almost unbearable. Staying in the relationship as it was seemed intolerable, but to pull away ... impossible. If I'd failed to involve the police or not acted when I did, heaven knows where or how it would have ended. I tried to tell Jai many times that I acted *for* myself and the children, not *against* him. He couldn't see that though, not back then in prison, or even months down the line. In his own tortured state, all Jai could feel was that I'd deserted him.

Why are you punishing me so harshly by sending me to prison? he wrote, *I can't write to you any more as I have no paper. I can't phone you as I have no money. I can't come and see you as I'm locked in a 10´ by 5´ cell all day and all night. They let me out twice to get food, but I can't eat. They let me out for one hour to walk around the yard, but when I get out you are not outside. They let me out for half an hour to have a visitor, but it is never you. They let me out for treatment, but the medicine is never you. Only two showers a week, but there is no cold water. Just drug addicts, murderers, thieves, child abusers, all sorts of criminals, but none of them are you.*

If I had your skills, I would shut my eyes and come and visit you, but I don't. You know I love you more than any man loves any woman on the planet. What do I have to do to prove my love to you ... tell me and I will do it, but please don't cage me, don't leave me here ... as death would be better. I am yours truly, waiting, praying, coping, dying, suffocating, hoping and ever loving, Jaya.

I couldn't bear it; I had to see him and booked a visit for the 16th May. Two days earlier, he had telephoned me twice … in tears. "My ego and my pride has been broken, Jacky," he told me. "I'll do whatever you ask, see whoever you want me to see. All I should have been was a good father to my son and a good husband, lover and friend to you. I'm so sorry; I will never ever hit another woman as long as I live. I will never make you feel like that again. You are the last person I wanted to hurt. All I care about now is winning back your love."

This time I knew I couldn't just rush back into his arms simply because he was asking me to; there was more at stake here than just me and Jai. Jessica was now in counselling as a result of what I'd put her through and I had Temujin to think about. Apart from that I'd been down this road once before; the promise that it would never happen again, the resolution to change … I needed to look into his eyes and see for myself if he meant it … *and somehow I had to get him to accept once and for all that he needed help.*

I had that chance two days later in my pre-scheduled prison visit. Knowing the arguments it would evoke, I didn't tell a soul that I was going and so I was left with no choice but to take Temujin with me. Thankfully, at five months old, he slept through the entire visit and was blissfully unaware of the experience. Seeing Jai left me deeply upset for days and, in a way, I wished I hadn't gone. Just as he had looked on his return from his India trip, the weight loss was horrific. The standard prison issue shirt hung loosely from his body, and there was a gaping divide between his neck and the collar that once fitted.

As the guard motioned me towards where he was sitting, waiting behind the wooden partition that divided us, I noticed he had his arms cradled around his midsection and was rocking his body backwards and forwards in the chair. The sight of him reminded me of one of those disturbing patient images you see in a psychiatric ward.

The allotted half an hour seemed to race by and we said very little to each other. He told me he wouldn't block any psychiatric referrals the courts might want to make this time. "Just tell them I'm not mad, Jacky," he said to me with a desperate look in his eyes. "Tell them I really did have the visions and it was only in trying to make others understand that I've landed myself here."

He gave me the address of his solicitor and urged me to write to him and explain that there were mitigating circumstances for his actions. "You have to make them understand I'm not a criminal, Jacky … you *have* to get me out of here."

I agreed on that day to do what I could to get him the appropriate help. "Promise me you will write every day and visit me again tomorrow," he pleaded as I got up to leave. I couldn't make a promise like that. I had a life outside those prison walls in which Jai had played a minor part for a very long time. It was a life full of daily pressures, work commitments, responsibilities, domestic routines … and ever increasing financial concerns.

I needed to talk to someone and that night I telephoned Hazel. It had been months since I'd spoken to her and, although there had been many occasions when I'd felt the desperate need to ring her, Jai viewed any contact of this nature as some kind of betrayal. His first letter to me from prison had included this paragraph: *'I used to be able to tell you anything without you analyzing me, condemning me, judging me, discussing me with the world, diagnosing me, baby handling me, prosecuting me, ridiculing me, undermining me, fighting with me, arguing with me and not trusting me.'*

With those thoughts going round in his head, I knew he would always view any outside help I tried to enlist with suspicion and it seemed the longer the 'emergency' went on the greater the paranoia grew.

Hazel was great, sympathetic as ever. "I'm sorry that things have got so out of control, Jacky" were her opening words. "When a spiritual emergency goes untreated, it can easily turn into a psychotic episode." She reminded me again of her words almost a year before, that when the emergency hits it can be mind-blowing. It is so powerful the recipient believes and feels that they can do *anything*.

"Remember the basic personality doesn't change. Whatever shadow aspects were under the surface, they will be doubly amplified," she said. She remarked how she knew that this was going the wrong way when, in a brief conversation with Jai the previous year, he'd told her, "Sai Baba will have to kneel at *my* feet."

She related to me a story of a twenty-year-old Birmingham girl who literally that week had ended up on medication up to the hilt and in a psychiatric ward after telling her parents in a manic episode, "You will have to kiss my feet and the ground I walk on. I am above God."

Please God, don't let Jai end up that way, I remember thinking.

Hazel urged me to ring Tony Neate, the Principal of the College of Healing in Malvern, Worcestershire. I hadn't met Tony personally, but I had undergone the foundation course with the College of Healing through the local adult education scheme, so I was familiar with the marvellous work that went on at the college.

"Tony has a panel of experts," she told me. "They include psychiatrists who are specially trained to identify and deal with spiritual emergencies. Between them they have fifty-five years experience and Tony will know just by talking with Jai whether this *is* spiritual emergency or a psychotic episode."

Once again I thanked Hazel for her help. She told me to contact her if things got too unbearable and said she would include Jai and me in her prayers. She urged me to read a book by Christina & Stanislav Grof called 'The Stormy Search for The Self' which she said would help me understand what was happening.

I remember the tears rolling down my face as I put down the telephone. A part of Hazel knew Jai's condition had gone untreated for far too long and I'd detected the despondency in her voice.

I managed to track Tony down after a couple of days. He had a very supportive but no bullshit quality about his advice. "Spiritual awakening is a very unsatisfactory term for what actually happens," he told me. "An opening up of consciousness is a more appropriate description. In the opening up, where there are unresolved issues such as trauma and pain from childhood, all of this will come to the surface." *I remember thinking how true this was in Jai's case.*

Like Hazel, Tony confirmed that if the emergency is not resolved and treated over long periods of time with deep healing and deep psychotherapy, then the 'episodes' will keep resurfacing and get more and more perilous. When I outlined Jai's childhood trauma, his life experiences and the background of events leading up to his imprisonment, Tony said, "Well, Jacky, when you put all of that into the melting pot … you have one hell of a dangerous concoction."

I asked him if he would be prepared to see Jai whilst he was in prison but he understandably declined; he added that he and his group would work with him 'psychically' from a distance, to remove whatever 'entities' and 'attachments' were with him. "The light and the shadow are pulling at him, Jacky," said Tony. "You have to understand that on another level his spirit has chosen this and what his spirit is saying to him is what inside is motivating him."

He agreed to see him on his release, if Jai was willing. He also said something very insightful, "Just beware of the manipulations, Jacky. The ego will do anything to get out of its present situation."

I'll try to keep that in mind, I thought … and then he delivered a final remark which I've never forgotten. *"The moment of finding his importance … is the exact moment of losing it."*

There was nothing else I could do whilst Jai was in prison …

other than get on with life. The only problem with that was that my life was full of mounting pressures. Another month had passed without the rent being paid and the landlord was understandably getting twitchy. Jai told me to tell him that he was in India for a couple of months and would settle everything on his return. He wasn't happy with that at all of course and I found myself dodging his telephone calls.

I was barely earning enough through my therapeutic work to cover the household bills and, with the workshops draining all my available resources, my bank balance now stood at zero. I had no choice other than to pour my energies into attracting new clients and increasing the Q.E.D membership. Despite the fact that I was passionate about my work, the pressure just to stay afloat was beginning to take its toll.

On top of that I couldn't seem to let go of Jai in my mind. The second date for his bail application was approaching and his letters conveyed a growing sense of panic and fearfulness. Later that week I missed one of his calls from prison because I was out of the house taking Temujin for a routine health check. To Jai that evoked in him the same feeling as a small child who loses sight of its mother in the middle of a crowded shopping centre and was as dire in its consequences. I'd confirmed everything he already knew and felt deep down inside *'that only God is truly there for me … only God comes with me all the way'*. No one else could be trusted, not even me.

I was overwhelmed with the burden of Jai's problems, but I somehow knew that my own peace of mind was intrinsically linked to his capacity to heal. I couldn't abandon him knowing the turmoil he was going through; neither could I leave him facing a longer prison term without trying to make the courts understand that he needed a psychiatric assessment.

It was 29th May, one week before Jai's scheduled court appearance. Together that morning, Kate and I sought some legal advice. I wanted to somehow strengthen Jai's defence but not lose sight of the need for a psychiatric referral. The solicitor explained that, as I was the injured party, she didn't automatically have the 'right of audience' on my behalf in court. The only advice she could offer me was to write to the CPS and Jai's solicitor in an attempt to influence the sentencing. My only hope was to push for a rehabilitative sentence rather than a punitive one.

On the same afternoon later that day, I was booked in for a prison visit and I hoped the information I had gained from the solicitor might lift Jai's spirits a little.

But I wasn't given the chance. Despite organizing a babysitter, writing letters to the CPS and his solicitor and moving heaven and earth to get there with time to spare … Jai blocked my visit completely.

The guards told me he was sitting by himself in the chapel and, even after three requests by them, he refused to take my visit. It was to be another five days before I heard from him again. *I knew I was being punished for not being there to receive his telephone call … at the exact moment he needed me.*

Eventually I got a letter from him on the Friday before his bail hearing. He told me about some lay preachers from America who'd visited the prison and how, during a healing from them, he'd felt Jesus Christ and The Holy Ghost enter him. He believed it was another part of God's plan, he told me; that God had brought him to prison to find Jesus's love and that this love would be a source of strength and guidance to him in his life.

'When He sent Jesus to me, I accepted Him and cried and cried. I fell on my knees and cried even more. And when God looks at me now all banged up in my cell and desperate to the point of suicide, He tells me, 'Don't worry, it will all turn out alright'.

God only knows how much I wanted it to turn out all right but, the more letters I received from him, the more convinced

I was of the *depth* of Jai's psychosis.

I desperately needed some answers and something that week made me turn to the book that Hazel had recommended: 'The Stormy Search for The Self' by C&S Grof.

It was one of those times in life that I call a 'light bulb' moment! Absorbing its contents was like having someone switch on the light in a room full of darkness ... and for the first time in over a year, I no longer felt alone with my experience.

The book contains glimpses into the life of one of its authors, Christina Grof, as well as personal experiences from other contributors who have either gone through a 'spiritual emergency' themselves or have lived through it with a loved one. Instead of looking at this non-ordinary state of consciousness as though it were a prelude to some pathological illness, the Grofs highlight the transformative and, indeed, healing effect that 'spiritual emergency' can ultimately provide for the sufferer.

I couldn't believe the parallels with Jai's experience. On pages 38 and 39, Stanislav identifies the contributing factors that can trigger such a crisis. He writes:

'It can be some primarily physical factor, such as a disease, an accident, an operation, extreme physical exertion, or prolonged lack of sleep...' He adds, *'Occasionally, a psychospiritual transformation can begin during intense and emotionally overwhelming love-making ...'*

'At other times', writes Stanislav, *'the beginning of a spiritual emergency can be traced back to a strong emotional experience, particularly one that involves a serious loss.'*

Deep spiritual practices, he notes, are also responsible for acting as a catalyst in spiritual emergencies, as well as active forms of worship such as *'... trance-dancing, Sufi whirling, powerful drumming, gospel singing or continuous chanting.'*

Of the list of triggers, nearly all of them applied to Jai. Every page I turned not only gave me a deeper insight into the extent of his experience but also made sense of every aspect of the bizarre behaviour. I couldn't put the book down!

On page 42, Stanislav says, '*When spiritual emergence is very rapid and dramatic, however, this natural process can become a crisis, and spiritual emergence becomes spiritual emergency. People who are in such a crisis are bombarded with inner experiences that abruptly challenge their old beliefs and ways of existing, and their relationship with reality shifts very rapidly.*

Suddenly they feel uncomfortable in the formerly familiar world and may find it difficult to meet the demands of everyday life. They can have great problems distinguishing their inner visionary world from the external world of daily reality. Physically, they may experience forceful energies streaming through their bodies and causing uncontrollable tremors.'

I remembered back to having seen the energy literally pouring from Jai's body when he'd showered. This confirmation brought such relief with it; at the time I thought *I* was going mad!

Stanislav continues, '*Fearful and resistant, they might spend much time and effort trying to control what feels like an overwhelming inner event. And they may feel impelled to talk about their experiences and insights to anyone who is within range, sounding out of touch with reality, disjointed or messianic.*'

I shuddered at the memory of Jai's 'vision' on the tape recording and how the tone of his telephone call had sent shock waves throughout my body. Jai believed he was the only person on the planet who'd gone through his experience and yet the similarities described in the book were astounding.

Undoubtedly the severity of the symptoms varies from one individual to another, but the book confirmed what I'd long suspected: that Jai had undergone a major spiritual crisis but it was an experience that was by no means unique.

Stanislav also provided the confirmation for me that what

inevitably happens in the state of emergency is that *'numerous old traumatic memories and childhood wounds tend to surface from the psyche.'* These then get added to *'deeper visions which seem to be coming from other cultures and other centuries.'*

On page 88 he comments on how people act out such visions and insights, *'If they have connected with what they feel to be God or a Higher Power, or with a celestial being such as Jesus or Buddha, they may allow this state to distort their ego or their sense of personal identity. Rather than understanding that they have tapped a universal reality that is potentially available to everyone, they feel that it is exclusively their own. Instead of emerging from the experience with the understanding that they are divine and so is everyone and everything else, they feel that they are God and have a message for the world. Such people may develop Messianic tendencies, which, when expressed, may alienate them from others.'*

Hazel's words echoed in my mind, *"He will tell you he is God and believe he can do anything."*

It was all there in Stanislav's book: the 'exclusivity' and Jai's belief that no one in the history of mankind had shared an experience like his; the 'luminosity' and the need to shield 'these eyes that have seen God' from the intensity of the light; the 'egocide' and the confusion over the drive to kill the ego with the drive to kill oneself; 'the belief that there is nothing to heal' or, if there is, as Stanislav suggests, that the full profound effect of the experience will be lost and life will once again become mundane and meaningless.

I have said before that I never doubted for a second that Jai experienced the visions. I knew that what he went through was profound, mystical, prophetic, and almost incomprehensible and I didn't set out to take his experience away from him. But Jai had made the tragic and dangerous mistake of taking the visions literally and, by doing so, had allowed them to distort his view of reality.

The only thing that was important now, if he was to resume any sense of normality, was that the visions, along with other material from the psyche, be explored for the healing potential they offered. Jai's condition was serious but, if nothing else, the book allowed me to believe that, no matter how difficult, there was the hint of a possible way forward.

It felt as though a window to the heavens had been opened in my mind.

CHAPTER SEVEN: 'GROUNDHOG DAY'

'You have ravish'd me away by a Power I cannot resist;
and yet I could resist till I saw you;
and even since I have seen you
I have endeavoured often to reason
against the reasons of my love'
Keats, John (1795-1821)

'Insanity is doing the same thing over and over and expecting a different result'
Albert Einstein (1879-1955)

On 5th June 2001, the courts granted Jai conditional bail. He was ordered to take up temporary residence at another address and one that was outside a hundred miles radius from our previously shared home. I knew the decision would antagonize him. Jai would kick against any move to block his access to us and I didn't think for a single moment he would stick to it. Even though I knew keeping a distance between us was the best thing, I viewed it as time wasted and time that he wasn't spending on his own healing. After all, I now believed I held the key to his recovery!

What I couldn't have known at this point was that the spiritual emergency aspect of Jai's condition … *was merely the tip of the iceberg.*

The resolve to stay apart lasted less than two weeks! And in our mutual desperation to see each other, I broke the court order to visit him at his temporary address in the south of England.

I'll never forget the sight of him, painfully thin, as we were led into the sitting room where he was waiting. I could sense the body tension, like a tightly coiled spring waiting to unfold and, as the day wore on, I got the distinct feeling he was using every ounce of energy to control it. After all, in Jaya's mind, all he'd done was swap one set of prison bars for another and, as I've said often in the pages of this book, he lived by his own code of rules. *No one*, not even the courts, told him what he could and couldn't do.

In the afternoon we were left on our own for an hour or two to talk and I was desperate to tell him my news. Surely now that I had a 'label' for his difficulties and a strategy to overcome them, would he not share in my relief? I began quoting eagerly from Stanislav's book, telling him how most people are completely unprepared for the onslaught to the senses that occurs during a 'spiritual emergency'. The analogy Stanislav relates is the one used by the American spiritual teacher, Ram Dass. Such a person, he says, can be compared to a toaster and the reaction you get when you 'stick a plug into 220 volts instead of 110 volts and everything fries'.

I went on and on, quoting from a pile of carefully scribbled notes and feeling like a scientist who'd just discovered a long awaited cure to some terminal disease.

Although he remained quiet … something inside me suspected he wasn't *truly* listening.

In fact, there was only one thing on Jai's mind that day and it wasn't sharing in my discovery, miracle cure or not! All *he* wanted was a reassurance of my love for him as he made several attempts to arouse me sexually. "Forget all of that, Jacky," he whispered over and over, kissing and caressing me tenderly. "Your love is all I need to heal me." *Oh, for heaven's sake, Jai, wake up, will you! If only that were true, I remember thinking …if only that were true.*

The problem was my *desire* for Jai was and always had been my Achilles' heel and it was a desire that kept coming back to wound me. Of all the relationships I'd had before Jai, I had never given myself over to a man so wholeheartedly … I don't think before him I'd ever fallen so deeply in love with anyone.

There were times, when looking back, I realized he exploited that desire as a way of getting what he wanted … It somehow gave him a sense of power over me … and this was one of those times. As much as I wanted him and dared to hope that my love would heal him, I could no longer be ruled by my emotions. I needed a commitment from him to accept some form of healing and stick with it… and I needed the hope of a way forward through all the chaos he'd created.

He was full of promises, just as he had been from his prison cell and I believed him … *again*. In the belief that I now had a diagnosis and a cure for his problems, I wanted so much just to wipe the slate clean and start all over, but I knew I had to stay firm. Despite him wanting to travel back with us then and there, I urged him to stay longer.

I had a 'Shamanic Healing' day planned at the workshops on the following Sunday. It was a small group and I knew the facilitator to be a skilled shaman. I invited Jai to join it and he agreed.

All he wanted now, he told me, was a chance to win back my love for him and that any decisions I made, he would stand by.

Finally, I thought, we're on the right track.

Looking back I'm not sure how much Jai benefited from that day although I'm certain a 'healing' of sorts did take place. I just recall the facilitator commenting to me at the end of it that 'his energies were all over the place'. An *understatement*, I remember thinking at the time. Maybe a part of me back then believed that if I could involve him in some group work, where he would be invited but not compelled to share his 'innermost' thoughts, then this might act as a gentle prelude to the real work; in other words, the one-to-one work with a skilled therapist. I knew that finding someone to work with Jai was going to be a challenge in itself and something else that he'd left entirely in my hands.

Over the next month or so our interactions were kinder to each other, albeit guarded on my part. Jai observed my request to keep his distance, staying at his city centre address for the time being, even though we came together for the odd day out here and there. One such day, I remember, was in the middle of July when we drove down to Weston-super-Mare. It was a beautiful, warm summer's day and he picked us up early so as to take advantage of the weather.

I remember that day acutely as he took Jess for endless donkey rides, played with her on the swings and slides, and rode the bumper cars with her at the fairground. I remember our shared picnic together and watching him interact with Temujin, then eight months old, as he rolled him around on a blanket on the sand and lovingly shielded him from the heat of the sun … and I remember wondering how on earth had it gone so horribly wrong. That day I spent time with a grown man who had the ability to live in the moment more than anyone I'd ever known and a man whose intrinsic goodness in those moments shone through like a blazing sun.

By late July, the pressure to generate some financial security into our daily lives overtook everything. The unpaid rent was mounting and it was worrying me sick. I was doing my level best with the spiritual centre and had attracted an adventure group called 'Spice' to book my talks and workshops, aiming them at their members interested in personal growth. With 'Spice' on board, it seemed that for the first time since the workshops had opened I was properly valuing the work I was doing and even though breaking even was still a long way off, I knew I was on target.

Jai meanwhile had involved himself in another mission in order to generate cash and it wasn't one that filled me with ease. He planned to recoup back all the money he'd ever loaned to significant others in the past. His argument was simple; he needed the money now and they needed to pay up, regardless of whether they had the wherewithal to do so. Garry was back on the scene and another so-called 'friend', a thickset black man with six-foot wide shoulders and eyes that could freeze a fire. Jai told me he'd set up a debt collecting agency and, with those two in tow, I wondered how on earth he was going about it.

As always I was accused of jumping to conclusions. "I'm not an idiot, Jacky," he said. "I'm not going to create any more trouble for myself." I certainly didn't like what he was doing though and, as much as he assured me that he wasn't using aggressive or intimidating behaviour, I was worried sick about the one legacy on which he seemed particularly focused.

It didn't take me long to realize that Jai was determined to go to whatever lengths it took to reclaim what he perceived to be his by birthright ... Dove St News ... and from this point on a bitter dispute with his brother over ownership of the flagship was to ensue. It was a dispute that for Jai was to bring all of his past grievances to the surface ... and would be the kiss of death for their relationship.

Looking back, I cannot begin to count the number of times he tried to involve me in his arguments with other people. Jai's belief was that if I loved him then surely I should stand by him and argue his case for him.

The problem was though that he had seemingly made a lifetime occupation over falling out with people and it was difficult to know sometimes where the truth ended and a distortion of the facts began. He said one thing and his brother claimed the opposite.

Ever since his brother had bailed him out of prison, Jai's involvement with Dove St had been on Nara's terms. Nara held the control, seniority of position *and* the purse strings and although for a while Jai 'played the game', I knew underneath he was seething. Not fully knowing their history together and not wanting to get involved, I opted to stay well out of their arguments ... a stance that Jai viewed as a complete betrayal on my part.

Despite the strained nature of their relationship, they were duty bound in late August of that year to go to India and sort out a land entitlement dispute amongst the family. Jai saw it as an opportunity to make contacts and set some business ideas in motion. The only problem was he needed Nara's financial backing again and, frankly, that wasn't going to happen, not in a million years.

Inevitably a row over money took place whilst they were in their childhood village in India and they went their separate ways. For Jai it gave him an opportunity to 'strike out on his own' and he travelled on to Delhi. To this day, as far as I am aware, the dispute over the land in India remains unresolved.

On his return he seemed even more determined than ever to make his mark upon the world. In Jai's mind, mankind had still to recognize him and, if he was ever going to gain the respect and admiration he believed himself entitled to, he'd got wise to the fact that it wasn't going to come from his peers in the business world. All he seemed to evoke from them was their mockery.

From this point on, Jai cleverly changed tactics. He tried to convince me he'd opened a school in his name for the poor, half-starved children of some remote Indian village whilst he was out there. I wish there had been a grain of truth in it but, just like the businesses he claimed to have, it was a fantasy, a fabrication of the truth that served to fuel his ego and seemed to fit with his new found mission.

This was a mission which held a promise so sweet that he began to crave it like an addict craves a fix. Where better to start in his mind than amongst those with whom he felt a natural superiority to; those who, in their unquestioning obedience, would accept his truth as their own.

From this moment on, Jai focused on those amongst whom he could play out his role as benevolent leader, master and saviour of the planet. It was to the poor, starving and needy that he turned his attention and it was this oppressed populous of the world that for him held the potential adoring following… of millions.

Frankly, if he'd been truly coming from a place of unconditional love, if his roots had been firmly cemented in the material world and he'd had wealth to spare, his mission would have indeed held merit. But this was far from the case.

The sharp reality was Jai had become oblivious to the fact that he was failing to fulfil a fundamental responsibility and that was in providing for his own family. Whilst he began to focus on devising strategies to raise his own profile amongst the underprivileged of the world … we were sinking deeper and deeper into debt. Kate said to me the one day as I sat tearfully at my desk with a pile of unpaid bills, "What's the point of offering you heaven on a plate, Jacky … *when you starve in the meantime …*"

Exactly, what *was* the point! The rent had gone unpaid for several months and I was barely meeting our household bills. Over the last two years my credit card balance had slowly crept up as a result of Jai coercing me into buying things for the home that we didn't need and now, on top of that, the workshops were threatened with closure.

Whatever financial resource Jai managed to lay his hands on was bypassing the family home and was being spent on ego driven pursuits that failed to gather form in the physical world and only seemed to quench his unrelenting thirst for power. Nothing was getting better. If anything, Jai was slipping deeper and deeper into the illusory world he had created and I could feel myself heading towards a breakdown…

Life seemed out of control … and yet none of it seemed to matter when the devastating news of the September 11th bombings hit our TV screens. That heart-sinking moment for me, as I'm sure for millions around the globe, will stay in my memory forever. Suddenly my daily dramas seemed minor.

What happened was surely a reality check for all humanity and one which shockingly conveyed that this was a global crisis and not just one that touched the American population. Every day, in every pocket of the planet, senseless killings take place in the name of religion and as a result of racial hatred. The innocent have died in droves, victims of war, targets of oppression and hatred in some form or another.

I wanted us to do *something* as a group from the workshops, but what else could we do other than send prayers and healing to the families of the victims? Later in the wake of the crisis, on Monday 3rd October, I hosted a discussion group and I called it 'September 11th – A Turning Point'. Jai asked to attend and I let him.

I rationalized that he would surely realize there was no place for ego here and that such an event must not, dare not, be used as an opportunity for him to take centre stage and harp on about his claims.

The problem was I made the tragic mistake of thinking that whatever was wrong with Jai, spiritual emergency or otherwise, was something he could 'turn on and off' at will. *It was a mistake I made …many times.*

I'd invited the World Earth Healing coordinator, a gentle soul named Leigh who works tirelessly for global peace, to open the meeting. He made a statement along the lines of 'holding our stillness', working only with the vibration of love and seeking to heal the 'illusion of separation'.

Then Jai broke in. "Can anyone else in this room say that they are truly happy …because I am," he said.

Nothing wrong with that statement I remember thinking …and then, "Even when the news broke, I was still happy; it didn't affect my happiness at all."

Maybe it was a line to shake people; Jai was adept at that I'd discovered and, if that was the case, it worked. A stunned silence followed. "If we truly have inner peace," he continued, "not even a major war can shake us out of our stillness. Let us say my name is not Jaya for argument's sake, but say … Jesus Christ. Would I be able to be shaken out of my stillness then?"

Surely, I remember thinking at the time, he *cannot* know how startlingly provocative his dialogue comes across sometimes. In the next breath he was offering out company cars (that he didn't have) and bragging "Who needs extra cash, I've got plenty to spare," arguing that sharing skills and possessions was a great way to spread peace and happiness. As was the norm, no one interrupted him.

When Jai talked, everyone listened. But not for the reasons he thought. Quite simply, people were terrified of interrupting him; a fact I repeatedly pointed out to him and one he failed to grasp in all of our time together. He intimidates people and his demeanour when standing tall is nothing short of overpowering. On this occasion as his dialogue gained momentum, his voice grew louder and harsher and his physical presence more aggressive. It was the same familiar pattern; prison had changed nothing.

That evening, as he began to pick on each person one by one from his standing viewpoint, I watched them visibly squirm. "I've no opinion on that," said one person. "I'm not sure where I stand at the moment," said another.

An interruption from a sensitive member of the group was perfectly timed and she ushered him out of the room into the kitchen like a small child who'd just made a social disgrace of himself. Later he said to me rather cuttingly, "I can't believe I was pushed out of my own building, a building I pay for!"

But this had long been the scenario; put Jai in front of an audience, light the blue touchpaper, retreat and watch the sparks fly! I've often said before in the pages of this book, he is the most complex and misunderstood individual I have ever known.

Later, as we both reflected on the evening's events, his eyes suddenly became moist with tears. "I remember when we lived in Lancashire," he said, suddenly accessing a memory, "the next-door neighbours, an English family, would shout to me every day as I left for school, 'Go home, Pakis, go home,

Pakis'… that really *hurt,* Jacky."

Of *course* it hurt. Oppression and racial hatred; it's all part of the illusion of separation and the underlying cause for all human suffering…

By late October of that year I felt trapped in a catch-22 situation. I was torn between my need to maintain a distance from Jai for my own peace and sanity and my need to know what havoc he was creating on a daily basis. A part of me just wanted it all to end but I couldn't just turn my back on the financial mess he'd created and I'd convinced myself that there was a cure for his problems.

Apart from that I also knew from past history with him that, whenever the natural rhythmic cycles of the melatonin and serotonin levels in his brain were interrupted, it produced a heightened state and increased agitation in his mood.

These levels were at their lowest and most dangerous during March/April and November/December. The routine of prison, albeit for five weeks, had forced him to adopt more normal and regular sleeping patterns but now, as we approached November, I sensed he was back to his old routines, staying awake for hours and hours on end, night after night. His eyes, dark ringed and heavy, had taken on that glazed, faraway expression again. On top of that, the impending court case and the possible threat of further imprisonment were only serving to increase his anxieties. *In short, Jai was treading a fine line and I knew it.*

As always he rejected any advice I gave him and took it to mean that I was trying to control him or 'man-manage' him as he'd now taken to calling it. If I pressed him about seeking help or reminded him of the promises he'd made in prison, then I was accused of putting 'psychological pressure' on him and trying to cage his 'free spirit'.

In fact, the longer he went on avoiding the intervention of psychiatrists, therapists or help of any kind, the more he held this up as some kind of living proof that there was nothing wrong with him and that the problem was obviously mine.

"Look at me," he would exclaim. "I'm fine now; I've realized that force is not the way to get people to accept my visions. I have to find another way." But Jai was consistent in one thing and one thing only and that was his total inability to look at his own misgivings. He appeared to have made a full-time occupation out of pointing out everyone else's faults and negative character traits but displayed a total unwillingness to look at his own.

In truth, Jai was *anything* but 'fine'. Certainly the initial jarring intensity of the energy had subsided somehow, but he still believed himself to be the saviour of mankind and still on a mission from God; none of the words had changed. All he'd done was to swap the melody. The first time round he was 'out of tune'; there was far too much bass and the words jarred and grated. Now he was playing more in harmony; it was easier on the ears and the words flowed better. Same words though, just a different melody ... *and I wasn't buying it, not for a single second...*

Looking back I realize that the periods of time I spent away from Jai somehow lulled me into a false sense of security. It was as if the absence brought with it a renewed sense of peace and balance and often led me to overlook the painful interactions between us. Then, when I did spend time in his company, something would happen that would jolt me back to reality and remind me of the sheer severity of his problems. One such event came in late October at the marriage celebration of a family member.

I'd always wanted to attend a traditional Indian wedding and, as it was in London, I saw it as a way to spend a weekend away doing something special as a family. On reflection, I realize that weekend was a significant turning point in our relationship in that it made me realize how deeply rooted the psychosis had become.

The journey in itself was a nightmare. We'd barely even left our home town when he verbally attacked a seventy-year-old man for mistakenly pulling out in front of our car, leaving the man shaking and distraught. When I told Jai how callous and unnecessary I thought his actions were, he turned on me, treating me to a verbal onslaught that lasted the entire duration of the journey. Somehow he always managed to completely justify his behaviour and bully me into agreeing with him.

I've often said before in the pages of this book that it was impossible to defend myself against Jai. In our abusive exchanges, he always emerged the verbal victor, usually as a result of sheer bullying tactics or because, having placed me in the role of disobedient child, I was thereby in need of punishment. By the time we got to our destination, following another road rage scenario in the middle of London's Theatreland, I had a twisted knot in my stomach, felt sick and frankly just wanted to go home.

Somehow I managed to get through the reception, despite the embarrassment of watching him order bottle after bottle of champagne for everyone on our table at the groom's expense. I didn't say a word as he listed false achievements about himself and businesses we didn't have as though he were running through a daily shopping list. He was a master at turning on the charm when he had an audience. When I witnessed him giving a business card to someone on the adjoining table telling them that he'd opened a modelling agency and a sound recording studio, something inside me clicked.

Jai sounded so convincing that I realized he actually *believed* the lies he told himself. It dawned on me that he seemed to have very little control over the fantasy world he was creating and that this was a sickness … for which no easily obtained or readymade cure existed.

Something else that I've stressed before was the belief that my own safety was directly linked to my staying close to Jai. It's why I stayed in the relationship as long as I did and tried to get him the treatment I knew he needed. I'd known for a long time that he posed more of a danger and a threat to me in the outside world if left unhealed and unsupervised. This was the paradox. It made me even more determined this time around that I wasn't going to let him just talk his way out of seeking treatment, of whatever kind.

I told him over and over that it was part of the deal of him being near me and his son and, even though I hated the fact that that sounded threatening, it became part of my armoury. Back then, I think I was afraid to admit, even to myself, that I was terrified of the hold he seemed to have over me.

Thankfully through the prison authorities, he'd been assigned some supervision of sorts in the form of a probation officer whom I shall call Jill. From this point on I found myself probing him for details of their meetings and asking him what her recommendations were for him. I hated this sleuth-like behaviour but I'd learned a long time ago with Jai that, when questioned, he only ever gave *half* the facts.

I discovered after the event that Jill had recommended him for a six week 'Domestic Violence Perpetrators' Programme' which had begun in September. Jai had manoeuvred himself out of it, having given the excuse that he had urgent family business in India ... family business he told her that would involve him for several weeks. It was far from the truth and another example of the manipulations and his ongoing, steadfast refusal to look inwards.

When Jill scheduled him to attend on the next available date which was another three or four months away, I was screaming inside; couldn't *anyone* see that this man needed help and he needed it NOW! It was far from ethical but I made a decision to contact her and in a letter I sent on 1st November, I outlined my beliefs about Jai's condition.

I told her I knew him to be suffering from a 'spiritual emergency' that had gone untreated and that there were also severe chemical disruptions in his brain. Supporting the letter with extracts from Stanislav's book, I begged her to meet with me, believing her to be my last hope in trying to make the courts understand what had happened to Jai over the last eighteen months.

Even though Jill was open and sensitive to what I had to say, she knew I was in a stalemate situation. Despite the attempts I'd made to influence the courts in their decision, the CPS seemed hell-bent on a custodial sentence and completely unwilling to recognize Jai's 'frayed' mental state. Even his lawyer had prepared his entire defence strategy around an assassination of my character, ignoring the presence of any underlying psycho/spiritual disorder.

That he was suffering from an untreated 'spiritual emergency' looked highly plausible, Jill told me, but she doubted the courts would view it as mitigating circumstances. "You have to remember, Jacky," she said, "that he also perfectly fits the 'criteria' used in assessing the underlying driver behaviour of domestic violence perpetrators"... *Yes, he did and there was no getting away from that.*

All she could do, she said, was ask the courts for a post-trial psychological report on Jai, the results of which would be viewed and taken into account before sentencing was passed. It didn't seem enough, not by any means...

There was very little else I could do. It had never been my intention to punish Jai with prison; I always knew in his case that it would serve very little purpose. To involve the police and the judicial system was something I believed he gave me no choice over. We were travelling this road *together* now and it seemed there was no turning back.

Another spell in prison and the consequences that that held for me seemed almost inevitable.

The month of November 2001 turned into the month from hell, with one conflict-ridden situation after another... and I was strongly sensing the build-up of energy again. Whatever was driving Jai's behaviour was getting worse and I was beginning to realize that despite the promises he'd made, he wasn't going to change, at least not until *he* was ready. I knew I had to make some life-changing decisions ... and soon.

During that month his ex-wife accused him of assault and pressed charges. "She's learnt from you," he said to me cuttingly. He was sketchy of course about the exact details, only to tell me that some weeks earlier he'd been to her house demanding what he perceived she 'owed' him from the marriage. When she returned the visit and tried to reason with him, he'd used threatening behaviour and roughly manhandled her off his premises. The police had subsequently become involved. My heart went out to her; I knew *exactly* how that felt.

The ever-widening gulf between him and his brother was rapidly turning into the Grand Canyon. Jai was helping himself to huge sums of money from the shop, justifying it as *his* and merely the livelihood that had been stolen from him. What he was doing with it, I had no idea. Although a roll of cash would occasionally land on the mat by the letterbox to cover our living expenses, still all of our debts remained unpaid.

Eventually the rows between Jai and his brother gave way to one physically violent episode and sealed in the hostility between them for good.

As for Temujin's first birthday celebrations on 23rd November of that year, I'd planned very little and had just wanted to keep it quiet and low-key. Jai had had other ideas, telling me that he'd planned to host a party in his son's honour at the Sai Baba temple in Perry Barr and that over a *thousand* people would be attending. I silently dismissed it as wishful thinking on Jai's part but my reluctance to participate caused another huge row between us.

Despite all the emphasis he'd placed on his son sharing the same birthday as Sai Baba, the living God on the planet, he failed to show his face on the day or even acknowledge Tem's first birthday with a telephone call. Even though it hurt me, I knew I was simply being punished again for failing to take his outrageous claims seriously.

It was also around this time that Jai told me he'd set up a private consultancy business, offering small companies advice on how to turn their struggling businesses into an overnight success. The sheer irony was staggering considering the lack of success he'd had in getting his own ventures off the ground. What was even more unbelievable was the hourly rate he'd decided he was worth … *five thousand pounds an hour!*

His bullying tactics to get me to produce flyers and business cards to market his new talent failed. Of course, I wanted nothing to do with it. But, as I've said often before, "No" was not a word Jai responded to well and every time I refused to indulge him in his fanciful ideas, the consequences would always come back on me …in the veiled threats, the verbal abuse and the mind games.

In much the same way that a spoilt child reacts to another's refusal to play by kicking sand in their face, so Jai would react spitefully to my refusal to play the game. I remember him that month entering the house and taking back all the presents he'd ever bought Jess, including the karaoke machine that she loved. When I reacted with rage, calling him a callous bastard, he kicked down the bedroom door, *literally*, in his temper.

"That's the difference between you and me," he said to me often. "Whether I'm with George Bush, President Clinton or Cindy Crawford, I'm dropping everything to be with you … that's the measure of my love for you." It might well have been a fantasy world that he was creating but there was nothing remotely comical about Jai's claims … he believed wholeheartedly in *everything* he did and said … and therein lay the *danger*.

As if his inflated ego was not enough cause for concern already, his claims were becoming more and more outrageous and bizarre. "Steven Spielberg wants to do a mini-series about me," he told me, "entitled *'The Man Who Never Sleeps'*."

He said he had plans to go into the pop promotions industry with Chris Evans so that he could spread the Krishna energy through music ... and he'd also set up a meeting with Richard Branson.

"Since my enlightenment," he said, "no one can understand the level I'm working on. I need people like Branson around me; he's on my level."

From this point on, his pursuit for a public platform from which to expound his claim as 'the Saviour of the Planet' led to an utter obsession with power and fame...

Frankly, I didn't know where to turn my attention to first. Financially things were getting worse by the day and, as the debt mounted, I felt like I was sinking in quicksand.

By late November there were no other options left open to me and I knew I could no longer support my spiritual venture. It was work that I adored but, despite the growing membership and the steady increase in private clients, I wasn't meeting the overheads, not by a long chalk. I had to be realistic... the workshops had to go.

As if I didn't have enough problems, that month a demand for an outstanding invoice landed on my desk and I remember the stomach-churning feeling when I saw how much it was for ... the sum of nearly three thousand pounds. Jai had placed an advertisement on my behalf in, of all places, ... a football magazine!

How do you respond to that? They were hardly going to swallow an excuse that my partner was undergoing some temporary aberration and had completely lost his senses and yet it was the truth! All I could do was write a polite letter back to the director of the company, a Mr Woods, stating that, as the sole proprietor of the workshops, I had never seen, approved of or authorized such an advertisement. Apart from anything else, I added, I was running a 'spiritual centre' and would certainly not have selected a football magazine as an appropriate medium to advertise my work, even if I had been rolling in spare cash!

But, over the next eighteen months, Argon Publishing and, in particular, Woods were to become a thorn in my side. Jai had used my promotional material and signed an order on my behalf. As far as Argon was concerned, they didn't care who was responsible; business was business and someone was going to pay.

It took over a year and a half and numerous court appearances until finally, in June 2003, the judge ordered the case against me to be dismissed. Argon were ordered to reimburse me £97.50 in costs but, to this day, I have never received the payment … somehow I didn't expect to.

It felt like a bitter-sweet victory considering the hundreds of wasted hours in time and energy preparing papers for my defence, travelling to and from the courts and arranging childcare for Temujin.

As we were leaving the court room after the final hearing, I remember Woods turning to the judge and telling him that under any other circumstances he wouldn't have a problem with Jai; in fact he actually quite liked him, adding that if he ever found himself in Birmingham, he'd probably go and have a drink with him … *I remember thinking 'Like attracts like energy'.*

From this point on my life became plagued with court appearances, police involvement, meetings with probation officers, court liaison officers, family protection officers, social services and whatever else the judicial system could throw at me. As if Jai didn't pose a big enough threat with his behaviour, now my very livelihood was being threatened as I attracted bailiff orders, solicitors' letters, county court judgements and threatening letters from the bank and credit card companies.

Until I'd met Jai I'd never owed money, been overdrawn at the bank or accumulated any unpaid debts. Not being able to pay my way in life was anathema to me. Now blacklisted as a bad debtor, my reputation and credibility was sinking as low and as fast as my anxiety levels were soaring. It seemed that the greater the financial responsibility Jai had shifted on to me, the less chance he had to set *himself* up for failure. In that way when things got out of control he could point the accusing finger at me and not at himself.

In short, Jai had entered my life like a tornado, created immeasurable chaos and left havoc in his wake ... and somehow I'd allowed it all to happen.

Emotionally over those next few weeks, I think I sank as low as a person can go. Whether I saw him physically or just spoke to him over the telephone, the verbal onslaughts between us became a daily occurrence. He would call sometimes at one or two in the morning from a club or casino and screech his undying love to me down the telephone ... whilst all evening he'd gambled away money we badly needed and bought rounds of drinks for endless hangers-on and anyone whose company he could buy ...even the exotic dancers that I wasn't supposed to mind about.

I despised all of it and I despised the person I'd become with Jai. He would push and push the buttons until, like a 'ticking bomb', I would explode ... 'mirroring' exactly his punishing behaviour with anger and aggression.

Feeling violated by the injustice of it all, I knew I had to get away from him, and yet the power he wielded over me was as blatant in its intent as if he'd held a pistol to my head ... *and potentially as deadly.*

Christmas came and went that year and served as a mild distraction to my daily dramas. I don't know how it happened but sometime during that period Jai and I called a temporary truce between us, even though a part of me by now had become wary of the constant manipulations. A truce of sorts made my life more manageable; I hated the roller coaster I'd been riding for the last two years. Watching someone you love act in a way that is so hurtful and damaging to the relationship is heartbreaking. So far, trying to understand why and seek out the answers had left me caught in a blind alley and with nowhere to go.

Yet, despite everything, there were still times when the 'old Jaya' would surface and I would see a glimpse of the generous, open-hearted and loving man I had once known. I sensed deep down that he was screaming out for love and yet the things he said and did just drove a wedge between us and tore us further and further apart.

There had been so much that was *good* in our relationship at the beginning and I knew I *had* been subconsciously attracted to Jai's *goodness*. I remember saying to Kate on more than one occasion that it was just as though some dark, mysterious invader had swept down and hijacked Jai, leaving in his place … *a crazed and twisted bully.*

Sometime in late January I made the decision that the workshops would close and the last date for talks was scheduled for March 7th 2002.

Writing to my Q.E.D members announcing the closure was one of the most painful letters I've ever written. I felt *passionate* about my work. There was an aspect of 'I told you so' in Jai's response to my decision; I suspect he was secretly glad that I hadn't made a financial success of it. It allowed him to feel smug that my failure in his eyes had been wholly due to my pushing him out of the venture virtually from the start. The simple truth was that the workshops never had a hope of succeeding with his disruptive energy in there; I know that now.

Between us, Jaya and I lost over seventeen thousand pounds in the venture and I remember the bank manager commenting as he reviewed the final accounts that it had been "a financial disaster." "It may have been a financial disaster to you," I replied, *"but to me it was a spiritual victory!"*

Ironically, as I write this book, Q.E.D lives on! Owing to a small group of wonderful people who believed in my vision, it was salvaged almost immediately and I ran it successfully without the financial constraints of a building to maintain. Some two years later I passed it on to a willing soul by the name of Steve Yates whose enthusiasm and genuine desire to serve spirit, helped by my sister Jayne, ensured its longevity and success.

I guess at the time I was grateful for the space this decision gave me to concentrate on where my life was going. I still had the accumulated debts hanging over me and I knew the next parting would be with the roof over my head. We owed seven months in rent and the owners of the property understandably wanted me out. It was probably the best thing that could have happened to me because over the next two months it forced me to look for alternative accommodation for myself and my two children and gave me the opportunity to 'physically separate' from Jai ... at last.

Still, for now, I couldn't ignore the fact that the court case was pending and during one ugly conversation in early February of that year he bellowed at me down the telephone, "Are you looking forward to the court case, baby? ... NOW THE TRUTH WILL OUT ... NOW THE WORLD WILL SEE HOW YOU TRAPPED ME!"

I remember placing the receiver down, closing my eyes and quietly sobbing. I was secretly dreading going to court because I *knew* it would be a farce and Jai would lie and distort the truth to his advantage. I really couldn't take much more.

The problem was, I seemed locked in an endless loop of my own making. 'Groundhog Day', Kate called it ... that ridiculous scenario of waking up every morning and repeating the same day with the same mistakes over and over again. Believing Jai was going to change was my Groundhog Day ...

and, boy, did I need a wake up call!

As I sat at my desk in the workshops that day, I screamed to the heavens, "For God's sake, take me out of all this, just take me out!"

I don't know what I was waiting for; something to happen, I suppose; *anything,* and less than five minutes later an e-mail came through marked 'from an unknown recipient'. I opened it and these simple words loomed up on the monitor:

'Don't give up when you still have something to give…'

I stared at it in disbelief as my tears gave way to a wave of mild hysteria. I will never forget the timing and the essence of that message; it was nothing short of miraculous. In the last two years, my faith had been tested beyond belief and yet that brief message contained within it all the hope I needed in that moment and confirmed everything I always knew … that God would never give up on me and that somehow the Universe was guiding and supporting me … *It was always my underlying faith that drove me through those darkest days.*

There is always a greater plan unfolding … and sometime in late February of that year, after nearly two years of 'riding the waves', the information and the answers I'd been searching for finally found their way to me.

This marks the turning point in my story and for the first time in a long while … *I felt there was a way out of the blind alley I'd been stuck in.*

I'd been clearing out some files in readiness for vacating the workshops when Kate called in to see me. She was always working tirelessly on my behalf, researching the Internet for information, case studies … on spiritual emergency, mental illness and psycho/spiritual disorders … anything that might shed some light on what was happening to Jai.

That day she handed me twenty sheets or so of printed information, all stapled together. "I think this is finally what you are looking for, Jacky," she said, with a look of immense relief on her face.

On the front sheet was the heading: 'Narcissistic Personality Disorder'. It read:

'NPD is an all-pervasive pattern of grandiosity (in fantasy or behaviour), the need for admiration or adulation and a lack of empathy. Usually beginning by early adulthood, sufferers can be confrontational, believe they are unique and fly into a rage if their inflated sense of self-worth is challenged.

Five or more of the following criteria must be met:

Feels a grandiose sense of self-importance.

Preoccupied with fantasies about unlimited successes.

Believes self to be special and unique.

Requires excessive admiration, attention and adulation.

Has a sense of entitlement and expects 'special' and priority treatment.

Is 'interpersonally exploitative' i.e. systematically uses others to achieve his or her own ends.

Lacks empathy.

Often envious of others.

Displays arrogant, haughty behaviour.'

As summarized from the American Psychiatric Association. (1994). Diagnostic and statistical manual of mental disorders, fourth edition (DSM – IV). Washington, DC: American Psychiatric Association.

For a while I sat in stunned silence reading the words over and over again. Slowly they began to sink in.

"But, Kate, this is *exactly* …"

"I know," she said.

I flicked through the document; the controlling behaviour, the disproportional reactions, the unpredictability, the appalling lack of empathy and the abuse … it was all there. The criteria and the supporting information fitted Jai perfectly and a wave of relief … and then anxiety washed over me. *This was really serious.*

Narcissistic character disorder is one of the most complex and overlooked mental health disorders of our time. From that moment on, the more I read and researched, the more I came to understand. It wasn't an awareness that brought with it any comfort; in fact quite the opposite. The only positive aspect was that at long last I knew what I was dealing with. *I guess it was like being suddenly handed the manual after spending hours and hours staring blankly into the engine of a car.*

Rage and envy are the key emotions underlying the narcissistic character and I had come to know both of them well in my experience with Jai. Understanding this disorder made sense in a way of *everything* that had gone before. It also allowed me to stop making excuses for him and to finally accept the gravity of his condition.

I'm sure as my story unfolds, there have been many times, dear readers, when I imagine you have been screaming at the pages of this book, "Why on earth did she put up with this man for so long?" and "Why didn't she just walk away?" Believe me, these are questions I've asked myself a thousand times. To arrive at the answers is to fully understand the character of a narcissist and that can only be achieved by experiencing them firsthand.

The awareness that you are living with a narcissist creeps up on you like a stalking predator. Once captured, you are forced to spend each moment second-guessing their every move until your very existence feels under constant threat. Or else you can do nothing … *and wait for them to devour you…*

How could I have known when I first met Jai that I would spend the next five years walking a tightrope between normality and his narcissistic behaviour? I have tried to outline in the following chapter the nature of the disorder and the understanding that ultimately led to my own healing and my eventual release from the narcissist's grip …

PART TWO

'THE AWARENESS AND UNDERSTANDING'

CHAPTER EIGHT: 'NARCISSISM AND ABUSE

– THE INSEPARABLE LINK'

'What he sees he knows not; but that which he sees he burns for, and the same delusion mocks and allures his eyes. O fondly foolish boy, why vainly seek to clasp a fleeting image? What you seek is nowhere; but turn yourself away, and the object of your love will be no more. That which you behold is but the shadow of a reflected image and has no substance of its own. With you it comes, with you it stays, and it will go with you – if you can go'

Taken from: The Myth of Narcissus as translated by Louise Vinge and presented in Chapter II – 'The Mythology of Stage One', Narcissism and Character Transformation by Nathan Schwartz-Salant

'The need to dominate comes from fear'

Chuck Spezzano

Trying to fathom narcissistic personality disorder (NPD) was like staring into a kaleidoscope and trying to second-guess the complex patterns that appear from the myriad of geometric shapes. In NPD the delicate thought patterns of the mind are disturbed, thus creating disorder ... *and shaping a view of the outside world that no longer has any basis in reality...*

You can't *know* a narcissist until you live with one and it's almost impossible to diagnose the condition from a neatly drawn up list of criteria; rather you have to *experience* the person first-hand.

Looking back, I remember the frustration many times when I tried to explain what was happening to those around me using phrases like, "You don't understand ... but you needed to have been there ... it's impossible to convey what happened..."

Kate once described it as an 'illness by stealth', in that it creeps up on you unawares and you've no idea that you've entered the minefield ... *until you're standing right in the middle of it!*

Narcissism takes its name from the myth of narcissus and is 'love turned on the self'; in other words, extreme self-adoration leading to a grossly overdeveloped ego. At the height of the 'emergency', Jai saw himself above every person on the planet who held a position of superiority and power. The longer the disorder went untreated, the greater control the ego took and the more outrageous his claims became, culminating in his ultimate fantasy that even 'God worked for *him* now'!

It was an over-inflated sense of ego that Robin Sieger immediately picked up on and cautioned him against in their June 2000 meeting. When discussing how Jai was going to get his 'big news' out to the masses, Robin said to him, "I don't want you to be held up to ridicule, Jai. If the media get hold of this they will turn it into a joke. You've got to understand how it sounds to people: 'I would like to introduce you to the Birmingham shopkeeper who is God ... Yes, this is Jaya Daridra who has discovered in his spare time that he is the emperor of the universe ...' "

But his ego was so out of proportion that it would in itself act as a block to any words of warning, even if the question of his sanity came under scrutiny. "They'd better bring the psychiatrists to *me*," he told Robin. "I'm not going to *them*. I haven't got a problem. Because if I was Robert De Niro, they would take them to him, wouldn't they, and I'm bigger than Robert De Niro..."

His sense of self-importance became so extreme that he exaggerated to the point of blatant lies ... "Steven Spielberg wants to do a mini-series on me entitled, 'The Man Who Never Sleeps' " and, in conversations, he name-dropped to impress, telling people that he'd set up meetings with famous people, because 'they were on his level'.

Distorting the truth and making up false claims about people he'd either met or was interested in meeting became part of the grandiose fantasy world he lived in and one in which Jai wholeheartedly *believed*. Ironically, this world view of him, the wild fantasy world he'd created, was, of course, the biggest lie of all, a misconception based on a false sense of self and one which had no foundation in the real world.

In expecting to be treated like royalty everywhere he went, constantly *demanding* recognition and respect, Jai typified the narcissist's behaviour. He'd arrived at Sai Baba's ashram with all the expectations of the surrounding protocol that would normally be heaped upon a visiting dignitary. It was a constant sense of entitlement and demand for recognition that spilled over into his everyday life. I remember being out with him once at a club and, after demanding a drink that the bartender didn't know how to mix, he turned on him and bellowed venomously, *"Do you have any idea who you are dealing with … do you KNOW who I am?"*

It was always so embarrassingly over the top and aggressive. If Jai didn't get the respect he believed himself entitled to, then he 'opened up' on the person, 'dismantling' them with such a force that they would visibly shake. As I've said before, his rage was not something of which you ever wanted to be on the receiving end.

It was the same 'sense of entitlement' that he'd displayed to the guards at the Swaminarayan Mandir when he demanded to see their head devotee. *"You'd roll out the red carpet for President Clinton, wouldn't you … and I'm telling you I'm more powerful than President Clinton…"*

Respect is not something to be demanded, it has to be earned, but Jai demanded respect from *everyone* he came into contact with. It was a word in his vocabulary that he repeatedly used with me, over and over. *"Now you're starting to respect me"* … *"I need to teach you about respect."* But, in actuality, Jai was completely devoid of *self-respect*. The narcissistic behaviour served as an impeccable cover, an impenetrable wall and a defence he'd created to protect what really lurked beneath it … *his true self.*

Sadly, like every other narcissist gripped by this disorder, Jai's true self suffered from a chronic lack of esteem and a desperate craving for validation and acceptance. *"Grandiosity,"* says 'The Course in Miracles', *"is always a cover for despair."*

In one of his prison letters he wrote to me, '*The world has driven me to the point of suicide and self-disgrace because they don't want to believe me, because they think I'm just a Paki, or a peasant, or a thug, or an uneducated foreigner, or just a broken-down motorbike, or just a newsagent, or just a younger brother, or just a crazy guy, or a guy who's confused, or a guy who's lost the plot, or a guy who's gone mad...*'

His letters were loaded with statements like that. What Jai believed the *world* thought of him was actually what he thought about *himself.* Here was a man with a persecution complex so huge that he'd sought to defend against it with an over-inflated perception of himself. But it was a façade that required an enormous amount of energy to maintain and, if there was to be any hope of him emerging from this hell state, I knew at some point that he would be forced to address the pains of his earlier experiences.

It is not possible to demand love, approval and acceptance from others when you cannot first find it for yourself, and Jai did not love, approve or accept himself because the opposite had been his reality.

Anyone who has suffered oppression knows that addiction and oppression go hand in hand. Addiction is based on self-abuse and simply reinforces the idea that you are worthless and unimportant. Jai knew all about addictive patterns and believed that other people needed to see him rich and successful in order to take him seriously. *"When I have the Bentley … the house in Spain … the private plane, etc, then others will see me for the man I am."* It was the underlying driver behaviour behind his gambling...

It dawned on me that he measured his sense of self-worth on the clothes he wore, the car he drove, the places he was 'seen' at. Even I had become a possession, an object, his 'woman', a 'psychologist with ten degrees' who surely must be so desirous to all men ... so as to fuel his narcissistic view of himself. It was a misguided viewpoint and one which had its roots firmly cemented in a thorough lack of self-acceptance.

Ironically, when I first met Jai, he oozed confidence and charisma, a fact I have reiterated several times throughout this book. I began to learn that it was a clever mask and a way of being that he relied on thoroughly in order to feel himself attractive and desirous to the outside world. In those early stages of our relationship I suppose I was blissfully unaware of his appalling sense of 'self'. His oft-repeated phrase to me, whenever he felt the threat of abandonment was, "Jacky, you can't leave me, you are my credibility in this world."

When in October 1999, at the Westway's awards ceremony, Robin had given Jai the ultimate accolade, that he'd heard "more business wisdom from this man in ten minutes ...than in the past ten years" Jai had clung to that remark, mulling it over, *daring* to believe it.

Eight months later in the taped meeting with Robin, he commented how, on the day, everyone had laughed at him because of his dress, "because I'd chosen to wear traditional Indian dress and I could see them all laughing. Then you (*meaning Robin*) dropped those lines and all of a sudden I was famous. All the Pakis were saying 'I like your style' and all the English people were saying 'if Robin says that about him, then he *must* be the man' and it was only because of those few words that you gave."

To the narcissist, surrounding themselves with credible people is a basic underlying drive and serves to reinforce their narcissistic view of themselves. In a sense, Jai looked to others to make *him* feel credible and so derived his own sense of self-worth from being associated with successful people. On the tape he says about Robin's accolade, "In my darkest moments, when I'd feel low, I'd just think about what you said and think, well, if he had a bit of faith in me and he was a calibre character, then I must be on the right track."

I had certainly been guilty of fuelling Jai's ego in those early days. To me, he was the most exciting, charismatic, passionate and generous man I'd ever met and for all of that I'd fallen in love with him. Even so, I had sensed his lack of self-confidence, something that outwardly he tried so hard to mask. He'd given me telltale glimpses of his early childhood, taunted by classmates because he 'couldn't speak the language or even use a knife and fork'. On top of that, contracting rickets and tuberculosis as an infant had left him with the physical stature of an eight-year-old at thirteen, all of which had begun to lead to grave feelings of inadequacy, feelings I suspected he'd deeply internalized.

He hadn't chosen an easy path, but one that seemed strewn with harsh lessons along the way. Was it any wonder that at the point in his life when he met me, he soaked up with relish all the praise, admiration and confidence building I heaped upon him?

Sadly however, attention, flattery, praise and admiration are fundamental needs to the narcissist and he will go to any lengths to obtain them and keep them alive. In this respect he is no different in his craving for adoration and approval … than an addict who craves a fix. The ultimate fix in Jai's case was his personal, awe-inspiring and exclusive relationship with God. Claiming that all of mankind had to go *through* him in order to find God conveniently diminished the power of others and fed his own narcissistic thirst for power.

Oddly, the more I came to understand the narcissistic personality, the more sympathy I felt for Jai. I wasn't so emotionally sick myself that I'd actively gone out seeking someone with this disorder but I truly believe I connected to the vulnerable, injured child in Jai and the child who was inherently *good*. Over the months that followed and as my understanding of the disorder grew, I yearned to journey into Jaya's world. What was lurking in his psyche that was so injurious as to have caused such extreme defence mechanisms? *I longed to penetrate the wall of steel that divided us.*

At some point in our research on the narcissistic character, Kate purchased a book for me to read by Nathan Schwartz-Salant entitled 'Narcissism and Character Transformation'. It is probably the most illuminating analysis on the subject she could have found. In it the author explores the myth, the archetypal evidence to support the disorder and also offers a thorough, albeit complex, but highly readable examination of its clinical interpretations. I am indebted to his findings in the presentation of this chapter.

In order to understand the narcissistic character, it is essential to explore the myth. First recorded by Ovid in 8 AD, the following is a condensed version based on the translation of the myth by Louise Vinge and presented in chapter two of Schwartz-Salant's work, 'Narcissism and Character Transformation'.

'Narcissus was born of Liriope, who was ravished by Cephisus, the river-god. The blind seer, Tiresias, was asked if the child would live to a well ripened age and the seer replied, "If he ne'er knows himself." Youths and maidens sought his love, but his pride made him cold and unyielding and no one touched his heart. Then a nymph of strange speech beheld him, resounding Echo. She was voice with no form, Juno having reduced her to voice alone, only able to repeat the last phrases of a speech and returning the words she hears.

When she saw Narcissus she was inflamed with love, but she had to hold back from him until he made a sound to which she could give back her own words. Agreeably she answers to his words "Here let us meet" with "Let us meet" and emerges from the woods to throw her arms around him and embrace him. But Narcissus flees at her approach, repelling her with the words, "Hands off! Embrace me not! May I die before I give you power o'er me"… "I give you power o'er me," she says and nothing more.

Echo hides herself away in disgrace and retreats into a lonely existence. Though rejected, her love remains and grows on grief. She wastes away becoming gaunt and wrinkled until all moisture fades from her body into the air. Only her voice and bones remain, then only her voice as her bones were turned to stone.

A scorned youth, seeing what Narcissus had done to Echo, prayed to the heavens, "So may he himself love, and not gain the thing he loves." The goddess Nemesis hears the prayer.

Narcissus rests by the side of a clear spring and while drinking from the water to quench his thirst is smitten by the sight of his own beautiful form and instantly falls in love with himself. He pines away in love for a reflection that eludes him. Echo, despite her anger and her inability to forget, takes pity on his wasted form, so in love was she with Narcissus. Each time Narcissus proclaims "Alas", she gives his words back to him. And when he says "Farewell" … "Farewell," says Echo too and seals his fate.

But when his body is sought in preparation for his funeral, it is nowhere to be found, but in its place a flower of white petals with yellow centre…'

The myth speaks volumes about the narcissistic character, beginning with the insight that Narcissus is the product of a 'forced union', following the 'ravishment', (rape) of his mother Liriope by the river-god Cephisus. Schwartz-Salant points out that the overwhelming patriarchal force, 'characterized as Cephisus or the elk, is an essential attribute of the narcissistic condition'. This linked directly with Jai's upbringing and the dominant male presence of his own father.

Jai gave me glimpses into his parents' relationship, in that it was 'extremely volatile' and that his own father was not a man anyone dared to cross or argue with. Narcissism is almost always about control and Jai recounted to me a couple of violent arguments between his parents which contained particularly sadistic overtones.

The narcissist has a primary need to control. Control centres on self-preservation and usually manifests when an individual has experienced extreme distress in their life or where they may have been rendered powerless as a child. To be on the receiving end of these controlling energies is to experience the 'Cephisus-like force' first-hand. It is explosive and exploitative and almost always threatening. In the five years I spent with Jai I came to know it well. It was an energy so dominating and forceful that I physically shrank from it many times.

They are the controlling energies, Schwartz-Salant writes, 'which tend to flood the ego, but which could become a sense of felt power, real and valid effectiveness. In their negative form they are sadistic and ruthlessly controlling, senselessly destructive of relatedness, while they are fueled by an envious underside which insists that no positive mirroring relationship will ever exist…'

According to Schwartz-Salant, these controlling energies do have a purpose, in that they are a demand to "Shut up and listen!" and to "be with me!" They were the energies which punctuated the taped conversation in which Jai ferociously conveyed his 'vision' to me. "ARE YOU WITH ME, BABY?" he screeched several times down the telephone with a ferocity that made me want to retreat rather than join forces with him. In essence, the narcissist almost always resorts to bullying tactics by threatening or coercing his target and ultimately forcing them into submission.

In this respect, there is no distinction between the narcissist's behaviour and that which is present in situations of domestic violence and abuse. It was little wonder that the police failed to take my claims about his mental state seriously; to them, Jai was just a criminal… and fitted the profile of a 'wife-beater' perfectly.

It surely follows that a positive masculine role model is essential to healthy psychological growth and clearly this was absent in Jai's case. In essence, 'the masculine power drive crushes the feminine,' Schwartz-Salant writes, 'and the capacity for *being*, essential for the 'I am' awareness that is central to identity formation, is absent; in its place is compulsive *doing*. (Ask the narcissistic character who he is, and he will usually tell you what he does).'

Jai's daily existence was filled with 'compulsive doing'. One of the first things I noticed about him was his incapacity to still the mind and allow himself to just 'be'. He developed an obsession for writing his 'philosophies' down on paper, creating endless lists that he called 'The correct way to live', often duplicating the same material over and over. His twenty page letters written from prison were full of repetitious statements and it was in his first letter that he conveyed this feeling to me: '*No one knows how hard I'm finding this, especially with my ADD (Attention Deficit Disorder). I'm finding it one hundred times worse than a normal person as I can always think of one hundred things to do every hour, but I can't do any of them in here…*'

The experience of prison must have felt like sheer torture to Jai, being forced to sit in isolation whilst the hubbub of the outside world continued on the other side of his prison walls. Somehow he managed to 'busy himself' even in his cell with countless activities he wrote to me about: '*I wake, make my bed, pray, meditate, read my Gita, The Bible, read the papers, watch TV, eat, walk outside, chant, write, think, reflect, sleep and dream.*'

To Jai 'compulsive activity' was like a lifeline, even if it failed to produce any tangible results. In the five years I spent with him I lost count of the number of meetings, half abandoned projects and numerous ideas that failed to produce anything concrete in the outside world. Jai viewed himself as a high-profile businessman and a CEO of an empire ... *but it was an empire that didn't exist.* In truth, his days were mostly filled with meaningless activity. Sadly, Jai's whole sense of identity was based on what he *did*.

In the myth, we see the portrayal of Echo as representing the female counterpart to Narcissus. Ironically an 'echo', suggests Schwartz-Salant, is what she is reduced to when faced with the extreme controlling energies so characteristic of the narcissistic personality. So often I came up against this with Jai. Either I complied with his demand to "Shut up and listen!" and then was indeed reduced to a mere echo, or else I attempted a defence that was always weak and feeble in its response.

I could not, nor wanted to, compete with his sharpness of tongue, his bullet-like responses which, when they hit, burned and exploded into a million pain-filled splinters. I would either shout obscenities or else retreat into my shattered frame and cry ... reduced once more to an echo and with 'little voice' of my own.

There is also an aspect of 'unrequited love' in the depiction of Echo, points out Schwartz-Salant, and that whatever interest she pays to Narcissus, it is never enough. Similarly with Jai, whatever attention, praise or encouragement I heaped upon him in my genuine love for him, I could never fill the gaping chasm of need that existed inside him.

Schwartz-Salant comments, 'Like Narcissus, narcissistic characters are terrified of being controlled for they have so little sense of personal power. Hence the sadism and extreme cruelty that dominates their behaviour when in any way pressed, just as "Hands off! Embrace me not! May I die before I give you power o'er me!" is Narcissus's reply to Echo's advances.'

This was the sad, paradoxical nature of my relationship with Jai. On the one hand, I was terrified of his dominating behaviour and the power he wielded over *me* and yet, on the other, he was equally as terrified of the power my love held for *him*. In one of his first letters from prison he wrote this to me:

'You have got me in so deep it is scary ... because you could destroy me. I now understand why men like Samson and all others like him got destroyed by women, as I have felt first-hand how a woman can suck you in so deep that you can't get back out, even if you tried to ... and death would be easier. Your love is like quicksand and the minute I stepped into it I have been sinking deeper and deeper and enjoying every minute of being engulfed by you. But now I've reached a stage where I'm all the way to the top of my head, all covered and totally in your care and your hands, trusting you to either let me sink ... or destroy me.'

The narcissistic condition is full of paradoxes. In one sense Jai was desperate for closeness and intimacy and yet the things he said and did to achieve this just drove me further away from him. Schwartz-Salant writes, 'The experience of being with a person with a narcissistic character disorder is one of being kept away, warded off.' This left me in a constant state of flux and turmoil. I couldn't figure out why someone, whose declarations of love seemed so meaningful and so full of intensity, would then invest so much energy in shunning a similar response from their partner. *"Do you think I need you in my life?"* was his oft-repeated phrase and it would cut through me like a knife.

"God has told me I must walk alone," he said at the height of his visions. *"Like the Buddha, I have to leave behind my family, as I too am treading a lonely path."* It was as if he gained some sense of honour and pride in acting as though he needed no one.

It took me a while to fathom that the very opposite was true. This whole front of 'not needing' was all part of the condition, as if to express an emotional need for another human being would totally shatter his self-image. *"I can't be the man I say I am if I need another."*

Commenting on this, Schwartz-Salant writes, 'The narcissistic character rejects feelings of need for another human being, for experiencing such needs can unleash rage and envy that could flood the weak ego structure. Narcissistic characters often take pride in having no needs, while doing a great deal for others'. Oddly enough, Jai was always the first to say, "Is there anything you need?" to anyone and *everyone* he met.

As I've mentioned earlier, deep-seated envy and rage dominate the narcissist's 'inner world'. They are envious of everyone around them who appear to have the things they don't and even envy people their enjoyment with life. Jai envied others their success in the material world, their popularity and even their academic status. They were all the things he needed from them and struggled to achieve for himself. He would seek to avoid evoking this envy at all costs by denigrating or devaluing the object of his envy.

Schwartz-Salant writes, 'Envy can dominate the life of the narcissistic character. A man may envy his wife's activities, femininity and way of being. Whatever she has, he wants.'

This underlying envy brought an unhealthy competitiveness into our relationship. Jai wrote me in one of his letters from prison, '*Even though you're the most amazing woman on the planet and no one recognizes this like I do, you are still only a woman and will not have my energy, my pure physical masculine strength, my mental strength, my emotional strength, my spiritual strength or my financial strength...*'

I realized that Jai had been jealous of many things in my life: my friendships, my academic qualifications ... and *especially* the love of my family. This aspect of the condition also made sense of why I evoked the narcissistic rage every time I did something *well*. As Ram had succinctly pointed out, each time I had displayed my 'effectiveness', it had the same effect on Jai as shining a huge spotlight on what he perceived to be his shortcomings.

In a way, Jai envied my 'feminine power', seeing it as a source of real strength and, in some respects, he coveted it. Sadly, it dawned on me that this consuming envy had been the underlying factor in his complete lack of empathy towards me in those early post-pregnancy days, in that Jai had even been envious of my ability as a woman to give birth. Even in his narcissism, woman as the bearer of life was something that he would never be capable of, or ever be able to lay claim to.

Schwartz-Salant says the felt conviction about envy is 'anything I need will be withheld from me, so I will spoil or otherwise destroy the withholding object'. It is one of the most overpowering and destructive emotions to deal with in the narcissistic character.

Where these overwhelmingly destructive emotions originate from is a *terrifying* fear of abandonment. Commenting on his clinical studies, Schwartz-Salant says, 'Over and over again I have met the following attitude: "If I contact all that strength and effectiveness, no one will be able to be with me, I'll be too powerful and everyone will send me away."'

I remembered Jai's words at the height of the crisis, "I'm terrified of my own power…" On the occasions when he told me, "I have to walk alone" I realized what he was really saying beneath those words was 'abandon all ties before *being* abandoned'. It finally sank in that Jai's biggest fear was not that of finding love … but of *losing* it.

He was paranoid that I would leave him and yet his callous and unpredictable behaviour created the very thing he feared the most. Following his arrest after the second assault, he wrote me this from prison:

'They put me in a box in the van, three foot by three foot and locked me in with handcuffs. I have never been in such an enclosed space in my life, it felt like a funeral casket. I kept getting a feeling of suffocation and running out of air and

drowning in the box. I had to keep chanting and reading to survive the journey to prison. They drove me past the bottom of our road and I kept looking out of the window, looking for you because I felt it was my funeral and I would never see you again...'

The depressing and often suicidal feelings Jai conveyed in his letters were impossible to ignore and yet Tony Neate had warned me about the manipulations and that the ego would do *anything* to get out of its present situation. He once wrote me, *'Being here, not knowing whether God is with me, or am I on my own, my ADD syndrome, spiritual emergency, never having been in isolation before, the fear of the unknown, the uncertainty, each day feels like ten years in this space. Please don't cage me, Jacky, don't leave me here ... as death would be better...'*

Even though the experience of prison, feeling alone and out of control, must have evoked unbelievable terror and panic in Jai, what often appeared to the observer to be depression was actually a camouflage for the narcissistic fury that raged beneath the surface. One day he wrote to me telling me his heart was breaking and he would give *anything* to see my face again ... and yet the next day he blocked my visit ...

Ironically, observes Schwartz-Salant, the problem with the narcissistic character 'like Narcissus, is not self-love but self-hate'. When I first met him, Jai confided that he was always surprised when others told him of the 'awe-inspiring and overpowering' effect he had on them. In his obsession with the mirror at the height of the 'emergency', he was in effect attempting to muster up all this strength and power through his own reflection and actually *feel* it. It gave some rationale to such bizarre comments as, "I've been called the Buddhist Marlon Brando," whilst staring intently at his own self-image.

Schwartz-Salant writes, 'Psychologically, the shadow or reflection carries the image of the self, not the ego. It is interesting and even psychotherapeutically useful to have persons suffering from narcissistic character disorders study their face in a mirror. Often they will see someone of great power and effectiveness, precisely the qualities they feel a lack of. For even though they may overwhelm others with their energy and personality qualities, they themselves feel ineffective.'

In the mirror reflection, if the person can 'separate from the Self and respect its will' rather than identify with their own inner drive for power, they would be able to feel their true effectiveness, and realize that it didn't belong to them, 'but stemmed from the archetypal energy of the Self'. As Schwartz-Salant points out, this is the most difficult part to transcend for everyone faced with this disorder.

'Being confronted with the power of the Self', not through an act of conscious will, but by an 'opening up of consciousness' can give way to feelings of being reborn. At the height of the experience, Jai often talked about his 'rebirth' and marked the year 2000 as the year he was born anew. He explained away and excused his bad behaviour around that time, declaring, "You have to remember that I'm going through the terrible twos." In this heightened state he was simultaneously flooded with feelings of perfect joy and bliss, "You can put me anywhere now and I'd be happy," coupled with underlying feelings of acute anxiety, fear and confusion ... such feelings that would be part of the normal emotional apparatus of a small child faced with such an experience.

Faced with the power of the self arouses such emotions, notes Schwartz-Salant, 'which always and everywhere have been associated with religious experience'. I have never forgotten something Jai said to me very early on in the experience, "Jacky, I have to focus on God, because everything else is a tightrope..."

It's impossible to examine the narcissistic condition without also exploring its archetypal roots. Archetypes are the common themes stored in the collective unconscious which emerge over and over again in symbolic form and in myth and magic. Residing deep within the individual psyche, they fill our dreams and the realms of our imagination with potent symbols and images of legendary heroes and heroines, gods and goddesses.

In the overweening pride and vanity displayed by the narcissistic character, we can see the untamed ego as represented in the archetype of 'The Trickster', the anti-hero, full of guile and … master of deception.

Much can be learned by connecting to our archetypes and most of us resonate with at least one archetype that links to our true nature. In the course of our lives we may even fluctuate between one varying form and another. I thought back to my own life and the time I mark as the beginning of my spiritual journey, my round the world trip in 1991.

Freed from the constraints of the material world I had become 'the intrepid explorer', 'the fearless traveller', open to the endless possibilities and adventures life held. What then followed for the next seven year phase of my life was a journey of quite different sorts: a time of withdrawal and reflection, devoted to exploring my own inner healing. In this respect, I had become 'the hermit', 'the spiritual aspirant', 'the seeker'.

In order to identify with our archetypes, at some point in our lives we need to stop and address our soul's purpose for being here. When we actively strive for spiritual maturity, we begin to question the deeper meaning of our lives. It is in this striving that we access and are then able to release the realm of hidden potential within us.

For some of us it takes a life crisis, such as the death of a loved one, financial collapse or a life-threatening illness for us to take stock and readdress exactly what it is we want from our lives. It is often when we are at a crossroads in our life that we activate the archetypes within us and, as such, these role models can be a source of great creative power, change and transformation.

Jai's visions had linked to the heroic mythical figure of Arjuna, the central character depicted in the Bhagavad-Gita, the sixth book of the Indian epic poem, The Mahabharata. Considered a sacred text, the Bhagavad-Gita has influenced the religious and philosophical beliefs of the population of India more than any other writings. The Mahabharata was composed between the fifth and second centuries BC and is believed to be the longest poem ever written, spanning one hundred and six thousand verses.

It is in the story of the great warrior, Arjuna, that we can begin to understand the archetypal seeds of Jaya's experience...

Arjuna is the warrior hero, one of the five virtuous Pandava brothers whose karma has led him into battle against his own blood relatives, the evil Kauravas. Lord Krishna, of whom Arjuna is a friend and disciple, offers to serve as his charioteer. Just as the two families are about to wage war on each other, Arjuna is suddenly filled with dread at what he is about to do. How can he slay on the battlefield the very members of his family with whom he grew up? In that moment he drops his bow.

In identifying with Arjuna, Jai had also waged war on his own family. In the original story the battle is for the kingdom divided up by the blind king, Dhritarashtra. In Jai's bitter dispute with Nara, it was the battle for ownership of Dove St, the flagship unit. Against his uncle, a debt, a legacy owed to his parents which Jai felt duty-bound to reclaim. Horrifyingly, the inability to resolve this issue led at one point to Jai threatening his uncle with the words, "Repay the debt owed to my mother and father or I will destroy the thing that means the most to you." By that he meant his uncle's son.

Issues of ownership, the need to reclaim his 'kingdom', were, like Arjuna, enough to send Jai into battle against his own family. A battle that in reality would cost him the very love and respect that he craved …

The story continues with Krishna's spiritual instruction to Arjuna regarding the path of union with his higher self. He teaches him that it is through knowledge, devotion and selfless action that we become at one with our higher nature. Arjuna knows that Krishna is a God and the eighth incarnation of Vishnu, the supreme God. Yet Krishna in his compassion causes Arjuna to forget his divine nature because no common man can stand to be in God's presence for long and so Arjuna addresses him in many forms, sometimes as his equal, at others his superior and even as his subordinate.

At a significant point in the story, Arjuna asks Lord Krishna to reveal himself, so that he may look upon the face of God and know Him. God reveals His magnificent creation in all its resplendent glory to Arjuna and, in that moment, he is awestruck, gripped by the fear of his own mortal weaknesses and insignificance. Yet, at the same time, he understands that there is nothing to fear from his own mortality; life is eternal in God's creation and death is merely a passage through which all creatures ultimately return to the Source.

With this knowledge, Arjuna bows to his Lord in abject humility. Transforming himself back into his human self, Krishna fills Arjuna with renewed hope and courage to go forward on the battlefield, but this time instilled with new knowledge … from which all wisdom and understanding flows.

I reproduce this extract from chapter two to illustrate the striking similarity of Jai's experience when visiting Sai Baba's ashram a couple of years before I met him.

'… *As Sai Baba moved between the crowds giving darshan (blessings), Jai fixed his glance. 'Are you really God?' he asked of him earnestly in his mind. Baba's look ripped through him like a razor-sharp blade. 'Yes, I am' came back the silent response. And in that moment of searching, touched by divinity, Jai was paralyzed with fear ... the absolute fear of his own unworthiness.'*

During the height of his experience Jai was flooded with this archetypal energy which had the potential for deep and transformational healing. Without the underlying character disorder, the archetypal factor in Jai's case, in that he experienced himself as Arjuna, Krishna's right-hand man, might well have produced a positive outcome.

Moreover, had its emergence been handled by a skilled therapist, it may have provided the key for enormous potential growth for the future.

However, as Schwartz-Salant points out, narcissistic character structures 'can contain archetypal, healing powers and behave like the 'unborn God' or sadly, (*as it was with Jai*), be a consistent, demonic urge toward power through ego inflation.'

In identifying with the archetypal warrior, Arjuna, through whom God instructs all humanity, Jai held the potential to become a powerful and inspiring leader and one capable of some wonderful work in the outside world.

The story of Arjuna is loaded with deep philosophical truths. When I met Jai, one of the things that struck me most about him was his knowledge of the Vedic scriptures, knowledge that is rooted in the classic teachings of yoga. In Jai's case this wasn't head knowledge that he'd gained from books, but rather an inherent wisdom that when he shared came from the heart. My first thought was that he had the potential to become a great spiritual teacher. It was a belief that was shared and endorsed by Kenny Pask, the soul reader he visited at the beginning of our relationship.

What I believe happened to Jai was that the spiritual emergency gave birth to the dormant powerful archetype of Arjuna through an opening up of consciousness and the drama of five thousand years ago began to play out in Jai's life. In attempting to integrate his transcendental nature, through the myth, the narcissistic urge in Jai gave way to expressing a 'superhuman power' that had no basis in reality. His oft-repeated challenge was, "Take a knife to me, plunge it deep into my body. I am Arjuna, I cannot die, I am immortal. He has given me unlimited life." Sadly it was the narcissism, the ego driven urge that distorted Jai's reality and blocked any awareness to the healing potential or the wisdom that might have been gained from this archetypal link.

It is interesting to note that the entire drama, the tests given to Arjuna and the subsequent spiritual teachings, are woven around the scene of a battlefield. The battlefield can be seen as a powerful representation of the internal conflict between good and evil within each human being. This gives added understanding to what Tony Neate, the Principal from the College of Healing, said to me when Jai was in prison, "Both the light and the shadow are pulling at him."

There was no greater battle than the one that Jai was experiencing ... *his own personal battle for supremacy between his ego and his higher self.*

Of all the archetypal themes the hero is the strongest, having a universal appeal that has penetrated probably every culture and country throughout the ages. Joseph Campbell in his brilliant work 'The Hero with a Thousand Faces' identified that the hero's journey can be broken into three stages: separation, initiation and 'the homecoming'. The separation is usually attributed to some powerful external force; in Jai's case, the vision from God which revealed his mission 'to do God's dirtiest work' and cleanse the planet of negativity. "I am walking the path of righteousness," he said and it was a path he would have to "walk alone." It drove him to seek alternative living accommodation that separated him from his family.

The period of initiation encompasses the extraordinary ordeals and adventures encountered along the way in order for the individual to undergo his transformation and emerge as the hero. On a purely physical level between the years 2000 and 2005 Jai lost his businesses, ostracized himself from his family, made himself homeless and destitute, caused myself, Jessica and Temujin to forcibly separate from him, was charged for various crimes which led to a number of prison sentences … and, along the way, gathered innumerable enemies.

On a mental level, his mystifying descent into the depths of the unconscious led him to the gates of his own personal heaven and hell. On the one hand he was 'blinded by light' and greeted by angels whilst on the other he was left grappling with demons and encountering the forces of darkness. I find myself wondering if he will ever be able to sustain a fully functioning role in everyday society. Sometimes he displays the emotional apparatus of a six-year-old and I can see him hiding in the shadows of his emotionally disturbed world, just like a child gripped in some terrifying nightmare that seems to know no ending…

For Jai, the incredibly harsh tests he attracted to himself as part of his initiation might well, under different circumstances, have paved the way for the birth of a new personality. But the transformation can only be achieved if the individual sees the initiation through to a successful conclusion. Only then can the hero emerge.

Unfortunately, everything I read pointed to the narcissistic character being a 'stuck pattern' and difficult to treat. Owing to the 'special defensiveness' of the disorder, in that it is a defence against harm to an already weakened sense of identity, Schwartz-Salant says, 'the longer a narcissistic character disorder goes on, the more difficult it is to transform.' As I have said before in the pages of this book, it would take, on Jai's part, an acceptance of the problem and a willingness to undertake the work even if a therapist skilled enough could be found.

The 'homecoming' or hero's return, the third and last stage in the hero's journey, sees the individual reintegrated into society into a new and all-encompassing role, a leading light amongst his peers. Jai's homecoming was to be of significant importance. He was the awe-inspiring hero whom God had blessed with His unlimited power, the saviour of all mankind. It was a 'homecoming' fuelled by his own narcissistic view of himself and one which, once again, had no basis in reality.

Unable therefore to complete the journey and return home, Jai is left with the terrifying threat of being stuck, forever feeling useless and achieving little in the remainder of his lifetime. 'Thus the duplex nature of narcissism begins to appear' writes Schwartz-Salant, 'represented as a process that can lead to a new creation – psychologically an experience of the self – or to a dead end, a waste of talent and a morbid need for mirroring.'

On 9th July 2001, long before I explored the subject of narcissism and long before I had the full awareness of Jai's condition, I dreamed this dream:

Two horses were about to start a race. Both were sandy brown in colour but only one of them was fitted with a muzzle. A tall man whose face was concealed in a brown hooded cape which reached to the floor stood next to me. The lower half of his body was shrouded in mist. I turned to him and said, "Who do you think will win?" Pointing to the horse with the muzzle, he said, "He's afraid of winning. Not only will he not win, I'll go a step further and say … he won't even start the race…"

I didn't realize at the time what the dream was telling me but, in hindsight, I see that the muzzled horse represented Jai (he is actually a fire horse in Chinese astrology) and his inability to start the race was symbolic of the stunting aspect of the narcissistic condition.

Narcissism is an enormous and complex area of study and I have merely touched the tip of the iceberg in the information I have presented here. The more I read, the more I realized that the pattern of Jai's behaviour perfectly matched the disorder. It dawned on me that the man I had fallen in love with was not the man I thought he was … but an enigma, a host of contradictions … I was no mental health expert, not by any stretch of the imagination, but I also knew that he was a man … *in deep, deep trouble.*

In the beginning, I was for Jai his 'enamoured echo', resounding back to him the positive statements he yearned to hear, yet dared not believe. I fed his fragile ego with adoring phrases, "You are so much more than others see you" … "You are so incredibly talented, creative, a true visionary"…

And just as Narcissus, terrified of being controlled, shrank from Echo's advances, so too did Jai reject mine. Like Narcissus, he turned his back on love, consumed by the fear of being caught forever in love's grip and being forced to surrender his own power. As he turned away, so he was cursed, destined to desire his own reflection and to love only himself … and never to gain that which he loves.

And as his echo I was left with the flames of passion that burned in my heart … grieving not for a love I had lost…*but one I had never had.*

CHAPTER NINE: 'THE VOICE OF EVIL'

*'Evil is unspectacular and always human, and
shares our beds and eats at our own table'*
W.H.Auden (1907-1973)

*'Whoever enters the Way without a guide
will take a hundred years to travel
a two day journey'*
Mathnavi of Rumi

Narcissism has many layers. Understanding the condition made perfect sense of why, up until now, Jai had systematically shunned treatment of any kind.

Why on earth would a man who saw himself as perfect and above God seek to enter therapy? I realized the more I kept telling Jai that there was something wrong with him, the less I was helping and the more I seemed to be fuelling his anger and his guilt.

It is estimated that over one per cent of the population are affected by NPD. It is a staggering statistic when you consider that some sufferers are undoubtedly heading companies and holding positions of power, thereby wielding their influence over others ... a little like modern day tyrants.

Dr Scott Peck in his prolific work, 'People of the Lie', comments that even though the phenomenon of Narcissism is still relatively new to psychiatric study, 'the particular brand of narcissism that characterizes evil people seems to be one that particularly affects the will.'

Sometimes I shudder at the thought of what damage, in his

narcissism, Jai could have wielded in the outside world had his quest for power been made manifest...

Evil is certainly not a word I would apply to a person lightly and I'm somewhat wary of its use in everyday language, but Jai had become wonderfully adept at covering up his own lies and deception. As Dr Peck points out, 'The evil are masters of disguise; they are not apt to wittingly disclose their true colours – either to others or to themselves.' Frankly, Jai posed a dichotomy to me. On the one hand, I was convinced that he had at least some 'conscious' awareness of his actions, in that they caused pain to others and yet, on the other, I wondered how much actual control he had over the rage itself.

But just as a child becomes aware of the difference between right and wrong, I know there were many times when Jai could have *chosen* to act differently and I had to conclude that he simply didn't care enough. An evil person, says Dr Peck, is 'remarkably consistent in their ability to be destructive and has an inability to tolerate their own misdeeds.'

For the last two years he'd been hell-bent on avenging himself on the outside world, projecting his rage on all those he perceived were responsible for his suffering. It never occurred to him for a single second that his suffering was self-created and that the war he saw himself a part of in the outside world was merely a reflection of the inner war that raged inside him.

Without his acknowledgment that there was anything wrong, he seemed doomed to be a prisoner, locked forever within the confines of a disorder that was certain to destroy him.

I began to realize that my emotional 'attachment' to Jai wasn't serving him. The longer I stayed in the relationship, albeit at a distance, the less chance there was of him acknowledging his own misgivings. Each time I accepted him back into our lives, I was effectively saying, 'There are no consequences to your actions' and, in a way, reinforcing his bad behaviour.

I think there was also a part of me that had begun to *accept* Jai's condition as though it was just something you get used to and I didn't want that … I couldn't imagine spending the rest of my life tiptoeing around his crazy behaviour. In a sense, I was just as guilty, although not consciously, of contributing to the macabre dance playing out between us. One of us had to alter course and I knew it wasn't going to be *him*.

I also knew the grim consequences of vacating the home we once shared and turning my back on him for good, in that it would only trigger his abandonment fears and cause him to act out his narcissistic behaviour. It was a catch-22 as always. Do you walk out on someone when you discover they have a mental illness? As I've said often before, I didn't fall in love with Jai because I had some perverse desire to be destroyed. I fell in love with him for all the good qualities I saw in him.

I didn't know if I had a hope in hell of penetrating his narcissistic wall of defence and getting him to accept that he needed help but I resolved to try one last time…

I wrote yet *another* letter to him. It contained the awarenesses from Stanislav's book and conveyed what I believed had happened to him over the last two years. When Kate and I had begun to fit the pieces of the puzzle together, it made total sense to the both of us … but then we weren't the ones gripped by the disorder.

I knew with Jai that the narcissism would always act as a 'block' to any awareness he might have and I wondered if my words would even scratch the surface of his comprehension.

I said I believed he'd been suffering from an underlying personality disorder, probably for most of his adult life and that it was a tightly woven 'defence mechanism' against a damaged childhood. The endless fasting, meditation and rhythmic drumming had caused an 'opening up of consciousness' levels leading to what Stanislav had described as a 'spiritual emergency'. When the 'emergency' hit, it dredged up all of the unresolved childhood pain … a veritable

Pandora's box from deep within the 'psyche' and, in seeking to defend against this unresolved pain, the ego span out of control … giving way to the Narcissism … literally, *love turned on the Self.*

I told him that I was still committed to helping him if he could finally acknowledge that he was indeed in need of help. It was full of supportive statements like: *'having a personality disorder, Jai, does not make you unlovable, neither does it negate your essential spiritual nature, your intention and your desire to do good in the world.'*

I said I believed it could be worked through by CBT (cognitive behavioural therapy) or deep psychotherapy and added that I'd nurtured the misguided belief for the last two years that it could be cured by love alone.

I ended the letter with these words: *'Die, Jaya, (metaphorically) to all that is not real within you … die to all that is not real within you.'*

Sometime in early March 2002, I drove unannounced to his 'offices' to give him the letter. I suppose in a way I was asking for the impossible; it was one thing asking him to change his behaviour, but quite another getting him to agree with my latest assessment of him. I had no idea how I would be greeted but he seemed ecstatic to see me. He'd been meditating in the front room of his two bedroom terraced house which had been turned into a shrine to the Indian Avatar who'd come to invade our lives.

He began telling me excitedly that the Ganesha statue in his room was 'dripping vibhuti' every day. Vibhuti is a 'sacred ash' believed to be accessed by Sai Baba from another dimension and known for its healing powers. The room he told me had become a 'miraculous healing room' and with the aid of an acquaintance of his, a healer by the name of Mohammed, he was 'spontaneously curing cancers, blood clots from the heart, brain tumours, drug addiction and even blindness'… simply with the action of prayer. *Oh God, I remember thinking, what am I doing here?*

He told me that I should make an effort to meet some of the people he'd healed. "Then you'll know it for yourself," he said, "and you'll be able to tell the world that I'm the greatest soul that ever lived…and all my visions were true."

I handed him the letter with tears in my eyes. As he scanned the first couple of pages, clearly inflamed by my lack of interest in his 'miracle room', the sarcasm began to roll from his lips. It was obvious he'd concluded that as I'd failed with my 'spiritual emergency' theory… I'd now resorted to labelling him 'a mental case'.

When he tossed the letter to one side referring to the disorder as 'narcostic disorder', (a deliberate mix of the two words, narcissism and agnosticism) and I corrected him, his smug response came back quick as a flash. "See!" he said, "I can't even say it! If I can't say it or spell it … then I can't *be* it!"

The last thing I wanted was a full-scale confrontation and I could see I wasn't achieving anything. As I got up to leave, predictably he began backtracking and pleading with me not to go. "I'll read it, Jacky," he said. "I *promise*."

I agreed to stay for a drink and, as I followed him through into the kitchen, the energy of the room at the back of the house couldn't have been starker in contrast to the healing room I'd just passed through. Cluttered with files and papers haphazardly thrown into cardboard boxes, two things immediately caught my attention. To the side of the television set, a pile of videos lay in a heap, some separated from their cases and scattered around the floor, but all clearly bearing the same title. "You watch 'Third Reich' movies … films about Hitler?" I asked him incredulously.

"Not just watch him, *study* him. He wasn't a bad guy, you know … you've got him all wrong," he replied almost casually. "He was a Master, just carrying out God's orders … he sits in the same halls as Jesus Christ." I thought back to the many times in the past when I'd telephoned him during the day and disturbed him watching TV … and my stomach did a nervous flip. I'd remembered feeling relieved at the time that he'd been watching what I presumed to be 'normal' daytime television when, for part of that time, he'd probably been engrossed in some movie depicting Hitler and the Nazi domination of the Jews. Something for the last two years had been driving Jai's aggressive and antisocial behaviour and it didn't bear thinking about what dark, archetypal forces in the 'opening up of consciousness levels' he'd unwittingly exposed himself to…

You'd have had to be blind not to see the other thing that drew my attention. I stopped dead in my tracks, staring in disbelief at the picture that adorned and *filled entirely* the wall of the chimney breast.

It was a life-size head and shoulders picture of *him*, a look of deep intensity in the eyes, the brow wrinkled, the faint trace of a smile …whilst poised, underneath a red umbrella … on a grey and rainy day in Cannon Hill Park.

"People just can't handle my perfection, Jacky," he said as I was leaving. "That's the problem"…

And so, like Narcissus, Jai continued to burn with the love of his own self.

Why on earth I thought that I had a hope in hell of succeeding, I've no idea. With the understanding I now have, I can see how it was my own ego back then, my own wishful thinking that believed Jai was capable of such change. Perhaps there was a part of me that *wanted* and believed that I could save him. Certainly I'd read enough about NPD at this stage to know that his very existence depended on him seeing himself as 'perfect'. I just wasn't *getting it!* Newsflash! Jai is *incapable* of such insight because of the *nature* of the disorder.

I had no choice but to let it go for the time being and I turned my attention to the court hearing. I think I became adept at learning to focus my energy on simply getting through one day at a time.

The case that took almost a year to come to court was finally scheduled for early April and the night before the hearing, I had this dream:

I was sitting at a large dinner party, surrounded by guests I didn't recognize, but I instinctively knew them to be warm and loving people. The table was beautifully decorated and covered with a delicious and appetizing array of Indian dishes. I began to eat with relish. After only a few mouthfuls, I was aware I was spitting out the food, literally choking on it and vomiting it out all over the table. But it wasn't the Indian delicacies I was choking on. I realized I was spewing out ... hair ... great, choking handfuls of it.

On the way to court, relaying the dream to Kate, I asked her what she thought it meant. "You *know* what that dream is saying to you, Jacky. Hair represents vanity, pride and conceit". The message of the dream was simple. *I was literally choking on his narcissism...*

I knew I had to get away from Jai's energy but I also knew any decisions I made surrounding my immediate future would be partly influenced by the outcome of the hearing. Even though I was dreading it, I knew the relief would be enormous when it was finally behind me.

Ironically, there was no courtroom drama. As soon as we arrived, Jai's legal representative had the ear of my solicitor and, as a result of plea bargaining on their behalf, Jai agreed to plead guilty to the second charge of common assault as long as I agreed to drop the charge of indecent assault. It was all over within an hour.

The police told me that his lawyer planned to wipe the floor with me if I took the stand. How would it look that I was testifying against a man who for the last year I was obviously hell-bent on 'rescuing', who I'd obviously on numerous occasions accepted back into our lives ... and even in moments of weakness ... back into my bed.

Indeed how *would* it look? I hadn't used the system properly and, even though I'd had my reasons, Jai had twisted everything neatly to his advantage. *I didn't have a leg to stand on.*

Even the 'key' witness, Garry, had failed to turn up. I was later to discover that Jai had told him to 'lose himself' somewhere. The only favourable aspect to come out of the whole proceedings was that, before sentencing was passed, Jai would be subjected to a 'post trial psychological report'... the one thing I'd been fighting for ... for the last two years.

I knew I had to tread very carefully now. Not knowing the length of prison sentence he was facing would be enough to re-evoke the terror and panic in Jai and inevitably spark the monumental rage so characteristic of the narcissistic condition. To him, losing control in this way was earth-shattering and this time there was the added uncertainty of whether I was prepared to stick around on his release.

About a week after the hearing I wrote to him asking him to acknowledge my need to physically separate from him. I told him I felt I had no alternative. All I was trying to do, I said in the letter, was to create 'the right attitudes, behaviour and responses for our children to learn by' and I stressed once again that I was acting on behalf of them, not *against* him.

Roughly around the same time, I moved out of the house we'd shared and I cannot begin to convey the sense of relief and peace that moving brought me. Jai had left me with no choice this time. I knew I had to leave for the sake of my children and for my own protection and sanity. Having the key to a property that he didn't have access to was the first positive step I'd made to taking back my own power. I now had a place of safety and somewhere to retreat to where I could shield myself from the backlash of his mood swings...

It was short-lived. Having my own space didn't stop Jai turning up on my doorstep unawares a week after we'd moved in.

I'd left the house to get some shopping out of the boot of my car, leaving the front door open and he literally jumped out of the car parked next to mine, taking me by surprise. I hadn't recognized the car… it was a Bentley, a car he, of course, claimed was *his* and which turned out to be a vehicle he'd 'borrowed' thinking that it would impress me.

I ran to the front door and, not acting rationally and only at the time out of protection for my children inside, I quickly closed it to stop him from entering, leaving *me* standing outside on the front lawn with *him.* He asked why I was blocking him from seeing us, particularly as he'd now agreed to the psychological assessment. I remember thinking, Y*ou didn't agree, Jai, the courts are forcing it on you…*

He started to tell me about his latest 'visions', demanding once again that I acknowledge his omnipotence and perfection. The all black clothing and the wild, outlandish claims were back. He was performing miraculous healings on a daily basis and God was using him as an instrument through whom He fed His prophecies for all mankind.

I *tried* to listen, but quite frankly I was sick of it and, apart from that, all the manipulations of the court hearing were still echoing in my mind. I gently but firmly told him to go, telling him that I thought things were getting out of control again. When he demanded to see Temujin and I refused, he began circling me. "Maybe you need a couple more slaps," he said, clenching his fists and with a mild mocking tone in his voice.

Jess came to the upstairs window. I looked up catching her attention and in that brief moment there was an unspoken communication that went on between us. We had a safety drill by the side of the telephone, the number to ring, what to say. On the insistence of the Child Protection Officer, our telephone number had been placed on instant response; it meant that a police officer from anywhere within the area should theoretically drop what they were doing and respond to the call. I took a big deep breath. "I'd go if I was you, Jai," I said to him, desperately trying to hide any trace of fear in my voice.

He wasn't stupid; he knew he was still awaiting sentencing and, realizing I wasn't going to give in, he backed away.

"What *would* make me spiral out of control," he said through the open window of the car as he reversed it ... "is not being allowed to see my son."

It was a nice parting shot ... and one that once again succeeded in its intention. Predictably, the day after that ugly scene, I opened my front door to find two dozen roses sitting on the step, gift-wrapped and with a card saying 'Sorry'...

I waited the rest of the day for the police to arrive but, from a call that was logged on Tuesday afternoon, it took until Friday for an officer to show up at my house.

So much for instant response...

It was April and knowing the cyclical nature of Jai's condition, I recognized that, this time, the mania was going into overdrive. Frankly, the psychiatric assessment couldn't come fast enough and, even though I knew a psychiatrist wasn't going to wave a magic wand and make it all better, I suppose what I was looking for was *confirmation* and the hope, for all of our sakes, that some sort of treatment was possible.

Through Jai's probation officer, I learned that the courts were prepared to pay three hundred and forty pounds towards the cost of a consultation. A psychiatrist had been recommended whose fees amounted to six hundred pounds; Jai was expected to make up the difference.

He telephoned me positively incensed, asking me if I knew of a psychiatrist less expensive! The irony was staggering. "A few months ago, Jai," I reminded him, "you valued *yourself* at five thousand pounds an hour. This is your mental health we're talking about. Do you really want to cheapen it by being treated by someone who values themselves at less than six hundred?"

But even comments like this failed to penetrate the narcissistic core; as far as Jai was concerned, he didn't even need a psychiatrist, never mind the indignity of having to pay for one. He listened to no one. It was to take four or more psychiatric referrals before a full diagnosis of his condition was arrived at and one that I wasn't privy to until months down the line.

About three weeks later, Jai was sentenced to four months in custody and put on a three-year probationary period. It was immediately halved and, as he'd already spent five weeks in custody the year before, it left a prison term of just over three weeks to serve, commencing on the 10th May and with a release date set for the 31st.

On the day that Jai began his sentence, I knew the feeling I *should* have had was one of immense release ... a release from the prison I'd effectively created for myself. What I actually felt was the opposite: complete devastation. Even though there was a part of me grateful for the protection Jai's imprisonment afforded me, I was still in agony. I'd learned to take on his thoughts and feelings so well in our relationship together that I was incapable of identifying with anything other than the anguish he must have been going through. And on top of that, I was coming to terms with the grief, the grief that accompanied the realization that, in my total adoration and love for him, I'd served as little more than a narcissistic fix...

It was a grief that on many occasions overwhelmed me. The day after Jai went to prison, my brother, Martin, held a family party at his house. I didn't feel like going but Jess persuaded me that it might take my mind off things. The scene that confronted me was one of ... smiling faces ... love songs playing ...couples ... humming ... children's laughter ... pure joy ... and I felt it, acutely.

I remember my legs giving way and I slid down the wall, collapsing in a heap of uncontrollable tears. No amount of consoling from my family could erase that feeling in that moment ... the grief ...it was *crushing*.

Even though on an intellectual level I had some comprehension of NPD and its complexities, I knew it was going to take months, maybe even years to come to grips with it emotionally.

It felt like hell and I knew I was vulnerable but, despite that, I resisted the temptation to write to Jai, even though he wrote to me on a regular basis. His first letter was full of declarations of love: '*I still sometimes get scared. I have to work so hard at being strong, as it's not easy to walk alone as you know. I must, since my greatest support (you) and my only support pulled away eighteen months ago. Please consider to come back for the sake of our love which has always been true and intense, the most intense love the world has ever seen.*'

I had to keep reminding myself of Tony's words and that "his ego will do *anything* to get out of its present situation." It was so hard to ignore his pain and yet, once the realization came for him that I wasn't going to write, visit him in prison or receive his telephone calls, his letters became more and more blameful until, finally, they were loaded with hostilities. In his eyes, I'd committed the ultimate act of betrayal. Not only had I abandoned him and left him to rot in prison with no hope of reconciliation ... but I'd also left him with the threat of an uncertain future lying ahead.

Sometime in the second week he wrote this to me: '*I will not go to the solicitor's or the courts or my family or friends or yours to see my son, only to you as you are the mother and have the greatest right over him than I do as the father ... but be careful, baby, because God has a greater right over him than you do and can take away your blessings for keeping him away from me unnecessarily and vindictively for no other reasons than to prove a point and to pain me ...*'

Statements like this were typical of the kind of veiled threat that had come to punctuate Jai's communication every time I'd tried to pull away from him. To tell me that God could 'take my blessings away' for keeping his son from him might seem to be a mild and unambiguous remark on his part. Yet, at the time, the sinister undertone concealed within it caused my stomach to convulse in fear.

The potential threat of impending doom and danger always evoked a physical reaction in me; it was meant to. Sly remarks like this are typically used in the narcissist's language, in order to evoke panic and as a means of controlling their target. I *never*, in all the time I knew him, got used to it; I simply *learned* to recognize it.

The letter went on: '*You don't have the qualifications to judge me or figure me out as I am an enigma that can't be judged or figured out. If I could they would destroy me as they did with Christ and Buddha and Prophet Mohammed and all the other great souls who came down to help the world...*'

I knew that, for any transformation to occur, the powerful drive of the ego needed to be acknowledged and surrendered and Jai seemed incapable of either. Over the weeks that followed, I realized I was as blameful in trying to make him accept there was something wrong with him as he was in trying to make me accept his visions and his claims.

So many times he hooked me back in with the endless promises to change that came to nothing. I think what hurts the most, when I reflect back, is that we weren't important enough to him as a family to even *try*. It was obvious that Jai didn't want the journey... just the result.

During the second week of his confinement, I took the significant steps to protecting myself that I should have taken a long time before and I filed for non-molestation and occupation orders. From past history and from his hostile letters, it seemed that I'd become the main target for Jai's violent rages and I wanted to shield myself and my children from that at all costs.

The orders meant that Jai was forbidden to enter or attempt to enter my property or even be within a hundred metres of it. It also allowed for the power of arrest if he, or any other person instructed by him, threatened us with violence or used violence against us.

I was advised by the solicitor handling my case to seek a residence order which secured indefinitely the living arrangements for Temujin and guarded against Jai ever attempting to remove him from my care. They were steps that I took painfully and reluctantly … and steps that I knew would have brutal implications for me.

The orders were served on him, whilst he was in prison, on 27th May 2002, exactly three years to the day that he'd moved in with me … and they had been the longest and most tortuous three years of my life.

I suppose I didn't expect any other response than fury. Any attempt to take back my power and effectively say "Enough" was like giving Jai the kiss of death! During the last few days of his prison term he wrote me this: *'To say to me that I need supervised visits to see my son and tell me I have to go through my solicitor is not an option, baby. If I try to see you it's harassment and you want to put injunctions against me to keep me away …well, you don't have to because your hostility, your coldness, your vengeance, your hate, your fury, your loveless look, your cold voice makes me want to stay away. If I let you push me to this, the negativity wins again.'*

Jai's response to the orders was simple; that 'there should be no orders' and that, for me, meant more court appearances. I was served with a notice to attend a CAFACSS meeting on 12th June, following his release from prison, the aim of which was to clarify the issue of 'supervised' visits with Temujin.

Nothing got resolved. I was insistent that a third party be present on the occasions Jai wanted to see his son and he was unable to come up with anyone remotely suitable. He was outraged at the fact that I was now asking him to work with the legal system. Why should *he* see his son under supervised conditions?

But the system was all I could work with for the time being; I knew I had to protect Temujin from all the arguments, hostilities and blame, both now and in the long term.

Later that same week, I was summoned to another court hearing in order to renew the non-molestation and occupation orders. Once again, Jai opposed them and, on this occasion, he decided to act as his own defence.

This was the platform he'd been craving for a long time. My intuition had been right; I'd always known that at some point he'd use an opportunity like this to create his own courtroom drama and turn it into a circus event ... ... with him as the main attraction.

His defence strategy took the form of a brutal and public attack on me. Ironic really, considering that two days earlier at the CAFACSS meeting, he'd created a melee in the waiting room by holding on to my feet and announcing to the waiting public, "Can't anyone see how much I love this woman?" Now, here he was humiliating me with a web of lies, distortions and slander in an attempt to publicly discredit my name.

To the outside observer, such conflicting behaviour would appear unbelievable and, despite knowing that the worshipping and then devaluing was all part of the narcissistic condition, it still hurt ... terribly. He told the judge that I'd used my 'powers' to hypnotize him and lure him away from his wife and that I should be struck off the hypnotherapy register, a disgrace to my profession.

He said he'd invested over sixty thousand pounds into our three-year relationship, a 'joke' figure he'd plucked out of the air and one that was laughable considering how much debt we were in. He added that this was money I now *owed* him. Private and intimate details about my past history and my previous relationships were aired and, as always, my family, and in particular my father, failed to escape his wounding insults.

The final straw came with a malicious attempt to paint me as an uncaring and unfit mother claiming that, as a small toddler, Tem had fallen down the stairs at least three times and I'd failed to show concern or have him checked out by a doctor. I don't know how I kept from leaping out of my seat at this stage and attacking him violently. My solicitor, sensing the tension in my body, gently gripped my forearm and whispered, "Let it go. The judge will see right through him."

His whole defence centred on a deliberate and malicious attempt to denigrate my character, claiming that I was intentionally keeping Tem away from him out of some warped revenge. I remember thinking afterwards, 'Could he have controlled all of that?' 'Does he have any idea how much pain he causes?'

I just recall a feeling of revulsion... That day he'd even used his own son as a weapon.

The judge *did* see through him thankfully and called him to order many times throughout the proceedings. It took almost two hours to grant the protection orders, based on Jai's previous violent history towards me, in my favour ... and once again no one questioned or even considered his psychological status.

I was saturated with all the 'stuff' I'd been carrying around during my three-year relationship with Jai; the 'visions' and 'the mission', the bizarre behaviour, the lies, the abuse, the court dealings, the debt, the rage, the pain ...I knew all I wanted at this point in my life was some peace and what I needed, what *all of us* needed, most of all was some time away.

About three weeks later, sometime during July of that year, a friend of mine called Christopher Stone asked me if I wished to join him and his family on a week long holiday to the Costa

Blanca. The flights were cheap and Chris had generously offered to cover the cost of my accommodation. I jumped at the chance for a break from all the stress and it was a holiday that was to alter the direction my life was taking. Chris and I, to this day, remain firm friends and I will always be grateful for the lifeline he offered me at exactly the time in my life that I needed it. The call to distant shores was beckoning and this brief time away marked the beginning of my love affair with Spain …

I felt more rested and perhaps a little stronger on my return although I knew it was going to take a lot more than a week's holiday to heal the trauma of my relationship with Jai. Despite that, for another three or four weeks at least, an element of peace prevailed. After a brief gap following the closure of the workshops, I'd begun to resume my hypnotherapy sessions and had attracted one or two clients on a regular basis. Without the financial overheads of a building to maintain, I took my work into the home environment and with the small income it provided, I slowly began to pay off our debts.

Then, one September afternoon of that year, as I sat typing at my computer, something drew my attention to the back of the house. There at the patio window overlooking our communal gardens …was Jai's face … pressed against the glass.

A rather dishevelled-looking woman was with him, wandering around the garden. She had an odd, almost haunted expression in her eyes. Every so often she paused and stooped to pick up a daisy from the lawn.

Tem got up from where he was playing and tottered to the window, curious and then excited to see what his daddy was up to. Jai was pulling faces at him through the glass and making him giggle. I knew I should stick to the court order and ring the police immediately but, as soon as he saw me reach for the house telephone, he motioned with a pleading look for me to place it back on the receiver. I did and seconds later it rang as he pressed his mobile to his ear.

"You're not meant to be here, Jai," I said to him firmly. "Who is the woman? I want you both to leave."

He told me her real name, but I will call her Kay for the purpose of this story. Kay had recently discharged herself from a local psychiatric unit, having made several thwarted suicide attempts. Somehow or another she had connected with Jai, possibly through his 'miracle healing room' and now, according to Jai, he was her 'saviour', her 'guru'. "You need to hear what I've done for her," he said, asking if they could both come in. I refused, unable to believe the surreal scene playing out on my back lawn or the bizarre conversation I was having through a plate glass window!

Predictably the tone became more insistent. "I've cured her of paranoia and manic depression. She's off pills she's been taking for years ... because of me! They tried to break her like they tried to break my dad...These psychiatrists know *nothing*." The irony was staggering ... *oh, for heaven's sake, Jai, what are you now, an expert in mental health?*

He began banging the glass. Ours was a quiet cul-de-sac and the small terraced houses were mainly occupied by elderly people, I knew he was just seconds away from causing a furore and upsetting the whole neighbourhood.

"If you don't leave now, Jai, I'm calling the police!" I flared and with those words put down the telephone.

I walked over to Tem, swept him up in my arms and carried him up the stairs to my bedroom... without glancing back. It was a good half-hour that I sat on my bed, my heart pumping furiously, until I heard his car start up and I secretly watched him exit our road.

That night and over many nights that followed, I grew to recognize the low rumbling noise of the engine as his car passed by my house, sometimes waking me at three or four in the morning ...and I would lie there with a twisted knot in the pit of my stomach knowing that, with every passing day, Jai's condition was worsening and my own fears were growing.

Jai continued to intrude on our lives on a frequent basis, always unannounced and always claiming that he had a reasonable excuse, like presents for the children, or bags of fruit, flowers or confectionery for me. I knew the desperation on his part to 'keep in touch', was all part of the narcissistic pattern to maintain his control over us … because, to Jai, the opposite was unthinkable.

I know I could have had him arrested numerous times but, on every occasion, I failed to exercise the power the courts had granted me. Something inside me would shudder at the repercussions and I'd rationalize to myself, 'How can I have him arrested for turning up bearing gifts?' But even those I realized were all part of the manipulations, to keep us sweet, to placate us and to provide him with an excuse to visit. There was also a part of me that didn't believe for a single second that, in Jai's case, a further spell in prison would serve any purpose. In fact if anything, if the past was anything to go by, it had made him worse.

Eventually, over time, I began to view this 'harassing' kind of behaviour as a nuisance, in that I was always on my guard and forever trying to guess his moods from his demeanour and his language. I'd never set out with the courts to block him from seeing Temujin, but it was always on the provision that he came peaceably. When he did, I would afford him the normal courtesies and take a short walk with him or let him play with his son outside on the front lawn.

Then there were times when I sensed his mood to be hostile and, on those occasions, I would go to extreme lengths to maintain the boundaries between us, often pretending to be out or not answering the door or telephone. There were even times when my behaviour verged on the paranoid … and it was a way of being I found utterly loathsome and isolating.

Around 11 p.m. on one October evening in 2002, Jai startled me at the kitchen window, tapping it to get my attention. Waving some money at me he motioned for me to answer the door. As it was so late, I opened it leaving the chain connected and thanking him for the money, asked him to pass it through the gap in the doorway.

"Don't be unreasonable," he said indignantly. "I've got over a thousand pounds here. Surely that's deserving of a cup of coffee."

I didn't want to let him in but I badly needed the money; I was in debt up to my neck, debt that he'd created. "Five minutes for a coffee, Jai," I said. "That's all."

He placed the money on the top of my refrigerator and, clutching a bottle of wine in his hand, began going through my kitchen drawers looking for an opener. I told him not to bother as I wouldn't be drinking any of it with him. He was persistent and, finding the opener, began to drink from the bottle, downing it in less than fifteen minutes.

When at that point I asked him to leave, he shifted into evasion tactics. "The psychiatrists can't find anything wrong with me," he said, with an almost defiant air. "It's all in your mind, Jacky. All I've ever needed is your love to heal me."

"I gave that, Jai," I answered softly, "and you abused it."

"You'll take my money though," he said cuttingly, sweeping the cash from on top of the fridge and scattering it all over the kitchen floor.

"I don't want your money, Jai," I said slowly, "just your promise to get help."

Dismissing the comment with his usual flippancy, he began to tell me about his production team and how filming had begun in preparation for a 'mini-series' ... a one-man show, featuring *him* in the starring role. They'd taken to calling him the 'Buddhist Marlon Brando' and were making him 'experience everything on the planet, no matter how ugly or vile' and then it was his role to discuss it in front of the camera. After all, he told me, it *was* his God-given mission and how else could he cleanse the planet of negativity if he didn't expose himself to the darkest of places or offer to witness the most depraved acts of human behaviour?

I felt sick. "You disgust me," I said, choking back a lump in my throat. "What's happened to you, Jai? Do you think this is the sort of man I want as a father to my son?"

For a few seconds, his eyes misted over with tears and rested upon a framed picture of Tem that sat on the window ledge. "He's the most beautiful thing that ever came from me ... I can never taint him," he said, almost wistfully. I found myself questioning as I'd done many times of late if the emotion was genuine and the tears real. In truth, I could no longer tell.

"No, Jai," I answered, "and I will never give you the chance to taint him."

"Give me a year," he said, stooping to pick up all the money from the kitchen floor. "In a year I'll have healed myself and I'm only coming back to you when I'm the man I say I am."

"Okay ... okay," I said. He sensed from my tone that I didn't believe him for a second but had just agreed with him so that he'd leave. The conversation was over and as he headed towards the door he paused to count out sixty pounds and placed it in my hand. "I'm going to the casino with the rest of this," he declared, "and by tomorrow I'll have made you a millionairess..."

I opened the door and let out a big sigh. "Look at your life," I said to him pleadingly. "Why can't you accept that you need help, Jai, if for no one else's sake but your son's!"

"Fuck him!" he said. "What's *he* ever done for me!"

The words made me gasp for breath. *God almighty, Jai, where does that come from?*

Whether it was the way the porch light caught his expression as it contorted and twisted with the vile ugliness of his words, I cannot say. All I know is that in that split second ... a look I can only describe as *satanic* darted across his face.

"I didn't mean that," he said, hanging his head shamefully. Then, echoing my thoughts out loud, added, "God, Jacky, *where* does that come from?"

I couldn't answer him, but I remember distinctly the feeling of *revulsion* I was left with that evening and it was a feeling that was becoming all too frequent and familiar in my interactions with Jai. I locked the door behind me and quietly sobbed.

That night I dreamed a dream:

I was in a military camp, dressed in full army uniform. There were seven of us, five men and two women. One by one we were led into a tent on the far side of the camp; two of the men went before me and didn't return. An officer said; "It's your turn." I sat cross-legged in the tent and, about twenty metres in front of me, a sniper aimed a long barrelled gun at me and I could feel the infrared ray of the weapon burning my third eye.

I was paralyzed with fear as he focused one by one on my energy centres. If he aimed a shot at the centre and it missed, it meant I lived. The sniper moved down each chakra and, each time I took a deep breath, I knew that my breathing was an indication that I'd survived.

Finally I was released and thrown into the back of an army truck. I had this dejected look about me as if my spirit had been broken and as the truck drove away, I didn't dare to look back...

The next morning I awoke feeling lousy. My whole body ached with tension and at the solar plexus I had the feeling that my intestines had been ripped out. I didn't need to dissect the dream; I knew it was a warning of danger. I'd had enough experience personally and in the energy work I carried out with clients to know that I was under 'psychic attack'.

It was around this time that I had to admit an unpalatable truth to myself and one that marks yet another turning point in my story. I was forced to come to terms with a secret fear that I'd been concealing for a very long time. It was also a fear that in actuality evoked more terror in me than the threat of impending violence or any diagnosis of Jai's mental health and one that tested my levels of courage to the max ... it was the fear that Jai was gripped by some dark and malevolent force ... *that he was in fact ... possessed.*

Believe me, dear reader, this is not a conclusion I arrived at lightly, far from it. Just as my labelling a person as evil evoked wariness within me, so did the thought that Jai was gripped by some dark and satanic presence. But, on some level, I'd *known* from the beginning and on seven occasions in total, twice on his return from India and five more during the period 2002 and 2004, I was given 'glimpses' of the possessing entities, (I say entities because there were more than one). When I reflect on these occasions, they all took place immediately after there had been a significant gap between the times I saw Jai, just as if my emotional attachment to him when we were together somehow dulled my psychic senses.

I am not alone in the assessment I make about Jai and the possession aspect of his condition; six other people in the course of my relationship with him drew the same conclusions of their own volition and without any persuasion on my part. One of these individuals who is particularly gifted clairvoyantly saw the possessing entities with her psychic vision and, as such, withdrew her commitment from the workshops, not wanting to be anywhere in the vicinity of Jai's energy.

Perhaps the most wholly convinced is Kate, my friend, researcher and a PhD student in parapsychology. The unquestionable belief for her came at the time when she and I sat down to listen to the taped recordings of Jai's 'heavenly visions', in order to transcribe them for this book. It was May 9th 2002, the day when the possession manifested 'audibly' in our presence and over and above Jai's words. She and I can offer no scientific explanation for what we heard, but I can barely bring myself to recall the reaction it evoked in *both* of us at the time.

It was not until nearly two years later in the spring of 2004 and during the attempted 'exorcism', that the full extent of the possession revealed itself to me.

For the possession to have entered and taken hold in the first instance, Jai must at some point have 'sold out' or made an unconscious pact with the forces of evil. He *did*. Just after he came back from his first trip to India, he told me rather offhandedly one day that he'd 'handed over his soul'. I remember the feeling those words evoked in me at the time ... utter revulsion. I'd also stored away Pam's dream in the back of my mind, which took place at the same time that he was in India and which I relate in chapter four. I knew at the time, that the foreboding message it carried was intended for me and it had ended with the words, '*I don't want his blood ... I want ...his soul.*'

I remember asking him, "How can you give away your soul, Jai. What does that mean?" His response had been almost gleeful. "Sai Baba has my soul now," he said.

In his book 'People of the Lie', Dr. Scott Peck says, 'There has to be a significant emotional problem for the possession to occur in the first place. Then the possession itself will both enhance that problem and create new ones. The proper question is: 'Is the patient just mentally ill or is he or she mentally ill and possessed?''

Jai had been the perfect target. Add to an underlying personality disorder his 'unsupervised' journey into the realms of the unconscious and he was a sitting duck for any evil entity that had wanted to play tricks with his mind. It was Rumi who said, 'Whosoever enters the way without a guide will take a hundred years to travel a two day journey.'

In actuality, Jai had been 'confused', even 'duped'. Just as the spiritual emergency had done much to disturb the delicate nuances of his brain, he was misled as to the real guise of his communicator. Back in the year 2000, at the height of the emergency, whilst lying in bed one night, Jai had whispered to me in the darkness, "Friend means foe, doesn't it?"

"No, Jai," I replied. "A friend is a friend, someone you can trust ... a foe is your enemy." I remember how he disagreed with me at the time until I was forced to show him the dictionary definition as proof.

Jai believed that it was God, Sai Baba, who was talking to him from the highest realms, when the plain and disturbing truth was ... he was in cohorts with the devil.

And just as it was my own *fear* of evil that attracted evil into my life as some gigantic test through which I learned great strength and courage, so the forces of evil had been attracted to Jai's intrinsic *goodness* and been threatened by his overwhelming desire to do good in the world...

At some point I have to bring my story thus far to some sort of conclusion and I wrote this book primarily to highlight the narcissistic aspect of Jai's condition. Although the possession aspect is clearly interwoven and much happened between the years 2002 and 2004 to support my claims, any examination of the part this played in his journey is worthy of far more investigation that I can give here. It is an *entire* subject in itself and one that I have saved for the sequel to this book, 'God is definitely in charge'.

One thing I was certain of at this point in my life and that was for any deep psychotherapy to succeed or for the demonic possession to be exorcised largely depended on Jai's *willingness* to participate in both. Sadly, I also knew that the narcissism would always act as a block to the healing awareness he so badly needed. For weeks now I'd wondered what the psychiatrists had made of him. All I got from Jai was that they'd found nothing wrong. A few days after he paid me that late night visit, I contacted his probation officer in the hope that she would acquaint me with what conclusions, if any, had been drawn about his mental state.

For obvious confidentiality reasons I wasn't allowed to know the full details of the consultation, only that a diagnosis had been reached. Jai had been labelled with a 'Character Disorder – Untreatable', with 'the predominant disorder being one of mood' and a vitamin B12 complex suggested.

In some respects the label didn't seem enough, in that it

failed to conceptualize all that I knew to be wrong and yet, in another, I sensed the hopelessness contained within it. The word 'untreatable' lingered on in my mind. I remembered something Bernie Siegel (author of 'Love, Medicine and Miracles') once wrote. He believes 'all illnesses are curable … but not all patients'.

I'd spent the best part of three years believing that Jai's condition was in some way treatable; that, with deep psychotherapy, perhaps the added intervention of medication and the overriding ingredient of *love* most of all, … there was a way forward. Finally, I had to accept that until he cried from the depths of his soul to heal, nothing was ever going to get better and that, in the process of destroying himself, he would, if I allowed him … destroy me too.

Right at the beginning of my relationship with Jai, someone said to me, "It's all just one big play, Jacky. Don't get into the drama and don't get into the mind games. Just like a play, the scenery may change, but the actors remain the same." It was good advice.

I knew that by just changing the scenery and going to Spain, it wasn't going to be enough. I had to do the 'inner work' and if Jai wasn't prepared to alter his reality, then I certainly had to alter mine. In order to learn true courage, one of the spiritual tests I'd contracted to undergo in this lifetime was to come face to face with the forces of *evil*. I knew at this juncture that by my emotional attachment to Jai, I was laying myself wide open and had become a target for whatever powerful, malevolent force was working through him. I also knew that the longer the possession went untreated, the greater the risk of Jai harming himself and us in the process.

My ability to disengage emotionally from him had been as feeble as my spiritual faith is unshakeable. Whatever else transpired, I knew that from now on I needed to consciously work towards fully regaining my mental and emotional strength.

It was time to face up to the fact that there was something so unhealed in me that I'd become addicted to the highs and lows, the pain and the ecstasy, of a relationship so warped and dangerous … and one from which I subconsciously believed there was no escape.

It was high time this nightmare ended … and somewhere in the distance …Spain was beckoning.

CHAPTER TEN: 'THE PATH OF HEALING'

'There are as many pangs in love as shells upon the shore'
OVID (43 BC – AD 17)

*'We are not permitted to choose the frame of our destiny.
But what we put into it is ours'*
Hammarskjold, Dag (1905 – 1961)

I once read somewhere that *'the things people say and do to each other in anger, they can forgive ... but never forget'*. Women in abusive relationships will tell you that it is rarely the physical abuse but the pain of the emotional and mental abuse that goes with it that causes the scars to remain unhealed ... *bruises fade, slander stays.*

In my relationship with Jai, I began to view my excellent memory and ability to retain information rather as a curse than a blessing. Words have a deep psychological impact on the human body; sometimes the things he said cut so deep they paralyzed me to the core. Statements in the aftermath of giving birth like, "You only got through that because of me ... you need to go away and find out how a *real* woman gives birth" were incredibly callous, especially when my emotions were so raw.

Looking back I realized I'd minimized all of the abuse and had spent the best part of three years denying my own needs and wants. In the end, the overwhelming imbalance in our relationship and Jai's unwillingness to accept he had a problem and seek help became the final nail in the coffin. Perhaps if he'd gone down the road of self-healing, I might still be with him now, supporting him, helping him through, loving him ... *and, I suspect from time to time, still riding out the waves...*

Over the eighteen-month period following Jai's prison term in 2002, the desperate attempts to keep me in his life beggar belief. In hindsight I realize I was trying to wear far too many hats. I had become his 'wife', his lover, his mother, his therapist, his friend, his judge and even at times his worst enemy. The strain of wearing all of those hats eventually took its toll and I knew that if I was ever going to 'heal' from him, I needed to cut myself off from him physically *and* emotionally.

Disconnecting from Jai however was something far easier *said* than done. The narcissist doesn't let go easily and, for the recipient, the one who is left in bewilderment still trying to fathom the narcissist's behaviour even years later …well frankly … finding closure is … almost impossible.

I'd nurtured the romantic dream and I'd fallen *violently* in love … and it was a love I believed would last forever. The shattering of that dream not only brought with it the sadness and loss that usually accompanies the ending of a relationship but also, as in my case, the heartbreaking awareness that the person I'd fallen in love with was not the person I thought he was.

I was much *changed* by my relationship with Jai. For a while, my normally gregarious nature was virtually eroded and I temporarily lost my sense of humour; so much so that people were to comment on it months down the line. Jai wore the persona of 'much maligned mystic' and in some twisted way used it as a perverse excuse to engage in his wayward and antisocial behaviour. The psychological effect on me was devastating, to the extent that for a while I retreated into a reclusive world with little or no social life of my own.

It was only when I took the time out to stand back and really look at our relationship that I acknowledged I could not have attracted Jai into my life or a relationship as emotionally wounding as this had there not been something inside me crying out to be healed. He challenged every core belief system and every moral precept I had; to 'hold on', to not admit to failure, to not care about my image or reputation, to soldier on and not ask for help and, on top of all that, he brought much of my 'shadow' to the surface.

With time, reflection and insight I came to the grim realization that I too was emotionally damaged; certainly not as emotionally damaged as the man I was trying to heal, but nonetheless dysfunctional. Jai wasn't the only one who wore a mask; I was just as guilty as he was of adopting a false persona and one in which the public and the private face had been locked in conflict for a long time.

I'd kept a secret deeply locked away inside me for nearly forty years and it was time to acknowledge the part it had played in my life. I was molested ... as a child of six years, by someone outside but known to the family. The dictionary definition of 'molestation' is 'to interfere with so as to annoy or cause injury'. I wasn't raped or violated, but my boundaries, those boundaries that as a child you instinctively know to be sacred were crossed. Even worse, I subconsciously held the belief that my father *must* have known about it. It was a false belief and one upon which I'd created emotional barriers between us for most of my adult life.

I entered adulthood with a distorted concept of 'boundaries'. Even though on some level I recognized that my relationship with Jai was abusive and destructive, my boundaries were so weakened I allowed it to happen. I am not suggesting that this early childhood experience was the entire reason for my emotional dysfunction, but I knew the problems I had now and the emotional patterns that had created them stemmed back and had their roots partly in my childhood.

Sometime in the latter part of 2002, I addressed this memory with my father and between us we ironed out all the painful misunderstandings. It upset him naturally and whether it was the right thing to dump this knowledge on a man with severe health problems is a question I've asked myself many times. I do know, however, that somehow my relationship with my father today has benefited from my openness and the healing that has subsequently taken place.

My relationship with my father has never been an easy one. But the lack of ease did not just stem from that early experience. I remember as a growing child being 'supersensitive' and acutely affected by any form of criticism. I think what I perceived back then to be a *lack of love* from my father was predominantly a lack of attention and validation. I have very little recollection of him being present in my childhood. It was my mother who not only looked after our daily needs but also entertained us; it was something that came naturally to her. It wasn't that my father intentionally withheld his love, simply that I never *felt* loved. With the understanding I have now, I *know* my father did his best and loved *all* of his children, *including* me.

Certainly, however, he was the formidable, dominant and controlling force in our household and, like many kids who grew up in the early sixties, I was subjected to the 'wait till your father gets home' and 'little children should be seen and not heard' syndrome. His job was both stressful and demanding and often spilt over into a general irritability in his demeanour when he was home. With a temper quick to rise, I seem to remember most of my early childhood 'fearing and often shrinking from his wrath'.

By the time I reached my teens I had become independent and headstrong … and was frequently accused of wanting the last word. I think I began to kick against every form of control in the only way I knew how. Add to this two distressing and shameful experiences that took place in my early teens: the first at the age of fourteen when, after following me home from school one day, two boys attacked me. This terrifying assault, along with the cuts, scratches and ripped clothing … I conveniently *hid* from both my parents. The second was at the age of sixteen when my father walked in, *literally*, on my first sexual encounter. It was little wonder that by the time I'd reached early adulthood I had unconsciously heaped upon myself layer upon layer of guilt.

Eventually, all the guilt I was carrying around blocked any chance for the love to pour through in my relationship with my dad. I felt guilty for what happened to me at the age of six, believing *somehow* it must have been my fault. I felt guilty for my shame-based experiences in my teens believing I'd let myself and him down *badly*. I felt guilty for a whole heap of things and on top of the guilt I was angry, resentful and deeply anguished.

When I finally embarked on my own personal journey of self-discovery some fifteen years ago, my spiritual faith and my ever-growing closeness to God just seemed to dredge more guilt to the surface, confirming my belief that I was sinful and needed to be punished. I began to see that the addictive behaviours I'd adopted in my life, the excessive drinking, smoking, addiction to sex and compulsive work patterns were all outlets I'd used to hide from what I *unconsciously* felt about myself. *All* addictions are ways of punishing the self.

Sometime during that fifteen-year period I began the long and painful process toward self-healing. It has frequently been my experience, however, in working with clients that unless the 'core' issue is uncovered and healed, we continue to attract experiences into our lives that only serve to reinforce our warped and distorted view of ourselves. On top of that, many of us absorb and replay the patterns of our own parents and, if I've learned anything in the field of personal development, it's that many of these patterns don't actually *serve* our growth.

By the time I was ready to deal with my core issue, I had already attracted into my life a dominant, ruthlessly controlling and punishing partner in Jai. In identifying with the negative masculine force exhibited by Jai, I understood that I had drawn to myself a grossly exaggerated, almost caricature, form of my father in an unconscious attempt to heal the early wounds of our relationship. *And, in allowing myself to be punished … I could cleanse myself of guilt.*

The toll on my physical body, from a relationship as emotionally wounding as mine was with Jai, was immense. The spinal column supports the physical body, so if we feel unsupported or our livelihood feels threatened, we will feel the counter-effects in the lower back. Add to that the 'burdensome' quality of guilt which is an emotion carried in the middle back and my spine felt as though it would snap in two. I lived on a cocktail of alcohol and high-strength painkillers to dull the pain for a good six months in the latter part of my relationship with him, until I finally realized that what I was doing was 'numbing' out what really needed to be faced and worked through.

On top of that I privately suffered from vaginitis in varying degrees during the period between 2001 and 2003. In Louise Hay's book, 'You can Heal your Life', she outlines the emotional patterns responsible for a whole host of diseases and illnesses. Problems in the area of the female genitalia, she states, relate to sexual guilt, anger at a mate and being romantically hurt by a partner. Once, when I tried to share with Jai the discomfort my condition caused me, he responded, "That's the difference between you and me. You're unclean … and you have so much dirt inside you." Although it was a judgmental and twisted remark and carried with it a deplorable lack of empathy, I realized that Jai had unconsciously tapped in to all the 'sexual guilt' that I was carrying.

Ironically, in my relationship with him, he 'mirrored' back to me, albeit brutally, much of what at the time I didn't want to *see* and, as a result of the understanding that came with it, a great deal of healing took place.

A fundamental part of the eventual healing process is acknowledging and accepting the problem in the first place and making a conscious choice to let it go. I recognized that I was carrying a 'rescuer pattern' with Jai and that in my attempts to 'fix' him, I had unwittingly become victim … and if anyone needed to be rescued it was *me*.

As unpalatable a truth as it was to swallow, I realized I was running a pattern in my life whereby *'I interfere with my own healing'* and, although it has taken me most of my adult years, I finally *chose* to remove the masks I'd been wearing. Through the wonderful discovery of various healing modalities, I sought release and freedom from the guilt, shame and feelings of abandonment that I'd carried around for far too many years.

Sometime in 2001, in the early part of my relationship with Jai, I'd met a man called Amon-Ra Antares. Having faced extreme adversity in his own life, Amon-Ra had awoken to his own 'divine' nature and he now calls himself a 'planetary server'. Part of his message is to bring awareness to the so called 'controlling forces' on this planet aimed at keeping us in ignorance and captivity. What he has to say is not palatable to all souls, but I for one knew that I was ready to hear his message.

I am a firm believer that, when you ask from the heart with integrity and purity of spirit, the right teacher will always present themselves. Although I wasn't aware of it at the time of our meeting, Amon-Ra was to play a major role in empowering me to take responsibility for my own healing and assisting me in my eventual release from the karmic ties that bound me in my relationship to Jai. I have known Amon-Ra for six years in a professional capacity and have great admiration and respect for the work that he does. I also think of him as my friend and a member of my soul group, in that I *know* that we have travelled throughout time many times together.

Amon-Ra first approached me not long after I opened the workshops, asking to carry out a talk and introduce the members to the various healing systems he was involved in. It was Amon-Ra who first introduced me to Pleiadian Lightwork, an ancient healing modality which has its roots in Lemurian, Atlantian and Egyptian healing-temple practices.

Pleiadian Lightwork teaches us to open the 'Ka' energy channels, so as to bring in and anchor a higher frequency light and life force into the physical body.

I was first made 'clairvoyantly' aware of these fifth dimensional beings of light when, in early August 2001, Bryna Waldman visited the UK from the United States and used my premises to carry out a workshop on Pleiadian Lightwork. I remember that morning with amusement when she appeared at the door forty-five minutes late and in her loud American drawl began cursing British taxi drivers. "Don't worry," I said to her, "you might be late but the Pleiadians were here on your behalf." She became really excited and asked me if I'd really seen them. "Well, if you mean those eight foot angelic beings, blue-grey in colour, walking around upstairs, then yes!" I replied.

I hadn't known it at the time but sometimes these beings, thought of as guardians of the Earth and our solar system, make conscious links with healers and lightworkers when they feel it important to convey essential planetary information. They are here in this time of great planetary change to awaken us to our own place in our evolutionary process and guide us as to what steps to take in going forward.

I clearly remember that morning when I'd put the key in the entrance door to the workshops, smiling to myself at seeing a trail of white feathers that led up the stairs to the first floor. White feathers are believed to signify the presence of an angel. Looking back I realized the heavenly presence that stopped Jai's fist short of my face that day in the workshops was an angel. From that moment to this I have never stopped believing in the existence of these unearthly beings and live in constant awe and gratitude for the wondrous protection they have brought to my life. These days I routinely call upon the Pleiadians in my work and when I invoke them they bring an intense and wonderful joyous quality to the healing.

Periodically throughout the years of 2002 and 2003, I sought

Amon-Ra's help on several occasions. I'd made the conscious decision to pull away from Jai but was struggling to sever the energetic ties between us. They were ties that, with Jai and I, went back not just to this physical lifetime ... but aeons.

Have you ever met someone who on first contact leaves you spellbound and you've no idea why? Or perhaps during that first meeting you felt so instantly drawn to them that you found yourself flirting with the memory of them forever? That's how it was with Jai; on some deeper level I already *knew* him. The attraction was simply magnetic and so overwhelmingly strong that I firmly believe there was no way on God's earth I could *ever* have resisted him.

I remember asking Kate when I first decided to write this book, "Where do I start?" and she simply replied, "At the beginning." It seemed like an obvious statement, but one that I had a problem with, in that my problem was defining *where* in fact the beginning was for me and Jai. I truly believe we were 'split souls' and that our coming together this time around had a far deeper intention, in that we were here in this lifetime to work out our karmic destiny. Such soul unions are often those that carry with them the most severe lessons ... and yet the ones that also grow us the most.

I'd made a 'soul contract' in heaven to stay with Jai forever and I'd wished in this lifetime with every fibre of my being that it could be so. But it was an agreement that had traumatized me in every area of my life with him and one that was preventing me from moving forward. I have often wondered how two souls who were once so close to each other could have ended up in this lifetime, so far apart. Yet, as painful as I knew it was going to be, I had to let go of him.

Through Pleiadian Lightwork, I worked to release some of the emotional patterns I'd unconsciously created. I found it incredibly empowering work and I am certain helped me address the unconscious processes within myself that finally led to the changes in my external reality. This is one healing session I would like to share in the pages of this book.

Amon-Ra (A)   Jacky (J):

A: "Why are you trying to shield him?"

J: "I'm all he has left in the world, his parents are dead and his brother has turned his back on him. I have to protect him."

A: "You have misplaced love issues; it is part of what you are down here to heal. What are you shielding him from, Jacky?"

J: "From himself. I am afraid he will want to end it if he goes to prison again."

A: "If Jai chooses to go off planet that will be his choice. It is probably part of the soul contract he has made with you."

J: "I made a soul contract to help him heal."

A: "And probably a vow not to leave him until he does. If he resists the healing, there is nothing you can do. You have to learn to let go."

J: "I need to make the courts, the police, everyone understand what's wrong with him. It's not his fault."

A: "No, it's his belief pattern. His abuse has left him hating women (not consciously). The problem is also what's working with him, controlling him. He has an astral friend that feeds off his pain."

Amon-Ra called in the Pleiadian Beings of Light to infuse mine and his energy fields with violet light. He placed his hand over, but not touching, my third eye and in that instant I 'saw' a past life memory from the Ghengis Khan lifetime. Jaya and I weren't romantically linked or in a relationship in that lifetime, but I 'saw' that he raped me and slit my throat. For the first time I was able to look at this memory as a casual observer.

Amon-Ra asked me to make a 'still' of the scene in my memory as though creating a black and white photograph.

Then he asked me to stamp it 'cancelled', tear it into pieces and burn it in the violet flame. I felt intense heat and a sense of peace and calm. He guided me through replacing the belief system of 'I am shameful and deserving of punishment' to 'I am worthy and love myself exactly as I am'.

As he moved his hands to my heart centre, I felt a welling up of emotion so powerful and painful it felt as though my head would burst. An image of a desert, cracked, dry and desolate came into my mind's eye.

"What's going on here, Jacky?" Amon-Ra asked me. "You know what it's to do with."

Once again the memory arose into my conscious awareness sharp and clear. It was the Native American Indian life when, as an old woman, I'd watched the mortal remains of my dead husband (Jai) being ferried across the great lake in a stone canoe. I saw myself wailing on the banks, mourning his loss. This loss, this grief, felt like the image of the desert I'd depicted in my heart: vast, desolate and seemingly never-ending.

A: "What's the belief system?"
J: "If I give my heart, I end up losing love."
A: "Reframe the image and replace the belief system."

I 'saw' myself again as the old Native American Indian woman, but this time kissing the earth on the grassy banks as the ashes of Jai's mortal remains were blown and scattered in the wind. I made the affirmation, 'I do not fear losing love. Love is eternal.'

J: "There's another belief system under this. It is to do with clinging on too hard for fear of losing the man I love. It is not serving me in this lifetime and it makes men feel claustrophobic."
A: "Change it."

I changed that belief system to 'I do not need to hang on. It is safe to love. I stand in my own power.'

J: "I believe I should have died before him and I vowed in this lifetime to come back for him."

A: "Rewrite the contract."

I imagined drawing up a 'contract' in front of me and the words, *'Vows are made of man, I let the heavens divine my destiny'* appeared on the page.

All in all I released numerous belief systems that were not serving me and accessed other past lives in which Jaya and I had shared strong karma. Much of the self-healing I was engaged in between the years 2002 and 2003 centred on the severing of past life connections we'd made between us.

Past life therapy allows for profound healing to take place at the source of the problem. In dealing with our past lives, we cease to concern ourselves with the symptoms they have created in this incarnation but address the root from which they stemmed. Working in this way allowed me to disconnect from Jai emotionally and regain the control in my life that I'd surrendered in my relationship with him.

In addition to the healing that took place using Pleiadian techniques, around this time I also underwent a series of hypnosis sessions with a qualified hypnotherapist and dear friend of mine called Anita. I'd asked Anita to work with me because no amount of correct breathing or meditation would disperse the overwhelmingly strong and panicky feelings I had in my chest. She took me into hypnosis and asked me to re-experience the first time I'd had that very same feeling.

I immediately accessed a past life memory in which, as a follower of Christ, I was persecuted and imprisoned by Roman soldiers. This is the verbatim account of what took place during that session.

"I'm being chased. All around me are Roman soldiers. There is one in particular, his name is Octavius (*whom I instinctively knew was Jai*). He's rough with me … he's going to kill me. The fear. The panic. It's cold, I'm trapped. I'm in a prison cell and my wrists are tightly bound behind my back. They want me to renounce my faith."

Anita asked me to tell her what they were saying and a dialogue played out between us:

O: "What is it about this man? Why do you feel you have to die for him?"
J: "He is my salvation."
O: "There's no glory in sacrifice."
J: "I know no other way."
O: "How I wish to be so important that someone would sacrifice themselves for me…"

"There's bright sunshine now … it's coming through the bars. No, it's more than sunlight … it's God's light. I'm on my knees praying for my soul to be taken. My guide has come for me … he's taking me into the light. I am being spared an agonizing death. It's over. I am surrounded by light … the light of Heaven."

Anita guided me to 'reframe' the scene before I 'died.' Reframing is like changing the 'life script', so that it may contain an outcome that allows the client to view it from a higher perspective in the current lifetime.

I saw myself forgiving Octavius. He told me that he "was only following orders." "I know that now," I responded … "but yours is not my truth. Violence and destruction is the evil made of man; it is not God's will."

Suddenly in the 'scene' in my mind, Octavius dropped to his knees and gripped my feet begging for forgiveness.

Afterwards, Anita and I explored the session for the healing potential it offered and to identify the issues that were relevant in this lifetime. Anita was particularly struck by Octavius's desire to be so important that someone would lie down and die for him. On some level, Jai in this lifetime had wished for his life to be of such great consequence that others would follow him.

I also found it interesting that in the 'reframing' stage of the regression, I'd seen Jai as the Roman soldier holding on to my feet and asking to be forgiven. It was an exhibiting pattern that in my experience with him always accompanied the 'remorseful' phase of his behaviour.

The theme of 'sacrifice' and 'redemption' was one that had come up time and time again for me in much of the past life work I'd previously undergone. To 'sacrifice' myself for a belief, a cause or a person was a pattern that was not serving me in this lifetime and one that to a degree had played out in my relationship with Jai.

Enormous relief followed as a result of that session and the uncomfortable, emotionally charged feeling in my chest disappeared. I knew I'd accessed a significant soul memory and one which allowed deep healing to take place at the source of the problem.

Anita and I had chosen 30th September 2002 to carry out this session; oddly it turned out to be National Forgiveness Day...

Personally, I am wholly convinced of the therapeutic value of regression and it is a healing technique I frequently use nowadays in my work. Sometimes when we are struggling with some of life's toughest lessons, we can find the solutions in our past lives or in the messages that speak to us in our dreams.

In the course of my relationship with Jai, one of the things that never ceased to amaze me was the power of my subconscious to communicate through my dreams. In paying attention to them and learning to decipher their meanings, they became an incredibly healing tool. I kept a dream journal and, at the height of the 'crisis', I noticed my dreams became more frequent and profound with every passing day; some of them I have already shared in the pages of this book.

The following dream took place much later, in fact towards the latter part of 2003, and I share it in this chapter in order to illustrate its uplifting nature and the part it played in my eventual healing process:

I dreamed I was flying through the air unaided with my arms outstretched like wings. As I looked to the right side of me, Temujin, my son, had grasped my hand and was flying alongside me. We reached a mountainous region and I could see a hot spring water pool dug out of a ledge on the mountain, the steam cascading from it. Together we began our descent and 'flew' right into it, submerging ourselves in the warm, crystal clear water. Underneath the water I looked at Tem and motioned to him that it was alright to breathe. We realized we could breathe under water and it felt wonderful. The dream ended as we emerged from the pool to a waiting Angel who simply turned to Temujin and said, "And from now on you will be known as Gabriel…"

In the waking moments of that dream, I knew that Temujin and I had been through a baptism of sorts and, in some religious ceremonies, the submergence of the body in water represents rebirth and transformation. In Native North American tribes, steam is considered to possess the combined purifying powers of fire and water and when used in Sweat Lodge ceremonies is believed to cleanse and revitalize the mind, body and spirit.

The dream had a cosmic-like quality to it and it felt as though Temujin and I had gone through some kind of rites of passage or initiation ceremony. Above all, it felt cleansing and purifying and I remember the feeling stayed with me for many days.

I also knew without a shadow of a doubt that it was a message for me to replace Temujin's four middle names with the name of 'Gabriel'. In the heavenly realms Angel Gabriel is known as 'The Awakener' and his name stands for 'God is my strength'. I like to think that this dream heralded the ending of the soul lessons that Temujin's birth names had carried and it was the beginning of a new chapter in his … and all of our lives.

For many of us, I suspect, the healing process seems never-ending. I am no exception. Even six years on as I write this book, occasionally the hurt and anger from my relationship with Jai still surfaces and I deal with it in the best way I know how. To be truthful with ourselves, to express and release our emotions, and to keep our thoughts as pure as possible … is all any of us can do and as such we continue to grow and evolve spiritually.

I think I knew at this point in my life that, in order to reinforce and support the work I'd been doing, some major life changes were in order.

In the late summer of 2003, Christopher once again invited me to join him and his family in Spain and it was a holiday that further cemented my desire to make my permanent home there.

It's always been my belief that when we want something that is our heart's desire and this is in accordance with our Higher Self, then the universe will conspire to make it happen. Staying connected to our Higher Self allows us to flow with the universe and remain open to the coded messages that litter our forward pathway.

In our relationship together, Jai's oft-repeated phrase was "God grants us what we need." He was right. But there is a gulf of difference between *needs* and *wants*. We may *want* something badly in our lives, but it may not be what we actually *need*. It is as though the universe instinctively *knows* what experiences will ultimately serve us.

Unconsciously I'd attracted Jai into my life and somehow destiny had divined our union. In accepting and moving through the challenges presented by the universe in the course of my relationship with him, I was able to heal the many debilitating patterns in my current and past lifetimes and so move on. I also knew that if Jai was ever going to begin the process of self-healing and undertake the journey to 'wholeness', I needed at this point in *my* life, to withdraw from *his* completely.

For a three-year period, I'd tried on every level to help him view his life from a different perspective, but no amount of help or healing from me had shifted him into a better space. Finally, standing up for myself and not allowing him to project onto me the pain and anger from his past was an act of 'honouring' myself. I finally understood and accepted that I was not responsible for providing the love that he couldn't find for himself.

Knowing at this point in my life that I could do no more, I offered the situation up to God and for nearly ninety days, during the period from September 2003 to November 2003, I sent up a prayer, every single night … a prayer for Divine dispensation … *and for the release from the karmic ties that bound us.*

On the 25th November 2003, exactly five years after Jai had entered my life, I was taken in dream state to the Karmic board.

I dreamed I was ascending a stairway lighted with candles and which led across a courtyard to a beautiful white temple. The entrance to the temple was shielded by a large tree and its branches leaned over to form an archway through which I passed. A door, inlaid with gold carvings, opened and I was led into a large room. Seated around a magnificent table, seven celestial beings whom I took to be angels beckoned me to join them. They placed a book on the table; its cover carried the symbol of the Egyptian 'ankh'. I recognized the book to be my personal Akashic records. One of these Higher level beings touched my brow and said, "Your karma is ended; everything you do for this situation from now on is of your own free will…"

Enormous relief followed as a result of this experience and I was finally able to believe that my karmic debt with Jai had been discharged. It was to be another three months later, owing to the 'possession' aspect of his condition, that I engaged, under my own free will, in 'an exorcism'. The detailed account of this and the sequence of events leading up to it, I have saved for presentation in the sequel to my story.

In July of 2004, my father generously funded a month long trip to Spain. It was a holiday that allowed me to recharge my batteries and gave me the courage and strength to believe that I could take my work and my future there. The benefits of that break away were enormous and I was able to spend some time with my children, quality time that had been denied me throughout the roller-coaster ride of the last five years.

It took barely two days of a month long holiday to sort out schooling for both my children and secure a rental on a small inexpensive apartment on the Costa Blanca. *I guess some things are just meant to be…*

On my return, I spent my last five weeks in the UK selling every last possession I owned in order to fund the flights and secure the deposit on my one bedroom rented apartment. Leaving behind the security of my family, with just a thousand pounds in my back pocket and all the money I had in the world … I set out into the unknown.

Tem was just under four years old and Jess nearly thirteen. I knew it would be tough for them at first but I held on to the fact that we were all headed for calmer waters … and we'd been given the chance to finally close a chapter … one that for me had been the most extraordinary and heartbreaking chapter of my entire life.

CHAPTER ELEVEN: 'THE ROAD TO FREEDOM'

*'Freedom is not something that anybody can be given;
freedom is something people take and people are as free as they want to be'*
Baldwin, James (1924-1987)

*'You can't separate peace from freedom because no-one
can be at peace unless he has his freedom'*
Malcolm X (1926-1965)

I watch the waves lap against the shoreline from the balcony of my tiny one bedroom apartment on the Costa Blanca … and I thank God I had the good sense to follow my 'inner knowing' and come here. These days I view my life from quite a different perspective. In the last two years, I've gained a deep inner peace and contentment that comes from many valuable lessons learned, borne out of and earned from much pain and suffering.

I knew in the writing of this book I would undergo a kind of inner catharsis and, through the many tear-stained pages of the manuscript, there has been much healing. Many people have asked me how I came to remember so much of what happened over a five year period and I tell them that some of the events detailed in this book are so vivid in my memory it is as if they happened yesterday … such is the narcissist's power.

When I sat down to write my story, I realized I had notes everywhere, torn pieces of paper, taped conversations, police statements, diary notes, letters to the courts, solicitors, healers, therapists and probation officers, and a pile of love letters that passed between us. I'd even kept a journal recording the cyclical pattern of the disorder; it had become part of my armoury. Piecing it all together, I already had my story, written in part and written already in the fabric of the universe...

In a meeting with Hazel in June 2006 to discuss the final preparations for this book I also came to the realization that my story was in actual fact *a Trilogy* and that it is in the sequel to this book, *'God is Definitely in Charge'*, that I explore the 'possession' aspect of Jai's condition and the subsequent 'exorcism' that took place. It is a smaller book in volume, but no means thinner in its content. I hope you will be moved to read it.

It is only in recent months that I have finally acknowledged the courage and resolve it took within me to make the dramatic and life-changing move in coming to Spain. When I stepped onto the plane in September 2004 with my two children in tow, just a suitcase of clothes and enough money in my back pocket to last three months, most of my family and friends declared me a 'mad woman'. Despite that, I just *knew* it was the right thing to do.

Painfully thin and weighing less than seven stone, I looked back then like a puff of wind might blow me away. The whole of the right side of my body ached with pain and discomfort as the stress of the previous five years began to exit my physical system. I was physically and emotionally exhausted. It took the benefit of a more relaxed lifestyle, healthy diet, warm sunshine and the best part of a year to feel well again. Frankly, I felt as though I'd been through a 'crucifixion' of sorts.

Despite all of that, I followed my inner guidance and, had it not been for my experience, I would not be here, living my personal dream, being of service and fulfilling my destiny. Every day I place my trust in the universe to supply me with everything I need and every day, in many different ways, the universe supports me.

Within three weeks of arriving in Spain, I connected with the WIBC (Women in Business Club), a networking group of women spanning the entire business spectrum dedicated to raising awareness of global women's issues. Ironically, I discovered that their fund-raising events support the victims of domestic violence throughout the Costa Blanca area, providing a place of shelter and safety for those family members affected. It feels rewarding to be able to be part of such a worthwhile cause and one towards which I feel a particular empathy.

My client base and reputation slowly began to build and I have been privileged to meet some wonderfully warm and supportive souls along the way. Knowing that I'm doing exactly what I'm supposed to be doing is a liberating feeling and has given me a sense of freedom and well-being I didn't know existed.

This book is no longer who I am nowadays. I am a stronger person for my experience and I believe I learned courage in the face of evil and compassion in the face of adversity. It has made me a better person and a better therapist. These days, there are few presenting problems that my clients bring to me that I have not already experienced or do not have the empathy to deal with. Over the last two and a half years my client work has taken on a dimension and depth that I neither consciously attracted nor thought myself capable of dealing with and, in all cases, I have served as a concrete and positive catalyst for growth. It has proved to be the most rewarding period of my life.

Some clients mirror back to me issues in myself that I still have work to do around. It is how the process works. Recognizing and working on these specific 'mirrors' helps us to grow emotionally and spiritually.

I'm not claiming to be 'healed' nor am I claiming to be enlightened. If I was I would not be here on the earth plane, still learning from my experiences and still trapped in my limited form. But enlightenment is a state I am *consciously* working towards. Every day I offer up to God a belief system, a behaviour pattern or way of being that is not serving me and every day I grow a little further toward the light.

In the course of my relationship with Jai, I learned much about myself. I learned to let go of my stubbornness, a quality that both served and hindered me. At times it was my stubborn streak that got me through the darkest days, but it was also the same obstinacy that held to the belief that I could change things, a trait that, in my experience with Jai, prolonged my pain and suffering.

Jai could not have entered my life if I hadn't been carrying the guilt or the shame-based trauma that was deeply locked away inside me. In some perverse way I believed I needed to be punished and that, if I 'sacrificed' myself by allowing myself to be abused, then I could free myself from guilt. It was a belief system that served no one.

Choosing Jai was an unconscious motivation and one that stemmed from the unfinished business between my father and me. Sometimes, we misguidedly believe that we can heal the pains of our past through our relationships, as though in replaying the past we might gain a new perspective. Finally, healing these many layers allowed me to learn from the experience, free myself and move on.

I also learned enough to know that it was my ego that believed I could save Jai. What right did I have to think that I could alter the course of events and force him to seek therapy? He often accused me of using what he referred to as 'my psychobabble' on him. Looking back, there were many occasions when I slipped into the role of 'therapist', 'healer' … even *'saviour'* and, under my intense scrutiny, I suspect there were times when Jai felt like nothing more than some gigantic, challenging case study.

Perhaps there was also a part of him that feared and doubted the ability of his fragile 'self' to survive the rigorous route of therapy. It takes enormous courage to travel that road and he would have my admiration indeed if he ever began the journey. NPD is after all a defence mechanism and, to Jai, a way of being that allows him to cope and survive in the outside world. *Simply loving him* wasn't enough to alter the course of things and force him to seek therapy; only *he* had that power within himself.

Accepting that there are some things in life that you just cannot change was a hard lesson for me and one that I was forced to learn. I now know that there are some things in life... *that simply aren't meant to be changed.*

It was an awareness that allowed me to let go. Finally letting go of Jai and detaching with love was in itself an action of love. It hurt like hell, it still does sometimes, but I have learned that it is not possible to 'save' another human being.

If we are to effect change in our external environment, then we must first begin by changing ourselves. 'All healing is self-healing'. Many of us become disheartened when we witness the destruction and chaos in the outside world, yet fail to recognize the part we play in co-creating it. It is only when we consciously apply a reverence for all of creation in our everyday lives, when we release judgment and acknowledge the part others play in our own evolution, that we can truly claim to be coming from a place of love and light. I stopped judging Jai a long time ago. I have acknowledged that he is travelling his own journey in this lifetime and it is not a journey that I can travel for him.

Stanislav writes that many researchers in the field of transpersonal psychology 'believe the growing interest in spirituality and the increasing incidence of spontaneous mystical experiences represent an evolutionary trend toward an entirely new level of human consciousness.' Some, he comments, go even further to suggest that the upward trend towards spiritual growth 'reflects an effort on the part of the forces of evolution to reverse the current self-destructive course of the human race.'

Had Jai been willing and able to truly integrate his mystical revelations and grow from such a crisis then his contribution to this evolutionary process might well have been marked. Sadly, as the human race continues to feel the threat of possible war in the outside world, so Jai's 'internal war' continues ... a war that is fuelled by acute anxiety, poor self-worth, jealousy, rage and fear.

The overwhelming drive in him to feel powerful and superior manifested in a need to dominate and control everyone around him. His desperation to feel loved and respected drove him to 'act out' and typify the narcissist's outlandish behaviour. He is a perplexing host of contradictions, at times a visionary, perceptive and full of wisdom and, at others, a tortured soul, troubled and full of pain. There is a part of me that still wants to fix him, but I can't. We are each responsible for our own growth, for healing our own painful issues and for letting go of our own past.

In many ways Jai was my greatest teacher. In the often painful interactions of our relationship, he brought much of my 'shadow' to the surface and it is in healing these unconscious parts of ourselves, of which we fear acceptance, that we 'grow'. We all attract to ourselves the life experiences we need in order to develop spiritually. In that respect, Jai served me. *And, for that, I thank him.*

You may well be wondering what has become of him these days? Has he himself grown from the experience? Once I thought perhaps he had, a little, in inches ... by degrees. But sadly, in recent months, I fear the opposite to be the case. It was only in the writing of the closing chapter for this book that he left a desperate voicemail message on my mobile urging me to contact him ... as he believed himself to be facing yet another prison term.

In the two and a half years I have been in Spain, communication with Jai has been minimal. What little he has shared though further confirms my fears that his life continues to be fraught with difficulties ... run-ins with the police ... business ventures that have gone pear-shaped... more soured friendships …and all because he continues to project his anger on the outside world. All the while, he fails to see the devastation and destruction he brings to the lives of others in the process.

Real growth takes effort and Jai still refuses to acknowledge the negative and destructive side effects of his behaviour. Frankly, there were very few occasions in the course of my relationship with him when I detected a genuine awareness of the pain he inflicted on others. Narcissists have 'selective memories'; they *choose* not to remember the abuse or even consider that their behaviour is in any way abusive. To recover from his condition would require on Jai's part some intense self-examination and, as I have said before, probably an enormous amount of courage.

Even today with everything that I have read about NPD, I am still uncertain as to whether it's his stubborn refusal to accept any underlying mental disorder that blocks his healing or if he is simply incapable of such an awareness or insight. As such, then his condition must be deemed 'untreatable'. Kenny Pask, the soul reader, warned me that the universe "will keep breaking him and breaking him until the ego is smashed." So long as Jai remains slave to the ego, he will always be driven in self-serving pursuits that will fail to bring him lasting peace and happiness.

One thing is for certain, I didn't set out to write this book to discredit him, stab him in the back, or to seek some warped revenge. I wrote it primarily to bring awareness to a disorder that grips more than one per cent of the population and one that is as destructive and devastating to those affected by it as to the sufferer himself. I still cling to the vain hope that Jai may gain some awareness through its pages and at some point in his life begin the healing process.

Perhaps that awareness will come one day when, at some point in the future, he finds himself looking back at a trail of broken dreams and wondering why his claims failed to manifest in the real world. How low does a person have to sink before they realize that the things they dreamed about themselves didn't come to fruition? I don't know the answer to that. Certainly I am no longer naive enough to believe that love alone is the cure for everything ... even if there is *hope,* always, in any given situation.

Nowadays I am often asked by my family and friends why I don't hate him for the experience he put me through, and to that I respond, "Nothing I endured in our relationship can ever compare to the hell state he is permanently locked in."

Someone told me recently that "Forgiveness is an inside job." I believe them. Holding onto resentments would not have served me in my new life and I have learned to let go of Jai with forgiveness and understanding. I have also acknowledged the part I played in co-creating the dysfunction within our relationship. Very rarely does the anger surface these days but, when it does, there is a difference. I am angry at Jai's behaviour and actions ... I don't *hate* the man.

Sometimes I am angry at myself for having put my children and, in particular, Jessica through such a difficult and bewildering experience and one which forced her to grow up far too quickly. The one comfort I have is that ours is a close enough relationship these days for her to talk to me openly and honestly about her worries and her fears. I know she is stronger for the experience and shows wisdom and understanding beyond her years ... such wisdom and understanding have allowed on her part much forgiveness to pour towards me in our relationship.

Certainly the one thing Jess and I both try to do is to not dwell on the past. To say to ourselves that 'we are not our past' is an empowering truth I've heard many times in spiritual circles and one which holds a wealth of treasure within it. Everything that happened to me in my relationship with Jai was as a direct result of the choices *I* made... but it is *my past.* Our past only serves to teach us the lessons and the learning gained from our personal experiences, but it is our past nonetheless.

It is in the present moment that we can *choose* to invite wonderful people and create wonderful experiences into our lives. With the benefit of my experience, I now *choose* to create my wonderful reality with every waking day.

I began this book by saying that it was not a love story, but it was a story about love. Love stories traditionally have happy endings and the finale is not how I would have wanted it. It is, however, what the universe *intended* for me. There is a part of me that will always care about Jai and a part that will always be affected by the outcomes of his life.

I know, in Jaya's mind, he believed he truly loved *me*. But, in some respects, he is incapable of love. It's not possible to truly love another person until you can first love yourself. He was a man with a God-given mission to save the world … and, yet, the simple truth was he couldn't even save himself. Life is a precious gift surely and we shouldn't waste a single moment of it. The finale I wanted for Jai was for the completion of the hero's journey … and every day in my prayers … I pray that it's not too late.

In Robin Sieger's meeting back in the year 2000, there's a part on the tape where Robin shares this touching story with Jai:

'When I was a boy, I was dying of cancer. And a spiritual friend of mine introduced me to a Jesuit priest who said to me, "Robin, what's your biggest regret?"

I answered that my biggest regret was that I'd wasted my gift. The priest asked me what my gift was and I answered, "I have the gift of communication."

The priest said to me, "Robin, if you have your health back, don't waste it."

Thankfully, I did regain my health and, as a result, viewed my life quite differently, not wasting the precious gift of communication combined with humour that God had blessed me with.'

If I could pass on one lasting message to Jai, it would be to reiterate Robin's words. *Don't waste your gift, Jaya; 'You are a child of the universe and you have a right to be here ...'*

So, dear reader, for now my story draws to a conclusion. What Jai did in life was what his soul had *intended* for him and, in that, he was no different to the rest of us. I once heard somewhere that *'what we do in life ...echoes in eternity'*. We all make choices every moment of our lives and *how* we choose to act in any given situation rests entirely in our hands. Every action has a consequence ... that is the karmic law of the universe.

What you make of Jai and the journey he is travelling is up to you. I try to remember there is a polarity in all things. So Saint or Sinner? ... Mystic or Madman? ... You, dear reader, decide. There's one thing I've been certain of all the way along.......

God is definitely in charge...

AFTERWORD

For Kate and Jayne, the two people who shared my experience with me daily, there will never be enough words of gratitude. They shared my 'highs' and my 'lows', my tears of anguish and my tears of joy, my darkest nightmares and my wildest dreams. True friendship and sisterhood is not something you can ever put a value on. Whatever was happening for me, they shared objectively, without bias, with compassion and with love.

And for that I owe them my sanity.

When I left for Spain I wrote Kate a letter in which I said, 'I know that you take comfort as I leave that I have stopped 'riding the waves', hopefully for all time. I am learning on this part of the journey that we can choose our means of travel … and I now choose to soar like the eagle, holding in light a 'vision of earth' … and the promise of a better future'.

Namaste,

Jacky

BIBLIOGRAPHY

Kind permissions for extracts from their works were granted by the following authors:

Schwartz-Salant, Nathan. *'Narcissism and Character Transformation'* Inner City Books, 1982

'The Celestine Prophecy' by James Redfield, published by Bantam Books. Reprinted by permission of The Random House Group Ltd.

Christina Grof & Stanislav Grof, M.D. *'The Stormy Search for the Self'* Thorsons, 1995

Scott Peck, Dr M. *'The Road Less Travelled'* Simon and Schuster, 1978

Scott Peck, Dr M. *'People of the Lie'* first published by Arrow, 1990

Donald Walsch, Neale *'Conversations with God: Book 3'* first published by Hodder & Stoughton, 1999

In the course of our research on the subject of 'narcissism', Kate came across the website of a 'self-confessed narcissist' by the name of Sam Vaknin. I would like to acknowledge Mr Vaknin for his extensive, extremely thorough and highly articulate writings on the subject of this complex disorder. His insightful piece of writing entitled 'For the Love of God' along with some other brief 'extracts' gathered on NPD were especially helpful in my research and for the particular issues I address in this book.
For further information, visit his website
http://samvak.tripod.com/

I am also indebted to the following publications:

Courteney, Hazel *'Divine Intervention'* first published by Cico Books, 1999

Spezzano, Chuck *'If it Hurts, it isn't Love'* first published by Hodder & Stoughton, 1999

Beattie, Melody *'Codependent No More'* Hazelden, 1987

Cooper, Diana *'A New Light on Ascension'* Findhorn, 2004

Scott Peck, Dr M. *'Further Along The Road Less Travelled'* first published by Simon & Schuster, 1993

Scott Peck, Dr M. *'Glimpses of The Devil'* Simon & Schuster, 2005

Assagioli, Roberto, M.D. *'Transpersonal Development – The Dimension beyond Psychosynthesis'* Thorsons, 1993

Burnham, Sophy *'The Ecstatic Journey'* Ballantine Books, 1997

'The Rider Encyclopaedia of Eastern Philosophy and Religion' first published by Rider in 1989, paperback edition published by Rider, 1999

Mason, Paul T. M.S & Kreger, Randi. *'Stop Walking on Eggshells'* New Harbinger Publications, Inc. 1998

O'Sullivan, Terry & Natalia *'Soul Rescuers'* Thorsons, 1999

Quan Yin, Amorah *'The Pleiadian Workbook'* Bear & Company, 1996

Hay, Louise L. *'You Can Heal Your Life'* Eden Grove Editions – an imprint of Axis Publishing, 1988

Williamson, Marianne *'Return to Love'* Harper Paperbacks 1996

Sandweiss, Samuel H *'Sai Baba, The Holy Man and the Psychiatrist'* San Diego: Birth Day Publishing, 1975

Siegel, Bernie S *'Love, Medicine and Miracles'* first published in UK by Rider, 1986

Campbell, Joseph *'The Hero with a Thousand Faces'* Cleveland: World Publishing, 1970

SUGGESTED READING

No spiritual library would be complete without the following publications:

Sieger, Robin *'Natural Born Winners'* first published by Random House Business Books, 1999

Courteney, Hazel *'The Evidence for the Sixth Sense'* Cico Books, 2005

Chopra, Deepak *'Synchro Destiny'* first published by Harmony Books, 2003

Chopra, Deepak *'How to Know God'* Harmony Books, 2000

Bays, Brandon *'The Journey'* first published by Thorsons, 1999. First Pocket Books hardcover 2001

Macbeth, Jessica *'Moon Over Water'* first published by Gateway Books, 1990

Dreher, Diane *'The Tao of Peace'* first published in the US by Donald I. Fine, Inc, 1990

About the WIBC:

The WIBC, Women in Business Club, was formed in May 2004 by Suzanna Mace and Karla Darocas to create an Association of Women aimed at helping each other financially and emotionally. Through networking and building relationships, women of all nationalities are able to share their skills and talents with each other.

The WIBC focuses on global women's issues as well as promoting goodwill within the community. Domestic violence in Spain is a serious issue and one which is so widespread it is impossible to ignore. The WIBC through its fund-raising events supports regional women's shelters and assists those affected by the outcomes of domestic violence as well as helping them reintegrate into society.

For more information about The Women in Business Club, visit the website:

www.wibc-spain.com

Printed in the United Kingdom
by Lightning Source UK Ltd.
120666UK00001B/52-87